영어는 **후치수식**,
한중일어는 **전치수식**

영어는 **후치수식**, 한중일어는 **전치수식**

발행일	2017년 10월 27일

지은이	오 상 환		
펴낸이	손 형 국		
펴낸곳	(주)북랩		
편집인	선일영	편집	이종무, 권혁신, 최예은
디자인	이현수, 김민하, 한수희, 김윤주	제작	박기성, 황동현, 구성우
마케팅	김회란, 박진관, 김한결		
출판등록	2004. 12. 1(제2012-000051호)		
주소	서울시 금천구 가산디지털 1로 168, 우림라이온스밸리 B동 B113, 114호		
홈페이지	www.book.co.kr		
전화번호	(02)2026-5777	팩스	(02)2026-5747
ISBN	979-11-5987-793-3 13740 (종이책)		979-11-5987-794-0 15740 (전자책)

잘못된 책은 구입한 곳에서 교환해드립니다.
이 책은 저작권법에 따라 보호받는 저작물이므로 무단 전재와 복제를 금합니다.

(주)북랩 성공출판의 파트너

북랩 홈페이지와 패밀리 사이트에서 다양한 출판 솔루션을 만나 보세요!

홈페이지 book.co.kr • 블로그 blog.naver.com/essaybook • 원고모집 book@book.co.kr

영어는 후치수식,
한중일어는 전치수식

오상환 지음

후치수식은 영어 학습의 요체이자 관건이며 첩경이다.
후치수식이 없는 한중일 동양 3국의 영어 학습자들이 가장 어려워하는
후치수식을 자연스럽게 통달할 수 있는 학습서.

북랩 book Lab

머리말
Preface

한국, 중국, 일본, 동양 3국의 언어와 세계 공통어인 영어 사이의 가장 눈에 띄게 뚜렷하고 또한 상호 간에 습득하기 어려운 구문론적인 특징이자 차이점 중 하나는 문장이 하나의 명사를 수식하는 방식인 '수식 구조'일 것입니다. 즉, 동양의 한·중·일어는 문장이 하나의 명사를 수식할 때, 명사 앞에서 수식하는 전치수식(Pre-modification) 구조를 갖고 있고, 반면에 영어는 명사 뒤에서 수식하는 후치수식(Post-modification) 구조를 갖고 있다는 것입니다. 물론, 하나의 형용사가 명사를 수식할 때에는 네 언어가 공히 명사 앞에서 전치수식할 수 있습니다. 그러나 문장이 하나의 명사를 수식할 때에는 양자 간에 아주 커다란 전치수식과 후치수식이라는 구문론적인 차이를 보인다는 것입니다.

필자는 동양의 한·중·일어와 영어 사이에 문장이 하나의 명사를 수식하는 위치의 차이가 영어를 학습하는 한·중·일 동양 3국의 사람들에게 난관이자 의무이면서 동시에 관건이자 첩경이 될 수 있다고 생각합니다. 영어를 잘 구사하는 사람은 거의 예외 없이 후치수식 구조를 자유롭게 사용할 수 있는 사람이고, 반면에 영어를 잘 구사하지 못하는 사람은 후치수식 구조를 자유롭게 사용할 수 없는 사람이라고 말해도 틀린 말이 아닙니다.

실제로 유럽의 대학생들이나 대학을 졸업한 사람들은 일상대화를 하는 데 지장이 없을 정도의 상당한 영어 구사력을 갖고 있습니다. 이것은 그들이 우리보다 더 열심히, 더 많이 공부해서라기보다는 그들 자신의 언어가 영어와 똑같은 후치수식 구조를 갖고 있어서 한·중·일 동양 3국 사람들보다 더 쉽게, 더 빠르게 영어에 적응할 수 있기 때문입니다. 필자가 알고 있는 한, 로망스어(Romance Languages)인 불어, 스페인어, 포르투갈어, 이탈리아어, 루마니아어, 영어가 속해 있는 게르만어(Germanic Languages)인 독일어, 네덜란드어, 덴마크어, 스웨덴어, 노르웨이어, 아이슬란드어, 우랄어(Uralic Languages) 인 헝가리어, 핀란드어, 에스토니아어, 그리고 슬라브어(Slavic Languages)인 러시아어, 폴란드어, 체코어, 슬로바키아어, 불가리아어 등 모두가 영어와 같은 후치수식 구조를 갖고 있습니다. 이런 연유로 유럽인들이 한·중·일 동양 3국 사람들보다 일반적으로 훨씬 더 빠르게 영어를 습득하고 더 나은 영어 구사력을 갖고 있는 것입니다. 이것은 같은 전치수식 구조를 갖고 있는 동양 3국에서, 한국인들과 일본인들이 중국어를 배우는 데 있어서 후치수식 구조를 갖고 있는 유럽인들보다 더 유리한 언어적인 학습 환경에 처해 있어서 중국어를 더 빠르게 습득하는 것과 같은 이치일 것입니다. 영어를 외국어로 배우고 있는 학습자의 언어가 영어와 같은 후치수식 구조를 갖고 있는가 아니면 영어와 다른 전치수식 구조를 갖고 있는가에 따라서 학습자가 영어에 적응하는 데 필요한 시간과 영어 구사력에 상당한 차이가 있다는 것이 엄연한 사실입니다.

동양의 한·중·일어의 입장에서 구문론적으로 봤을 때, 일단 영어의 후치수식 구조에 익숙해졌다면, 이것보다 학습하기 더 어려운 영어의 구문론적인 구조는 없습니다. 사실, 하나의 명사를 긴 문장이 앞이나 뒤에서 수식한다는 것은 고도로 복잡하고 정교한 인간의 사고와 언어활동의 한 단면이자 증거라고 할 수 있습니다. 명사를 수식하는 속성은 모든 언어에 공통적으로 존재하는 보편적인 속성이지만, 영어 구사력에 있어서 후치수식 구조의 사용은 대화의 내용을 더 정확하고, 깊이 있고, 세련되며, 품위 있게 심화시켜주는 측면이 강해서 교육을 많이 받은 사람일수록 더 많은 후치수식 구문을 사용한다는 것도 사실입니다.

세계 공통어인 영어를 외국어로 배우고 있는 사람이라면 영어에 빨리 그리고 품위 있게 잘 적응할 수 있기를 희망하지 않는 사람은 아무도 없을 것입니다. 영어의 학습

과정이나 내용을 간략하게 살펴보면, 발음, 억양, 끊어 읽기, 어휘, 회화, 문법, 독해, 영작, 청취, 시험영어 등 헤아릴 수 없을 만큼 많은 학습 내용과 과정이 있습니다. 이러한 영어의 모든 내용과 과정의 목표가 학습자로 하여금 훌륭한 영어 구사력을 빨리 갖게 하는 것이라고 한다면, 필자는 특히 영어의 후치수식 구조가 없는 한·중·일 동양 3국의 사람들에게는 후치수식 구조를 가능한 한 빨리 정확하게 숙달하는 것이 그 어떠한 영어 학습의 내용과 과정보다 훨씬 더 쉽고, 빠르고, 중요하고, 절실하게 필요하다고 생각합니다.

본 교재는 쉽고 간단한 단문(Simple Sentence)을 후치수식을 이용해서 어렵고 복잡한 복문(Complex Sentence)으로 조작할 수 있어야 비로소 훌륭한 영어 구사력을 가질 수 있다는 언어학적인 기반 위에서 후치수식 구조가 없는 한·중·일 동양 3국의 사람들을 위해서 출간되었습니다. 영어의 단문을 복문으로 조작할 수 있다는 것은 후치수식을 자유자재로 사용할 수 있을 때라야 비로소 가능한 일입니다. 후치수식 구문을 조작할 수 있다는 것은 구문론적으로 영어에 마침내 완전히 적응했다는 것을 말해준다고 볼 수 있습니다. 물론, 단문을 명사절과 부사절을 가진 복문으로 조작할 수 있는 것도 중요하지만, 그러나 구문론적으로 봤을 때, 명사절과 부사절을 가진 복문을 만드는 것은 후치수식 구조인 형용사절을 가진 복문을 만드는 것에 비하면 훨씬 더 단순하고 쉽습니다.

또한 본 교재는 후치수식을 통해서 쉽고 빠른 영어 교육의 한 방법을 제시해줌으로써 영어 학습에 결코 식지 않는 열정을 갖고 막대한 노력과 비용을 치르면서도 큰 성과를 얻지 못하고 있는 한·중·일 동양 3국 학습자들의 영어 실력을 폭발적으로 향상시켜 줄 수 있을 것이라고 생각합니다. 필자는 한·중·일 동양 3국의 학습자들의 영어 실력을 쉽게, 빠르게, 그리고 폭발적으로 향상시켜 줄 수 있는 한 가지 확실한 방법은 보통의 쉬운 단문(Simple Sentence)을 후치수식을 사용해서 어렵고 복잡한 복문(Complex Sentence)으로 자유자재로 전환시킬 수 있는 능력을 가능한 한 빨리 습득하는 것이라고 확고하게 믿고 있습니다. 다시 말해서, 영어의 후치수식 구조의 학습은 후치수식 구조가 없는 한·중·일 동양 3국의 사람들에게는 필수 불가결하고, 불가피한 학습의 요체이면서 동시에 영어 학습의 성공으로 가는 열쇠와 첩경을 제시해줄 수 있다는 점을 다시 한 번 더 강조하고 싶습니다.

이런 취지에서, 본 교재는 900개의 쉬운 단문(Simple Sentence)을 3,524개의 후치수식 구문으로 만들어서 구문론적으로 분류·정리해 놓았습니다. 각 장에 있는 후치수식 구문을 동반하고 있는 50문장을 매일 소리 내어 꾸준히 읽어간다면 일정 수준의 영어를 정복하는 데 18일이라는 짧은 시간 내에 소기의 목적을 달성할 수 있을 것입니다. 특히 본 교재가 제공하고 있는 QR코드를 통해 영어 녹음물에 접근해서 리스닝을 훈련한다면 영어의 후치수식에 대한 적응과 효과와 속도는 크게 높아질 것입니다. QR코드를 통한 리스닝을 적극적으로 이용할 것을 강력하게 권장합니다. 비록 본 교재가 문법적인 용어를 사용해서 분류·정리돼 있지만, 이것은 교재의 내용 분류상 불가피한 측면이었다는 점을 이해해주었으면 합니다. 그러나 동시에 실제로는 이러한 문법적인 분류와 설명이 영어 학습자들이 후치수식을 이해하는 데 훨씬 더 수월한 학습 방법이 될 것이라고도 생각합니다. 어느 정도의 영어 문법에 익숙한 학습자라면 문제가 없겠지만, 영어 문법에 익숙하지 않은 학습자일지라도 문법 내용과 설명에 크게 신경 쓰지 않고 후치수식 구문에 중점을 두고 차분하게 소리 내어 읽어간다면 본 교재의 내용을 쉽게 소화해서 자연스럽게 활용할 수 있을 것입니다. 본 교재를 학습함으로써 후치수식 구문을 자유자재로 사용할 줄 아는 뛰어난 영어 구사력을 가진 한·중·일 동양 3국의 영어 학습자들이 많이 나오기를 진심으로 희망하고 기대합니다.

끝으로 중국어와 일본어의 교정을 위해서 수고해주신 중국어 원어민 쟝 홍(江 弘) 선생님과 리우 쿤(刘 坤) 선생님 그리고 일본어 원어민 시라이 마리(白井 万里) 선생님, 그리고 영어 녹음을 위해 수고해주신 미국인 원어민 Harrison Taylor 선생님과 제타 스튜디오의 정광섭 사장님께 지면을 통해서 깊은 감사의 마음을 전합니다. 또한 본 교재가 세상의 빛을 보도록 쾌히 출간을 허락해주신 북랩출판사 손형국 사장님과 출간을 위해 귀중한 조언을 아끼지 않으신 김회란 출판사업본부장님, 그리고 빈틈없는 교정과 세련된 편집과 디자인을 위해서 많은 수고를 해주신 권혁신 과장님을 비롯한 여러 편집부 직원분들께 진심으로 감사의 마음을 표합니다.

2017년 10월

오상환

목차
Contents

머리말 (Preface) ··· 004

01 관계 대명사 (Relative Pronoun)

1. 관계 대명사 Who (주격/Nominative) ································· 012

2. 관계 대명사 Whose (소유격/Genitive) ······························· 034

3. 관계 대명사 Whom / Who (목적격/Objective) ···················· 052

4. 관계 대명사 Which (주격/Nominative) ······························ 076

5. 관계 대명사 Whose / Of Which (소유격/Genitive) ············· 096

6. 관계 대명사 Which (목적격/Objective) ······························ 124

7. 관계 대명사 What (주격/Nominative) ································ 146

8. 관계 대명사 What (목적격/Objective) ································ 166

9. 관계 대명사 That (주격/Nominative) ································· 188

10. 관계 대명사 That (목적격/Objective) ································ 208

11. 관계 대명사 생략 (주격/Nominative) ································ 228

12. 관계 대명사 생략 (목적격/Objective) ······························· 246

영어는 **후치수식**, 한중일어는 **전치수식**

02 관계 부사 (Relative Adverb)

1. 관계 부사 When ·················· 268

2. 관계 부사 Where ················· 296

3. 관계 부사 How ··················· 318

4. 관계 부사 Why ··················· 346

03 분사 (Participle)

1. 현재분사 (Present Participle) ·················· 376

2. 과거분사 (Past Participle) ····················· 398

01

영어는 **후치수식**, 한중일어는 **전치수식**

관계 대명사
Relative Pronoun

1. 관계 대명사 Who
(주격/Nominative)

관계 대명사 who는 선행사가 사람인 경우에 사용하는 주격 관계 대명사이다. 구조는 대부분 '선행사 + who + 동사'의 형태로 되어 있다. 문법적으로 관계 대명사는 접속사와 대명사의 역할을 하고, 선행사를 후치수식하는 형용사절을 이끈다. 명사 후치수식 구조가 없는 우리로서는 '~하는 사람'을 표현할 때 사용하는 관계 대명사라고 이해하면 되겠다.

여기서 두 가지 주의할 점이 있는데, 하나는 주격 관계 대명사 who 대신에 that을 써도 된다는 것이다. 관계 대명사 that은 사람, 동물, 사물을 가리지 않고 모든 명사를 수식할 수 있기 때문이다. 선행사가 사람인 경우에는 관계 대명사 that보다는 who를 압도적으로 더 많이 사용하지만, 구어에서는 that도 많이 사용한다.

또 한 가지 주의할 점은 주격 관계 대명사 who와 다음에 있는 be 동사는 동시에 생략할 수 있다는 점이다. 왜냐하면 주격 관계 대명사 who와 be 동사 다음에 동격의 의미가 있는 명사가 오는 경우에는 명사 앞과 뒤에 콤마를 찍어서 관계 대명사와 be 동사를 생략할 수 있고, 이 경우를 제외하면 주격 관계 대명사 who와 be 동사 다음에는 형용사구가 오든지 현재분사가 오든지 아니면 과거분사가 오기 때문에 이것들은 주격 관계 대명사 who와 be 동사가 없어도 더 간단한 명사 후치수식 구조의 구문이 되기 때문이다. 주격 관계 대명사와 be 동사를 동시에 생략하는 것을 영문법에서 'Whiz Deletion'이라고 한다.

관계 대명사에는 제한적 용법(restrictive use 또는 defining relative clause)과 계속적 용법(non-restrictive use 또는 non-defining relative clause) 두 가지의 용법이 있는데, 전자는 주격 관계 대명사 who 앞에 콤마가 없는 것으로 관계 대명사 절이 앞에 있는 선행사를 직접 수식하는 용법을 말하고, 후자는 주격 관계 대명사 who 앞에 콤마가 있는 것으로 선행사에 대해서 부가적으로 기술적인(descriptive) 설명을 가하는 용법이다.

선행사가 사람인 단순한 한 명사를 수식하는 기능을 관계 대명사 who가 담당하고 있는데, 명사 후치수식 구조가 없는 우리에게 절실히 필요한 것은 보통의 일반 문장을 명사 후치수식 구문으로 자유자재로 만들 수 있는 구문 전환 능력을 기르는 것이다. 이러한 후치수식 구문을 이용한 구문 전환 능력을 기르는 것은 학습자들을 복잡하고 어려운 영문법의 굴레에서 벗어나게 해주면서도 동시에 영어 청취력과 구사력을 크게 향상시켜 주는 대단히 효율적인 영어 교육의 방법이라 하지 않을 수 없다.

이러한 점을 예를 들어 쉽게 설명하면, "모든 사람은 지금보다 더 행복해지려고 열심히 노력하고 있다."라는 문장을 '지금보다 더 행복해지려고 열심히 노력하고 있는 모든 사람'이라는 명사 후치수식 구문으로 만들 수 있는 것이 영어를 마스터하는 첩경이자 열쇠이며 핵심과제라는 것이다. 참고로 우리말이 명사를 앞에서 수식하는 전치수식 구조로 되어 있는 반면에 영어는 명사를 뒤에서 수식하는 후치수식 구조로 되어 있다. 이러한 두 언어 사이의 명사를 수식하는 방식의 전혀 다른 중대한 차이점을 깊이 인식하고 집중해서 학습하는 것이 영어정복의 지름길이자 열쇠이며 핵심과제라는 것을 깊이 명심하고 학습해주기 바란다.

> 여기서 "그들은 우리의 삶에 깊이 영향을 미치고 있다."라는 문장을 '우리의 삶에 깊이 영향을 미치고 있는 사람들'이라는 명사 후치수식 구문으로 전환시켜보면 다음과 같이 할 수 있겠다.
>
> They influence our lives deeply.
>
> 1. People who influence our lives deeply. (관계 대명사 who)
> 2. People that influence our lives deeply. (관계 대명사 that)
> 3. People influencing our lives deeply. (현재분사)

※참고: 본 교재의 각 기본 문장이 동반하고 있는 후치수식 구문들은 문장이 아니기 때문에 마침표를 찍어서는 안 되지만 영어 자동 읽기 프로그램을 실행하려는 학습자들을 위해서 부득이 마침표를 찍었다는 점을 밝혀둡니다.

1. 아주 많은 사람들이 대도시에서 살며 일한다.

   很多人在大城市生活工作。

   非常に多くの人々が大都市に住みながら働いている。

2. 나는 그 남자가 다재다능하다고 생각한다.

   我认为那个男人多才多艺。

   私はその男が多才多能だと思う。

3. 사람들은 습관적으로 담배를 피운다.

   人们习惯性地抽烟。

   人々は習慣的にタバコを吸う。

4. 사람들은 피가 물보다 더 진하다고 말한다.

   人们说血浓于水。

   人々は水より血の方が濃いと言う。

영어는 **후치수식**, 한중일어는 **전치수식**

1. **A great number of people live and work in large cities.**

    A great number of people who live and work in large cities.
    A great number of people that live and work in large cities.
    A great number of people living and working in large cities.

2. **I think the man is versatile.**

    I think the man versatile.
    I think the man to be versatile.

    The man who I think is versatile.
    The man that I think is versatile.
    The man whom I think versatile.
    The man who I think versatile.
    The man that I think versatile.
    The man whom I think to be versatile.
    The man who I think to be versatile.
    The man that I think to be versatile.
    The man I think versatile.
    The man I think to be versatile.

3. **People smoke habitually.**

    People who smoke habitually.
    People that smoke habitually.
    People smoking habitually.

4. **People say blood is thicker than water.**

    People who say blood is thicker than water.
    People that say blood is thicker than water.
    People saying blood is thicker than water.

01

관계 대명사 (Relative Pronoun)

5. 사람들은 해산물을 먹는 것을 무척 좋아한다.

    人们很喜欢吃海鲜。

    人々は海産物を食べるのが大好きだ。

6. 그들은 자신들이 받는 것보다 더 많은 것을 기꺼이 준다.

    他们乐于奉献出比自己得到的更多的东西。

    彼らは自分たちが受けたものより多くのものを喜んでくれる。

7. 그들은 중요한 것은 어떤 것이든 다 하려고 노력한다.

    他们努力做所有重要的事情。

    彼らは重要なものはどんなものでもしようと努力する。

8. 의사는 자신의 환자를 치료하는 것을 결코 포기하지 않는다.

    医生绝对不会放弃治疗他们的病人。

    医師は自分の患者を治療することを決して放棄しない。

9. 많은 자원봉사자가 가난한 사람을 위해서 일하고 있다.

    很多志愿者在为穷人工作。

    多くのボランティアが貧しい人のために働いている。

5. **People love to eat seafood.**

   People who love to eat seafood.
   People that love to eat seafood.
   People loving to eat seafood.

6. **They are willing to give more than they take.**

   People who are willing to give more than they take.
   People that are willing to give more than they take.
   People willing to give more than they take.

7. **They try to do anything important.**

   People who try to do anything important.
   People that try to do anything important.
   People trying to do anything important.

8. **Doctors never give up treating their patients.**

   Doctors who never give up treating their patients.
   Doctors that never give up treating their patients.
   Doctors never giving up treating their patients.

9. **Many volunteers are working for the poor.**

   Many volunteers who are working for the poor.
   Many volunteers that are working for the poor.
   Many volunteers working for the poor.

10. 나는 그 여학생이 영어를 말하는 데 유창하다고 믿고 있다.

我相信那个女学生能流利地说英语。

私はその女生徒が英語を流暢に話すと信じている。

11. 그들은 당뇨병과 고혈압으로 고생하고 있다.

由于糖尿病和高血压他们有困难的时期。

彼らは糖尿病と高血圧で苦労している。

12. 그는 자기 혼자의 힘으로 그 문제를 해결할 수 없다.

靠自己的能力他不能解决那个问题。

彼は自分一人の力でその問題を解決することはできない。

13. 그들은 가난하다는 것이 무엇인지를 안다.

他们知道贫穷是什么。

彼らは貧乏というものが何かを知っている。

10. I believe the girl is fluent in speaking English.

I believe the girl fluent in speaking English.
I believe the girl to be fluent in speaking English.

The girl who I believe is fluent in speaking English.
The girl that I believe is fluent in speaking English.
The girl whom I believe fluent in speaking English.
The girl who I believe fluent in speaking English.
The girl that I believe fluent in speaking English.
The girl whom I believe to be fluent in speaking English.
The girl who I believe to be fluent in speaking English.
The girl that I believe to be fluent in speaking English.
The girl I believe fluent in speaking English.
The girl I believe to be fluent in speaking English.

11. They suffer from diabetes and hypertension.

People who suffer from diabetes and hypertension.
People that suffer from diabetes and hypertension.
People suffering from diabetes and hypertension.

12. He can't solve the problem on his own.

The man who can't solve the problem on his own.
The man that can't solve the problem on his own.
The man not able to solve the problem on his own.
The man unable to solve the problem on his own.

13. They know what it is to be poor.

People who know what it is to be poor.
People that know what it is to be poor.
People knowing what it is to be poor.

14. **그 종업원들은 훌륭한 영어 구사력을 필요로 한다.**

那些职员需要出色的英语表达能力。

その従業員たちはすぐれた英語駆使力を必要とする。

15. **중년의 남자들이 극도의 스트레스로 고통받고 있다.**

中年男人因极大的压力饱受折磨。

中年の男たちが極度のストレスで苦しんでいる。

16. **몇몇 학생들은 자신의 손톱을 깨무는 버릇이 있다.**

某些学生有咬指甲的习惯。

若干の生徒たちは自分の爪をかむ癖がある。

17. **그녀는 그 후보자가 가장 적격이라고 생각한다.**

她觉得那个候选人最合适。

彼女はその候補者が一番適格だと思っている。

14. **The employees need a good command of English.**

The employees who need a good command of English.
The employees that need a good command of English.
The employees needing a good command of English.

15. **Middle-aged men suffer from extreme stress.**

Middle-aged men who suffer from extreme stress.
Middle-aged men that suffer from extreme stress.
Middle-aged men suffering from extreme stress.

16. **Some students have the habit of biting their nails.**

Some students who have the habit of biting their nails.
Some students that have the habit of biting their nails.
Some students having the habit of biting their nails.

17. **She thinks the candidate is most qualified.**

She thinks the candidate most qualified.
She thinks the candidate to be most qualified.

The candidate who she thinks is most qualified.
The candidate that she thinks is most qualified.
The candidate whom she thinks most qualified.
The candidate who she thinks most qualified.
The candidate that she thinks most qualified.
The candidate whom she thinks to be most qualified.
The candidate who she thinks to be most qualified.
The candidate that she thinks to be most qualified.
The candidate she thinks most qualified.
The candidate she thinks to be most qualified.

18. 그들은 스마트폰에 중독되어 있다.

    他们沉迷于智能手机。

    彼らはスマートフォンに中毒になっている。

19. 그들은 충분한 수면을 갖지 못하고 있다.

    他们没有足够的睡眠。

    彼らは十分な睡眠をとれていない。

20. 그는 자신이 행동하는 것과 말하는 것에 책임을 진다.

    他对自己的言行负责。

    彼は自分の行動と言動に責任を持つ。

21. 모든 사람은 대통령 선거에 깊은 관심이 있다.

    所有人对总统选举都很关心。

    すべての人は大統領選挙に深く関心がある。

22. 그들은 한자를 읽고 쓸 줄 모른다.

    他们不会读和写汉字。

    彼らは漢字を読み書きすることができない。

23. 그들은 온갖 종류의 시험으로 인해 스트레스를 받는다.

    由于各种测试他们受到压力。

    彼らはあらゆる種類の試験によってストレスを受ける。

18. **They are addicted to smart-phones.**

   People who are addicted to smart-phones.
   People that are addicted to smart-phones.
   People addicted to smart-phones.

19. **They don't get enough sleep.**

   Students who don't get enough sleep.
   Students that don't get enough sleep.
   Students not getting enough sleep.

20. **He is responsible for what he does and says.**

   The person who is responsible for what he does and says.
   The person that is responsible for what he does and says.
   The person responsible for what he does and says.

21. **Everyone is deeply interested in the presidential election.**

   Everyone who is deeply interested in the presidential election.
   Everyone that is deeply interested in the presidential election.
   Everyone deeply interested in the presidential election.

22. **They don't know how to read and write Chinese characters.**

   People who don't know how to read and write Chinese characters.
   People that don't know how to read and write Chinese characters.
   People not knowing how to read and write Chinese characters.

23. **They get stressed out because of all kinds of tests.**

   People who get stressed out because of all kinds of tests.
   People that get stressed out because of all kinds of tests.
   People getting stressed out because of all kinds of tests.

24. 그들은 너무 바빠서 식사할 시간도 없다.

　　他们太忙连吃饭的时间都没有。

　　彼らはとても忙しくて食事をする時間もない。

25. 한 어린이가 하마터면 차에 치일 뻔했다.

　　一个孩子险些被车撞了。

　　ある子供が危うく車にひかれるところだった。

26. 그들은 자신의 감정을 숨기지 않는다.

　　他们不隐藏自己的感情。

　　彼らは自分の感情を隠さない。

27. 많은 사람이 체중 문제를 갖고 있다.

　　很多人有体重问题。

　　多くの人が体重の問題を抱えている。

28. 그들은 이런 풍습에 익숙해 있지 않다.

　　他们不习惯这种习俗。

　　彼らはこのような風習に慣れていない。

29. 그들은 이런저런 이유로 직업을 바꾸고 싶어 한다.

　　他们想通过这样那样的理由换工作。

　　彼らはそんなこんな理由で職業を変えることを望んでいる。

24. **They are too busy to have time to eat.**

    People who are too busy to have time to eat.
    People that are too busy to have time to eat.
    People too busy to have time to eat.

25. **A child was nearly hit by a car.**

    A child who was nearly hit by a car.
    A child that was nearly hit by a car.
    A child nearly hit by a car.

26. **They do not hide their feelings.**

    People who do not hide their feelings.
    People that do not hide their feelings.
    People not hiding their feelings.

27. **Lots of people have a weight problem.**

    Lots of people who have a weight problem.
    Lots of people that have a weight problem.
    Lots of people having a weight problem.

28. **They are not used to this custom.**

    People who are not used to this custom.
    People that are not used to this custom.
    People not used to this custom.

29. **They want to change jobs for some reason or other.**

    People who want to change jobs for some reason or other.
    People that want to change jobs for some reason or other.
    People wanting to change jobs for some reason or other.

30. 그들은 다른 사람의 사정과 감정을 이해하려고 노력한다.

他们正在努力试图了解别人的情况和感情。

彼らは他人の事情と感情を理解しようと努力している。

31. 그는 결코 나를 추호도 실망시키지 않을 것이다.

他绝不会让我感到丝毫的失望。

彼は決して私を微塵も失望させないだろう。

32. 그녀는 나에게 더 열심히 노력하라고 격려해준다.

她鼓励我要更加努力工作。

彼女は私にもっと一生懸命努力しなさいと励ましてくれる。

33. 수의사는 우리의 말 못하는 아픈 동물 친구들을 치료해준다.

兽医对我们的不会说话的动物朋友们进行治疗。

獣医は痛いと話すことのできない動物を治療してくれる。

34. 모든 사람은 지금보다 더 행복해지려고 열심히 노력하고 있다.

所有人都在为了比现在更幸福积极地努力着。

すべての人は今よりもっと幸せになろうと一生懸命努力している。

35. 보행자들이 이어폰으로 음악을 듣고 있다.

行人在用耳机听音乐。

歩行者がイヤホンで音楽を聞いている。

30. **They try to understand other people's situations and feelings.**

People who try to understand other people's situations and feelings.
People that try to understand other people's situations and feelings.
People trying to understand other people's situations and feelings.

31. **He will never ever let me down.**

The person who will never ever let me down.
The person that will never ever let me down.

32. **She encourages me to work harder.**

The woman who encourages me to work harder.
The woman that encourages me to work harder.
The woman encouraging me to work harder.

33. **Veterinarians treat our silent sick animal friends.**

Veterinarians who treat our silent sick animal friends.
Veterinarians that treat our silent sick animal friends.
Veterinarians treating our silent sick animal friends.

34. **Everyone is working hard to be happier than now.**

Everyone who is working hard to be happier than now.
Everyone that is working hard to be happier than now.
Everyone working hard to be happier than now.

35. **Pedestrians are listening to music through earphones.**

Pedestrians who are listening to music through earphones.
Pedestrians that are listening to music through earphones.
Pedestrians listening to music through earphones.

36. 그들은 친절과 배려를 실천한다.

    他们实践亲切和关怀。

    彼らは親切と配慮を実践する。

37. 그들은 항상 클래식 음악을 들으면서 일한다.

    他们总是听着古典音乐工作。

    彼らはいつもクラシック音楽を聞きながら働いている。

38. 그들은 자신의 삶에 만족한다고 말한다.

    他们说他们满足于他们的生活。

    彼らは自分の人生に満足していると言う。

39. 그는 남들보다 더 사려 깊게 생각하고 행동한다.

    他比别人要更沉思地想过后才行动。

    彼は他人よりもっと思慮深く考えて行動する。

40. 우리 부모님이 오늘날까지 우리를 길러주시고 지원해주셨다.

    我们的父母直到今天养育支持我们。

    私たちの両親が今日まで私たちを育て、支援してくれた。

41. 그 비서는 영어와 중국어를 둘 다 말할 줄 안다.

    那个秘书英语和汉语两种语言都会说。

    その秘書は英語と中国語の両方を話すことができる。

36. **They practice kindness and consideration.**

People who practice kindness and consideration.
People that practice kindness and consideration.
People practicing kindness and consideration.

37. **They always work while listening to classical music.**

People who always work while listening to classical music.
People that always work while listening to classical music.
People always working while listening to classical music.

38. **They say that they are content with their life.**

People who say that they are content with their life.
People that say that they are content with their life.
People saying that they are content with their life.

39. **He thinks and acts more considerately than others.**

The person who thinks and acts more considerately than others.
The person that thinks and acts more considerately than others.
The person thinking and acting more considerately than others.

40. **Our parents have reared and supported us until today.**

Our parents who have reared and supported us until today.
Our parents that have reared and supported us until today.

41. **The secretary can speak both English and Chinese.**
The secretary is able to speak both English and Chinese.

The secretary who can speak both English and Chinese.
The secretary that can speak both English and Chinese.
The secretary who is able to speak both English and Chinese.
The secretary that is able to speak both English and Chinese.
The secretary able to speak both English and Chinese.

42. 그들은 초만원인 지하철을 타려고 애를 쓰고 있다.

    他们正在试图乘坐拥挤的地铁。

    彼らは超満員の地下鉄に乗ろうと頑張っている。

43. 사람들은 여러 가지 이유로 다른 나라로 이민을 간다.

    人们由于各种原因移民到其他国家。

    人々はさまざまな理由で他の国へ移住する。

44. 그 철학자는 인간의 마음에 대한 예리한 통찰력을 가지고 있다.

    那位哲学家对人的心灵有敏锐的洞察力。

    その哲学者は人間の心に対する鋭い洞察力を持っている。

45. 그들은 비상사태가 발생할 경우에 무엇을 해야 할지 알고 있다.

    他们知道在紧急情况下该怎么办。

    彼らは非常事態が発生した場合に何をすべきか知っている。

46. 그들은 이상적인 남성이나 여성을 찾고 있다.

    他们正在寻找理想的男人和女人。

    彼らは理想的な男性や女性を探している。

47. 그 학자는 지적인 즐거움이 가장 지속적인 것이라고 말한다.

    那位学者说知识的乐趣是最持久的。

    その学者は知的な楽しさが最も持続的なものだと言う。

42. They are trying to get on the overcrowded subway.

People who are trying to get on the overcrowded subway.
People that are trying to get on the overcrowded subway.
People trying to get on the overcrowded subway.

43. People move to other countries for various reasons.

People who move to other countries for various reasons.
People that move to other countries for various reasons.
People moving to other countries for various reasons.

44. The philosopher has a keen insight into the human mind.

The philosopher who has a keen insight into the human mind.
The philosopher that has a keen insight into the human mind.
The philosopher having a keen insight into the human mind.

45. They know what to do in case of an emergency.

People who know what to do in case of an emergency.
People that know what to do in case of an emergency.
People knowing what to do in case of an emergency.

46. They are searching for Mr. or Ms. Right.

People who are searching for Mr. or Ms. Right.
People that are searching for Mr. or Ms. Right.
People searching for Mr. or Ms. Right.

47. The scholar says that intellectual pleasure is the most lasting.

The scholar who says that intellectual pleasure is the most lasting.
The scholar that says that intellectual pleasure is the most lasting.
The scholar saying that intellectual pleasure is the most lasting.

48. 그들은 자신의 세계보다 더 큰 세계가 있다는 것을 모르고 있다.

他们不知道有比自己的世界更大的世界。

彼らは自分の世界よりもっと大きな世界があるということを知らずにいる。

49. 그들은 교육이 인생의 성공으로 가는 열쇠라고 믿는다.

他们认为教育是人生成功的钥匙。

彼らは教育が人生の成功への鍵だと信じている。

50. 그는 자신이 지금까지 직접 보지 않은 것은 어떤 것도 믿지 않는다.

他不相信不能直接看到的任何东西。

彼は自分が今まで直接見なかったことはいかなることも信じない。

48. **They don't know there is a larger world than their own.**

People who don't know there is a larger world than their own.
People that don't know there is a larger world than their own.
People not knowing there is a larger world than their own.

49. **They believe that education is the key to success in life.**

People who believe that education is the key to success in life.
People that believe that education is the key to success in life.
People believing that education is the key to success in life.

50. **He doesn't believe anything he hasn't seen for himself.**

The person who doesn't believe anything he hasn't seen for himself.
The person that doesn't believe anything he hasn't seen for himself.
The person not believing anything he hasn't seen for himself.

2. 관계 대명사 Whose
(소유격/Genitive)

여기서 말하는 관계 대명사 whose는 선행사가 사람인 경우에 사용하는 소유격 관계 대명사를 뜻한다. 구조는 '선행사 + whose + 명사'의 형태로 되어 있고, 해석은 '누구의 ~이/가 ~한 사람' 또는 '누구의 ~을/를 누가 ~한 사람'으로 할 수 있겠다.

여기서 주의할 점은 관계 대명사 whose는 선행사가 동물이나 사물인 경우에도 사용될 수 있다는 점이다. 선행사가 동물이나 사물인 경우에도 구조는 선행사가 사람인 경우와 같다.

관계 대명사 who와 마찬가지로 관계 대명사 whose도 접속사와 대명사의 기능을 하면서 선행사인 명사를 후치수식하는 형용사절을 이끈다.

관계 대명사 whose를 쓰는 경우가 관계 대명사 who를 쓰는 경우보다 빈도가 더 낮아서 우리에게 익숙하지 않아서인지 학습자들이 관계 대명사 whose를 사용하는데 좀 더 신경이 쓰일지 모르겠다. 하지만 우리가 인칭 대명사의 소유격을 사용하는 것을 어려워하지 않는 것처럼, 소유격 관계 대명사도 단순한 구조이므로 문법적인 설명보다는 여기에 있는 많은 예문들을 통해서 원어민처럼 자연스럽게 듣고 말하고 읽고 쓸 수 있도록 연습해주기 바란다.

여기서 "그의 세계 평화에 대한 기여는 지금까지 두드러지게 돋보였다."라는 문장을 '세계 평화에 대한 그의 기여가 지금까지 두드러지게 돋보였던 외교관'이라는 명사 후치수식 구문으로 전환시켜보면 다음과 같이 할 수 있겠다.

His contribution to world peace has been outstanding.

The diplomat whose contribution to world peace has been outstanding. (관계 대명사 whose)

학습자들의 영어 실력을 쉽고 빠르게 그리고 폭발적으로 향상시켜 줄 수 있는 확실한 한 가지 방법은 보통의 일반 문장을 명사 후치수식 구문으로 자유자재로 전환시킬 수 있는 능력을 가능한 한 빨리 습득하는 것이라는 점을 깊이 인식하고 많은 연습을 해주기 바란다.

1. 그들의 마음은 순수하다.

    他们的心是纯洁的。
    彼らの心は純粋だ。

2. 그 학생의 아버지는 물리학자이다.

    那个学生的父亲是物理学家。
    その生徒の父親は物理学者である。

3. 그 어린이의 부모님은 돌아가셨다.

    那个孩子的父母去世了。
    その子供の両親は亡くなった。

4. 그의 아들은 유명한 정치인이다.

    他的儿子是一个著名的政治家。
    彼の息子は有名な政治家だ。

5. 피의자의 진술은 완전히 믿을 수 없다.

    嫌疑人的陈述是完全不可靠的。
    被疑者の供述は完全に信じられない。

6. 그녀의 이름은 내 이름과 똑같다.

    她的名字和我的名字一样。
    彼女の名前は私の名前と同じだ。

7. 그들의 모국어는 영어가 아니다.

    他们的母语不是英语。
    彼らの母国語は英語ではない。

1. **Their hearts are pure.**

   People whose hearts are pure.

2. **The student's father is a physicist.**

   The student whose father is a physicist.

3. **The child's parents are dead.**

   The child whose parents are dead.

4. **His son is a famous politician.**

   The man whose son is a famous politician.

5. **The suspect's statement is totally unreliable.**

   The suspect whose statement is totally unreliable.

6. **Her name is the same as mine.**

   The friend whose name is the same as mine.

7. **Their native language is not English.**

   People whose native language is not English.

8. 그녀의 아들은 감옥에 수감되어 있다.

   她的儿子被关押在监狱。

   彼女の息子は刑務所に収監されている。

9. 그녀의 인생은 슬픔과 후회로 가득 차 있다.

   她的生活充满了悲伤和悔恨。

   彼女の人生は悲しみと後悔に満ちている。

10. 그들의 취미는 꽃을 재배하는 것이다.

    他们的爱好是种花。

    彼らの趣味は花を育てることだ。

11. 그 미국인 교수의 중국어는 내 중국어보다 더 낫다.

    那位美国教授的中文比我的还好。

    そのアメリカ人教授の中国語は私の中国語よりましだ。

12. 그녀의 미모는 대적할 만한 사람이 없다.

    她的美貌是无与伦比的。

    彼女の美貌に太刀打ちできる人はいない。

13. 그들은 자신의 이름을 한자로 쓸 수 없다.

    他们不能用汉字写自己的名字。

    彼らは自分の名前を漢字で書くことができない。

14. 그들의 생일은 1월 1일이다.

    他们的生日是1月1日。

    彼らの誕生日は1月1日だ。

8. **Her son is in prison.**

   A mother whose son is in prison.

9. **Her life is full of sorrow and regret.**

   A woman whose life is full of sorrow and regret.

10. **Their hobby is growing flowers.**

    People whose hobby is growing flowers.

11. **The American professor's Chinese is better than mine.**

    The American professor whose Chinese is better than mine.

12. **Her beauty is unequalled.**

    The woman whose beauty is unequalled.

13. **They cannot write their own names in Chinese characters.**

    People whose own names they cannot write in Chinese characters.

14. **Their birthdays are on January 1.**

    People whose birthdays are on January 1.

15. 그의 어머니는 지금까지 약 한 달 동안 병원에 입원해 계셨다.

迄今为止他的母亲已经在医院呆了大约一个月。

彼の母親はこれまで約一ヶ月の間病院に入院していた。

16. 그들의 생각은 대다수의 사람과 다르다.

他们的想法与大多数人不同。

彼らの考えは大多数の人と違う。

17. 그들은 살날이 얼마 남지 않았다.

他们生活没剩下多少活的日子了。

彼らの余命はあまり残っていない。

18. 그녀의 사진이 지금 잡지 표지에 나왔다.

她的照片如今出现在杂志封面。

彼女の写真が雑誌の表紙に載った。

19. 그들은 자신의 어려움을 스스로 극복해야 한다.

他们必须克服自己的困难。

彼らは自分の困難を自ら克服しなければならない。

20. 그 작가의 소설은 찬사를 받고 있다.

那位作家的小说受到敬佩。

その作家の小説は賛辞を受けている。

21. 그들의 비자는 이번 달에 만료될 예정이다.

他们的签证将于本月过期。

彼らのビザは今月に満了になる予定だ。

15. **His mother has been in hospital for about a month.**

    The friend whose mother has been in hospital for about a month.

16. **Their thoughts are different from the majority of people.**

    People whose thoughts are different from the majority of people.

17. **Their days are numbered.**

    People whose days are numbered.

18. **Her picture has appeared on the magazine cover.**

    The girl whose picture has appeared on the magazine cover.

19. **They have to overcome their difficulties on their own.**

    People whose difficulties they have to overcome on their own.

20. **The writer's novel is admired.**

    The writer whose novel is admired.

21. **Their visas are due to be expired this month.**

    People whose visas are due to be expired this month.

22. 그 학자의 친구들은 전 세계에 흩어져 있다.

    那位学者的朋友们分散在世界各地。

    その学者の友達は全世界に点在している。

23. 그의 아버지는 지금 폐암으로 돌아가셨다.

    他的父亲死于肺癌。

    彼の父親はいま肺がんで亡くなった。

24. 그녀의 부모님은 거액의 돈을 자선단체에 기부했다.

    她的父母向慈善机构捐赠了大量的钱。

    彼女の両親は巨額のお金を慈善団体に寄付した。

25. 그녀의 우산에는 구멍이 나 있다.

    她的伞有一个洞。

    彼女の傘には穴があいている。

26. 그 군인들의 시신은 지금까지 결코 발견되지 않았다.

    那些军人的尸体至今还没有被发现。

    その軍人たちの遺体は今まで決して発見されなかった。

27. 그 운동선수들의 세계기록은 지금까지 깨지지 않았다.

    那些运动员的世界纪录迄今为止没有被打破。

    その運動選手たちの世界記録はこれまで破られなかった。

28. 그들의 풍습과 문화는 우리와 크게 다르다.

    他们的习俗和文化与我们的有很大的不同。

    彼らの風習と文化は私たちのものと大きく異なる。

22. **The scholar's friends are scattered all over the world.**

    The scholar whose friends are scattered all over the world.

23. **His father has died of lung cancer.**

    The student whose father has died of lung cancer.

24. **Her parents donated a large sum of money to a charity.**

    The girl whose parents donated a large sum of money to a charity.

25. **Her umbrella has a hole in it.**

    A girl whose umbrella has a hole in it.

26. **The soldiers' bodies have never been found.**

    The soldiers whose bodies have never been found.

27. **The athletes' world records have not been broken.**

    The athletes whose world records have not been broken.

28. **Their customs and cultures are greatly different from ours.**

    People whose customs and cultures are greatly different from ours.

29. 그 대통령의 연설은 아주 훌륭하다.

那位总统的演讲非常精彩。

その大統領の演説は非常にすばらしい。

30. 그녀의 개가 길에서 보행인을 물어버렸다.

她的狗在街上咬了行人。

彼女の犬が道で歩行者を噛んだ。

31. 그의 얼굴은 땀으로 뒤범벅이 되어 있다.

他满脸都是汗水。

彼の顔は汗でぐちゃぐちゃになっている。

32. 그 가수의 노래는 많은 면에서 나의 마음을 감동시킨다.

那位歌手的歌在许多方面打动我的心。

その歌手の歌は多くの面で私の心を感動させる。

33. 그 난민들의 국적은 시리아이다.

那些难民的国籍是叙利亚。

その難民たちの国籍はシリアだ。

34. 그의 조국에 대한 헌신은 너무 훌륭해서 믿어지지 않게 보인다.

他对祖国的奉献非常出色简直不能相信。

彼の祖国に対する献身はあまりにも立派で信じられない。

35. 그들의 성격은 항상 쾌활하다.

他们的性格总是快乐。

彼らの性格はいつも陽気だ。

29. **The president's address is excellent.**

   The president whose address is excellent.

30. **Her dog bit a pedestrian on the street.**

   The woman whose dog bit a pedestrian on the street.

31. **His face is covered with sweat.**

   The man whose face is covered with sweat.

32. **The singer's songs touch my heart in many ways.**

   The singer whose songs touch my heart in many ways.

33. **The refugees' nationality is Syria.**

   The refugees whose nationality is Syria.

34. **His dedication to his country appears too good to be true.**

   The man whose dedication to his country appears too good to be true.

35. **Their personality is always cheerful.**

   People whose personality is always cheerful.

36. 그들의 사고방식은 성리학에 기반을 두고 있다.

他们的思维方式是基于性理学。

彼らの考え方は性理学に基づいている。

37. 저 젊은이들의 행동은 우리의 눈살을 찌푸리게 한다.

那些年轻人的行为使我们皱眉。

あの若者たちの行動は我々の眉をひそめさせる。

38. 그 범인의 강도질을 저지른 동기는 아직 밝혀지지 않았다.

那个罪犯抢劫的动机还没有被揭露。

その犯人の強盗を犯した動機はまだわかっていない。

39. 그들의 부모는 그들을 재정적으로 지원해줄 수 없다.

他们的父母不能在经济上支持他们。

彼らの両親は彼らを財政的に支援することはできない。

40. 그들의 일상생활은 미세먼지로 위협받고 있다.

他们的日常生活受着微尘的威胁。

彼らの日常生活はPM2.5に脅かされている。

41. 그 의사의 이 분야에서의 명성은 타의 추종을 불허한다.

那位医生在这个领域的声誉是无与伦比的。

その医者のこの分野における名声は他の追随を許さない。

42. 그 정치인의 국민에 대한 애정은 유난히 강하다.

那位政治家对人民的爱非常强烈。

その政治家の国民に対する愛情はとりわけ強い。

36. **Their way of thinking is based on Neo-Confucianism.**

People whose way of thinking is based on Neo-Confucianism.

37. **The young people's behavior makes us frown.**

The young people whose behavior makes us frown.

38. **The culprit's motive for committing a robbery is not yet revealed.**

The culprit whose motive for committing a robbery is not yet revealed.

39. **Their parents can't support them financially.**

The students whose parents can't support them financially.

40. **Their daily lives are threatened by fine dust.**

People whose daily lives are threatened by fine dust.

41. **The doctor's reputation in this field is unsurpassed.**

The doctor whose reputation in this field is unsurpassed.

42. **The statesman's love for the people is exceptionally strong.**

The statesman whose love for the people is exceptionally strong.

43. 그 축구선수의 지구력은 돋보인다.

那位足球运动员的耐力非常突出。

そのサッカー選手の持久力は目立つ。

44. 그 민족의 조상이 문자 체계를 만들었다.

那个民族的祖先创造了书写系统。

その民族の先祖が文字体系を作った。

45. 그들의 모국어는 더 이상 사용되지 않는다.

他们的母语不再使用。

彼らの母国語はこれ以上使用されない。

46. 그들의 학업성적은 지금까지 상당히 많이 향상되었다.

他们的成绩提高了不少。

彼らの学業成績は今までかなり向上した。

47. 그 피겨 스케이팅 선수의 연기는 폭넓은 찬사를 받고 있다.

那位花样滑冰运动员的表演受到广泛好评。

そのフィギュアスケート選手の演技は幅広い賛辞を受けている。

48. 항공 교통 관제사들의 역할은 항공 안전에서 대단히 중요하다.

空中交通管制员的作用在航空安全方面非常重要。

航空交通管制官の役割は航空安全において非常に重要だ。

49. 우리는 그분들의 사랑과 헌신을 말로 다 표현할 수 없다.

我们无法用言语描述他们的爱和奉献。

私たちは彼らの愛と献身を言葉ですべて表現できない。

43. The soccer player's endurance is outstanding.

The soccer player whose endurance is outstanding.

44. The people's ancestors created the writing system.

The people whose ancestors created the writing system.

45. Their native language is no longer spoken.

People whose native language is no longer spoken.

46. Their school grades have improved quite a lot.

The students whose school grades have improved quite a lot.

47. The figure skater's performances receive widespread acclaim.

The figure skater whose performances receive widespread acclaim.

48. Air traffic controllers' role is critical in aviation safety.

Air traffic controllers whose role is critical in aviation safety.

49. We cannot describe their love and devotion with words.

People whose love and devotion we cannot describe with words.

50. 그들의 영어 구사력은 흠잡을 데 없다.

他们的英语运用能力是无可挑剔的。

彼らの英語の駆使能力は完璧だ。

50. **Their command of English is flawless.**

People whose command of English is flawless.

3. 관계 대명사 Whom/Who
(목적격/Objective)

관계 대명사 whom 또는 who는 선행사가 사람인 경우에 사용하는 목적격 관계 대명사이다. 구조는 '선행사 + whom/who + 주어' 또는 '선행사 + 전치사 + whom + 주어'로 되어 있고 동사의 목적어나 전치사의 목적어로 사용된다. 해석은 '주어가 ~하는 사람'으로 하면 되겠다. 문법적으로 관계 대명사 whom 또는 who는 접속사와 대명사의 역할을 하면서 선행사인 명사를 후치수식하는 형용사절의 기능을 담당하고 있다.

여기서 몇 가지 주의할 점이 있는데, 첫째, 목적격 관계 대명사 whom 또는 who는 주격 관계 대명사 who처럼 관계 대명사 that으로 바꿔 쓸 수 있다. 이 점은 주격 관계 대명사 who에서도 언급했듯이 목적격 관계 대명사 that은 선행사가 사람이든 동물이든 사물이든 명사는 모두 다 수식할 수 있기 때문이다.

둘째, 목적격 관계 대명사 whom 또는 who는 생략할 수 있다. 그 이유 중 하나는 선행사와 목적격 관계 대명사가 이끄는 형용사절이 매우 밀접한 관계에 있어서 관계 대명사를 생략하여도 의미의 혼란이 일어나지 않기 때문이다. 또 하나의 이유는 같은 말을 두 번 반복하고 싶어 하지 않는 경향 때문이다.

셋째, 관계 대명사 whom 또는 who가 전치사의 목적어일 경우에는 전치사가 관계 대명사 whom과 붙어 있을 수도 있고, 관계 대명사 whom 또는 who와 떨어져서 뒤에 올 수도 있다.

넷째, 목적격 관계 대명사 that 앞에는 전치사를 쓸 수 없다. 다시 말하면, 목적격 관계 대명사 whom 또는 who 대신에 that을 쓸 경우에는 that 앞에 전치사를 쓰지 못하고 전치사를 뒤에 두어야 한다는 것이다.

마지막 다섯째로, 북미 영어권에서 특히 구어체에서 관계 대명사 whom과 의문 대명사 whom은 거의 사용되지 않고 대신에 who를 사용한다는 점이다. 그러나 이것은 구어체에서 얘기고 문어체에서는 문법에 맞는 글이라는 것을 보여주기 위해서 정확하게 whom을 쓰는 것이 더 좋겠다. 특별히 주의할 것은 전치사 다음에는 반드시 whom을 써야지 who를 써서는 안 된다는 것이다.

여기서 "나는 그들과 지금까지 긴밀한 접촉을 유지해 오고 있다."라는 문장을 '내가 지금까지 긴밀한 접촉을 유지해 오고 있는 사람들'이라는 명사 후치수식 구문으로 전환시켜보면 다음과 같이 할 수 있겠다.

I have kept in close contact with them.

1. People whom I have kept in close contact with.
2. People who I have kept in close contact with.
3. People with whom I have kept in close contact.
4. People that I have kept in close contact with.
5. People I have kept in close contact with.

1. 목적격 관계 대명사 whom
2. 목적격 관계 대명사 who
3. 전치사 + 목적격 관계 대명사 whom
4. 목적격 관계 대명사 that
5. 목적격 관계 대명사 생략

위의 다섯 가지 예문 가운데서 구어체에서는 5번과 2번, 4번 예문이 일반적으로 더 많이 사용되고, 1번과 3번은 주로 문어체에서 사용된다. 하지만 거리끼지 말고 위 다섯 가지 예문을 모두 다 자유롭게 사용할 수 있도록 충분히 연습해주기 바란다.

1. 나는 그 선생님을 존경한다.

    我尊敬那位老师。

    私はその先生を尊敬している。

2. 나는 지금까지 그 학생들과 얘기했다.

    我跟那些学生谈话一直到现在。

    私は今までその生徒たちと話した。

3. 나는 어제 그 친구와 같이 영화관에 갔다.

    我昨天和那位朋友一起去电影院了。

    私は昨日その友達と一緒に映画館に行った。

4. 나는 그에게 의지할 수 있다.

    我可以靠他。

    私は彼に頼ることができる。

영어는 후치수식, 한중일어는 전치수식

1. **I admire the teacher.**

   The teacher whom I admire.
   The teacher who I admire.
   The teacher that I admire.
   The teacher I admire.

2. **I have talked with the students.**

   The students whom I have talked with.
   The students who I have talked with.
   The students with whom I have talked.
   The students that I have talked with.
   The students I have talked with.

3. **I went to the movies with the friend yesterday.**

   The friend whom I went to the movies with yesterday.
   The friend who I went to the movies with yesterday.
   The friend with whom I went to the movies yesterday.
   The friend that I went to the movies with yesterday.
   The friend I went to the movies with yesterday.

4. **I can depend on him.**

   The man whom I can depend on.
   The man who I can depend on.
   The man on whom I can depend.
   The man that I can depend on.
   The man I can depend on.

5. 나는 그녀와 같이 가고 싶다.

　　我想和她一起去。
　　私は彼女と一緒に行きたい。

6. 나는 그들을 좋아하고 존경한다.

　　我喜欢并且尊敬他们。
　　私は彼らが好きで尊敬する。

7. 나는 매주 일요일마다 그들과 함께 축구를 한다.

　　我每个星期天和他们一起踢足球。
　　私は毎週日曜日に彼らと一緒にサッカーをしている。

8. 나는 술 한잔하기 위해서 그들을 불러낼 수 있다.

　　我为了喝一杯酒可以叫他们出来。
　　私は一杯のお酒を飲むために彼らを呼び出せる。

9. 사람들은 그녀를 천사라고 부른다.

　　他们称她为天使。
　　人々は彼女のことを天使と呼ぶ。

5. **I want to go with her.**

   The woman whom I want to go with.
   The woman who I want to go with.
   The woman with whom I want to go.
   The woman that I want to go with.
   The woman I want to go with.

6. **I like and admire them.**

   The people whom I like and admire.
   The people who I like and admire.
   The people that I like and admire.
   The people I like and admire.

7. **I play soccer with them every Sunday.**

   People whom I play soccer with every Sunday.
   People who I play soccer with every Sunday.
   People with whom I play soccer every Sunday.
   People that I play soccer with every Sunday.
   People I play soccer with every Sunday.

8. **I can call them out to have a drink.**

   The friends whom I can call out to have a drink.
   The friends who I can call out to have a drink.
   The friends that I can call out to have a drink.
   The friends I can call out to have a drink.

9. **They call her an angel.**

   The girl whom they call an angel.
   The girl who they call an angel.
   The girl that they call an angel.
   The girl they call an angel.

10. 그는 그 젊은 매력적인 아가씨와 결혼했으면 한다.

他想和那位年轻有魅力的女孩儿结婚。

彼はその若い魅力的な女性と結婚することを望んでいる。

11. 나는 그에게 커다란 존경심을 갖고 있다.

我非常尊重他。

私は彼に大きな尊敬心を持っている。

12. 나는 어제 길에서 나의 한 옛 친구를 만났다.

我昨天在路上遇见了我的一个老朋友。

私は昨日道ばたで私の昔の友達に会った。

13. 나는 항상 그에게 속마음을 털어놓을 수 있다.

我可以经常向他透露我的心。

私はいつも彼に本心を打ち明けることができる。

14. 그녀는 그를 회사 자금을 횡령한 것 때문에 해고했다.

因为挪用公司资金她解雇了他。

彼女は彼を会社の資金を横領したことで解雇した。

10. He would like to marry the young attractive girl.

The young attractive girl whom he would like to marry.
The young attractive girl who he would like to marry.
The young attractive girl that he would like to marry.
The young attractive girl he would like to marry.

11. I have great respect for him.

The person whom I have great respect for.
The person who I have great respect for.
The person for whom I have great respect.
The person that I have great respect for.
The person I have great respect for.

12. I met an old friend of mine on the street yesterday.

An old friend of mine whom I met on the street yesterday.
An old friend of mine who I met on the street yesterday.
An old friend of mine that I met on the street yesterday.
An old friend of mine I met on the street yesterday.

13. I can always confide in him.

The friend whom I can always confide in.
The friend who I can always confide in.
The friend in whom I can always confide.
The friend that I can always confide in.
The friend I can always confide in.

14. She fired him for embezzling company funds.

The man whom she fired for embezzling company funds.
The man who she fired for embezzling company funds.
The man that she fired for embezzling company funds.
The man she fired for embezzling company funds.

15. 나는 그 선생님을 잊을 수 없다.

我不能忘记那位老师。

私はその先生を忘れられない。

16. 모든 사람은 이름만 들으면 그를 안다.

任何人只要听到他的名字就知道他。

すべての人が名前を聞いただけでも彼を知ることができる。

17. 나는 그들과 함께 캐나다에 갔었다.

我和他们一起去过加拿大。

私は彼らとともにカナダに行った。

18. 그녀는 예전에 자신의 손주들에게 기저귀를 갈아주곤 했었다.

她以前经常给自己的孙子们换尿布。

彼女は以前に自分の孫のおむつを取り替えてあげたりしていた。

19. 나는 어젯밤 파티에서 그녀를 만났다.

我昨晚在聚会上见到她了。

私は昨夜パーティーで彼女に会った。

15. I cannot forget the teacher.

The teacher whom I cannot forget.
The teacher who I cannot forget.
The teacher that I cannot forget.
The teacher I cannot forget.

16. Everyone recognizes him by name.

The person whom everyone recognizes by name.
The person who everyone recognizes by name.
The person that everyone recognizes by name.
The person everyone recognizes by name.

17. I went to Canada with them.

The friends whom I went to Canada with.
The friends who I went to Canada with.
The friends with whom I went to Canada.
The friends that I went to Canada with.
The friends I went to Canada with.

18. She used to diaper her grandchildren.

Grandchildren whom she used to diaper.
Grandchildren who she used to diaper.
Grandchildren that she used to diaper.
Grandchildren she used to diaper.

19. I met her at the party last night.

The girl whom I met at the party last night.
The girl who I met at the party last night.
The girl that I met at the party last night.
The girl I met at the party last night.

20. 나는 그에게서 스키 타는 법을 배웠다.

   我从他那儿学会了滑雪的方法。

   私は彼からスキーの滑り方を学んだ。

21. 나는 결코 도대체 그들에게 보답할 수 없을 것이다.

   我永远不可能报答他们。

   私は決して彼らに恩返しできないだろう。

22. 그들은 그 정치지도자를 무척 존경한다.

   他们非常尊敬那位政治领导人。

   彼らはその政治指導者をとても尊敬している。

23. 그는 지금까지 자신의 부모님에게 반항해왔다.

   他到迄今为止都在反抗他的父母。

   彼は今まで自分の両親に反抗してきた。

24. 그 사람보다 그 주제에 관해서 더 훌륭한 권위자는 없다.

   关于那个主题没有比他更优秀的权威人士。

   その人よりそのテーマに関して優れた権威者はいない。

20. **I learned to ski from him.**

   The person whom I learned to ski from.
   The person who I learned to ski from.
   The person from whom I learned to ski.
   The person that I learned to ski from.
   The person I learned to ski from.

21. **I could never possibly repay them.**

   People whom I could never possibly repay.
   People who I could never possibly repay.
   People that I could never possibly repay.
   People I could never possibly repay.

22. **They admire the political leader so much.**

   The political leader whom they admire so much.
   The political leader who they admire so much.
   The political leader that they admire so much.
   The political leader they admire so much.

23. **He has defied his own parents.**

   His own parents whom he has defied.
   His own parents who he has defied.
   His own parents that he has defied.
   His own parents he has defied.

24. **There is no better authority on the subject than him.**

   The scholar whom there is no better authority on the subject than.
   The scholar who there is no better authority on the subject than.
   The scholar than whom there is no better authority on the subject.
   The scholar that there is no better authority on the subject than.
   The scholar there is no better authority on the subject than.

25. 우리는 그 운동선수를 자랑스러워한다.

   我们为那位运动员感到自豪。

   私たちはその運動選手を誇りに思っている。

26. 그녀는 지금까지 그들과 오랫동안 교제해왔다.

   她一直和他们长期交往。

   彼女は今まで彼らと長い間付き合ってきた。

27. 나는 지금까지 그들이 예의 바르다고 생각했었다.

   我认为他们很有礼貌。

   私は今まで彼らが礼儀正しいと思っていた。

28. 우리는 그들이 행복하다고 말할 수 있다.

   我们可以说他们很幸福。

   我々は彼らが幸せであると言える。

29. 나는 그와 내가 할 수 있는 어떤 식으로든 협력하고 싶다.

   我想和他合作用任何我可以的方式。

   私は彼と私ができるどんな形であれ協力したい。

25. **We are proud of the athlete.**

   The athlete whom we are proud of.
   The athlete who we are proud of.
   The athlete of whom we are proud.
   The athlete that we are proud of.
   The athlete we are proud of.

26. **She has kept company with them for a long time.**

   People whom she has kept company with for a long time.
   People who she has kept company with for a long time.
   People with whom she has kept company for a long time.
   People that she has kept company with for a long time.
   People she has kept company with for a long time.

27. **I have considered them to be courteous.**

   People whom I have considered to be courteous.
   People who I have considered to be courteous.
   People that I have considered to be courteous.
   People I have considered to be courteous.

28. **We can call them happy.**

   People whom we can call happy.
   People who we can call happy.
   People that we can call happy.
   People we can call happy.

29. **I want to cooperate with him in any way I can.**

   The person whom I want to cooperate with in any way I can.
   The person who I want to cooperate with in any way I can.
   The person with whom I want to cooperate in any way I can.
   The person that I want to cooperate with in any way I can.
   The person I want to cooperate with in any way I can.

30. 그녀는 그들과 빈번하게 접촉하고 있다.

　　她频繁地与他们接触。

　　彼女は彼らと頻繁に接触している。

31. 나는 그들에게 편안함을 느낀다.

　　我对他们感到很舒服。

　　私は彼らから安らぎを感じる。

32. 나는 그 친구들과 같은 마을에서 같이 자랐다.

　　我和那些朋友们在同一村庄一起长大的。

　　私はその友達と同じ村で一緒に育った。

33. 나는 그 친구들과 함께 같은 초등학교에 다녔다.

　　我和那些朋友们一起上同一所小学。

　　私はその友達と一緒に同じ小学校に通った。

34. 나는 지금까지 항상 그를 부러워했다.

　　我一直羡慕他。

　　私は今までいつも彼を羨ましがった。

30. She comes in frequent contact with them.

People whom she comes in frequent contact with.
People who she comes in frequent contact with.
People with whom she comes in frequent contact.
People that she comes in frequent contact with.
People she comes in frequent contact with.

31. I feel comfortable with them.

People whom I feel comfortable with.
People who I feel comfortable with.
People with whom I feel comfortable.
People that I feel comfortable with.
People I feel comfortable with.

32. I grew up with the friends in the same village.

The friends whom I grew up with in the same village.
The friends who I grew up with in the same village.
The friends with whom I grew up in the same village.
The friends that I grew up with in the same village.
The friends I grew up with in the same village.

33. I went to the same elementary school with the friends.

The friends whom I went to the same elementary school with.
The friends who I went to the same elementary school with.
The friends with whom I went to the same elementary school.
The friends that I went to the same elementary school with.
The friends I went to the same elementary school with.

34. I have always envied him.

The person whom I have always envied.
The person who I have always envied.
The person that I have always envied.
The person I have always envied.

35. 나는 지금까지 오랫동안 그들을 알고 지냈다.

我已经认识他们很长时间了。

私は今まで長い間彼らを知っていた。

36. 나는 사무실에서 그들과 함께 일한다.

我在办公室和他们一起工作。

私はオフィスで彼らと働いている。

37. 나는 지금까지 그가 정직하다고 믿었다.

我一直相信他是诚实的。

私は今まで彼が正直だと信じていた。

38. 나는 그 친구들과 흉금을 터놓고 함께 얘기할 수 있다.

我可以和那些朋友们推心置腹交谈。

私はその友達と胸襟を開いて話すことができる。

39. 우리는 미국 원주민을 인도인이라고 잘못 알고 있다.

我们错误地认为美国原住民是印度人。

私たちはアメリカ先住民をインド人だと誤解している。

35. I have known them for a long time.

People whom I have known for a long time.
People who I have known for a long time.
People that I have known for a long time.
People I have known for a long time.

36. I work with them at the office.

People whom I work with at the office.
People who I work with at the office.
People with whom I work at the office.
People that I work with at the office.
People I work with at the office.

37. I have believed him to be honest.

The person whom I have believed to be honest.
The person who I have believed to be honest.
The person that I have believed to be honest.
The person I have believed to be honest.

38. I can have a heart-to-heart chat with the friends.

The friends whom I can have a heart-to-heart chat with.
The friends who I can have a heart-to-heart chat with.
The friends with whom I can have a heart-to-heart chat.
The friends that I can have a heart-to-heart chat with.
The friends I can have a heart-to-heart chat with.

39. We wrongly believe native Americans to be Indians.

Native Americans whom we wrongly believe to be Indians.
Native Americans who we wrongly believe to be Indians.
Native Americans that we wrongly believe to be Indians.
Native Americans we wrongly believe to be Indians.

40. 나는 여행 동안에 한 매력적인 캐나다 아가씨와 사귀었다.

我在旅途中与一个有魅力的加拿大女孩交往过。

私は旅行の間ある魅力的なカナダ人女性と付き合った。

41. 나는 지금까지 내 인생에서 결코 그들을 만난 적이 없다.

我从来没有在我的生活中遇到他们。

私は今まで人生で決して彼らに会ったことがない。

42. 나는 예전에 그 친구들과 같이 수영하러 다니곤 했었다.

我曾经和那些朋友们经常一起去游泳。

私は以前その友達と一緒に水泳しに行ったりした。

43. 나는 지금까지 그녀에게 결코 말도 걸어보지 못했다.

至今我从来没有和她说过话。

私は今まで彼女に決して言葉もかけることができなかった。

44. 우리는 그가 대단히 창의력이 있다고 생각했었다.

我们认为他很有创意。

私たちは彼が非常に創意力があると考えていた。

40. I made friends with an attractive Canadian girl during the trip.

An attractive Canadian girl whom I made friends with during the trip.
An attractive Canadian girl who I made friends with during the trip.
An attractive Canadian girl with whom I made friends during the trip.
An attractive Canadian girl that I made friends with during the trip.
An attractive Canadian girl I made friends with during the trip.

41. I have never met them in my life.

People whom I have never met in my life.
People who I have never met in my life.
People that I have never met in my life.
People I have never met in my life.

42. I used to go swimming with the friends.

The friends whom I used to go swimming with.
The friends who I used to go swimming with.
The friends with whom I used to go swimming.
The friends that I used to go swimming with.
The friends I used to go swimming with.

43. I have never even spoken to her.

The girl whom I have never even spoken to.
The girl who I have never even spoken to.
The girl to whom I have never even spoken.
The girl that I have never even spoken to.
The girl I have never even spoken to.

44. We thought him most creative.

The friend whom we thought most creative.
The friend who we thought most creative.
The friend that we thought most creative.
The friend we thought most creative.

45. 나는 그들과 거의 공통점이 없다.

我和他们几乎没有共同点。

私は彼らとほとんど共通点がない。

46. 나는 지금까지 그를 단 하루도 잊지 않았다.

我从来没有忘记过他。

私は今まで彼のことをたった一日も忘れなかった。

47. 나는 지금까지 5년 이상 동안 한 아일랜드 아가씨와 서신 교환을 해왔다.

我至今和一个爱尔兰女孩书信交往五年多了。

私は今まで5年以上の間、あるアイルランドの女の子と文通をしてきた。

48. 나는 그에게 아주 많은 애정과 존경심을 갖고 있다.

我对他有很多爱心和敬意。

私は彼にとても多くの愛情と尊敬心を持っている。

49. 나는 같은 고등학교에서 동료 교사들과 함께 영어를 가르쳤었다.

我在同一所高中和我的同事老师们一起教了英语。

私は同じ高校で同僚教師らとともに英語を教えた。

영어는 **후치수식**, 한중일어는 **전치수식**

45. I have very little in common with them.

People whom I have very little in common with.
People who I have very little in common with.
People with whom I have very little in common.
People that I have very little in common with.
People I have very little in common with.

46. I have never forgotten him even for a day.

The person whom I have never forgotten even for a day.
The person who I have never forgotten even for a day.
The person that I have never forgotten even for a day.
The person I have never forgotten even for a day.

47. I have corresponded with an Irish girl for over five years.

An Irish girl whom I have corresponded with for over five years.
An Irish girl who I have corresponded with for over five years.
An Irish girl with whom I have corresponded for over five years.
An Irish girl that I have corresponded with for over five years.
An Irish girl I have corresponded with for over five years.

48. I have a great deal of affection and admiration for him.

The man whom I have a great deal of affection and admiration for.
The man who I have a great deal of affection and admiration for.
The man for whom I have a great deal of affection and admiration.
The man that I have a great deal of affection and admiration for.
The man I have a great deal of affection and admiration for.

49. I taught English with the fellow teachers at the same high school.

Fellow teachers whom I taught English with at the same high school.
Fellow teachers who I taught English with at the same high school.
Fellow teachers with whom I taught English at the same high school.
Fellow teachers that I taught English with at the same high school.
Fellow teachers I taught English with at the same high school.

관계 대명사 (Relative Pronoun)

50. 나는 그 법적인 문제에 대해서 변호사와 상의할 필요가 있다.

有关那个法律问题我需要咨询律师。

私はその法的な問題について弁護士と相談する必要がある。

50. **I need to consult with a lawyer about the legal matter.**

A lawyer whom I need to consult with about the legal matter.
A lawyer who I need to consult with about the legal matter.
A lawyer with whom I need to consult about the legal matter.
A lawyer that I need to consult with about the legal matter.
A lawyer I need to consult with about the legal matter.

4. 관계 대명사 Which
(주격/Nominative)

관계 대명사 which는 선행사가 사람이 아닌 동물이나 사물인 경우에 사용하는 주격 관계 대명사이다. 구조는 '선행사 + which + 동사'로 되어 있고 해석은 '~하는 동물/사물'로 하면 되겠다. 주격 관계 대명사 which도 문법적으로 말하면 접속사와 대명사 역할을 하고, 선행사인 명사를 후치수식하는 형용사절을 이끄는 관계 대명사라고 이해하면 되겠다.

여기서 주의할 것이 두 가지 있는데, 하나는 주격 관계 대명사 which 대신에 관계 대명사 that을 쓸 수 있다는 점이고, 또 하나는 주격 관계 대명사 which와 그다음에 오는 be 동사는 동시에 생략할 수 있다는 점이다. 이것은 주격 관계 대명사 who에서도 언급한 것과 마찬가지로, 주격 관계 대명사 which와 be 동사 다음에 동격의 의미가 있는 명사가 오는 경우에는 명사 앞과 뒤에 콤마를 찍어서 관계 대명사와 be 동사를 생략할 수 있고, 이 경우를 제외하면 주격 관계 대명사 which와 be 동사 다음에는 형용사구나 현재분사, 과거분사가 오기 때문이다. 이것들은 관계 대명사를 사용하는 것보다 더 간단한 명사 후치수식 구조이기 때문에 할 수만 있다면 더 간단하게 말하고 쓰려는 경향 때문이라고 보면 되겠다. 주격 관계 대명사와 be 동사를 동시에 생략하는 것을 영문법에서 'Whiz Deletion'이라고 한다.

주격 관계 대명사 which를 쓸 경우와 that을 쓸 경우를 비교해보면 that을 쓰는 빈도가 훨씬 더 높다. 아울러서 관계 대명사 who, whom, which는 문어체에서 더 자주 사용되고 관계 대명사 that과 관계 대명사 생략은 구어체에서 훨씬 더 자주 사용된다는 것도 알아두면 좋겠다.

문법적인 설명보다는 실제로 많은 예문들을 보고 익혀서 원어민들처럼 자연스럽게 듣고 말하고 읽고 쓸 수 있도록 연습하는 것이 무엇보다도 중요하다.

여기서 "항공 산업은 전 세계를 조그만 마을로 만드는 데 크게 도움을 주고 있다."라는 문장을 '전 세계를 조그만 마을로 만드는 데 크게 도움을 주고 있는 항공 산업'이라는 명사 후치수식 구문으로 전환시켜보면 다음과 같이 할 수 있겠다.

The aviation industry is vastly helping to make the whole world a small village.

1. The aviation industry which is vastly helping to make the whole world a small village.
2. The aviation industry that is vastly helping to make the whole world a small village.
3. The aviation industry vastly helping to make the whole world a small village.

1. 주격 관계 대명사 which
2. 주격 관계 대명사 that
3. 현재분사

명사 후치수식 구조가 없는 우리에게 있어서는, 보통의 일반 문장을 관계 대명사를 비롯한 명사 후치수식 구조로 자유롭게 전환시킬 수 있는 능력을 기르는 것이 영어를 정복하는 지름길이자 열쇠이며 핵심과제이고, 학습자들의 영어 학습을 지루하지 않게 하면서도 영어 실력을 쉽고 빠르게 그리고 폭발적으로 향상시킬 수 있는 좋은 방법이다.

1. 그 차는 전속력으로 달리고 있다.

   那辆汽车在全速行驶。

   その車は全速力で走っている。

2. 신발이 내 발에 잘 맞지 않는다.

   鞋子不适合我的脚。

   靴が私の足に合わない。

3. 풍부한 천연자원이 우리의 해안에 매장되어 있다.

   在我们的海岸上储藏着丰富的自然资源。

   豊富な天然資源が私たちの海岸に埋蔵されている。

4. 영어는 어떤 다른 언어보다 더 광범위하게 사용되고 있다.

   英语比任何其他语言使用更广泛。

   英語はほかのどんな言語より広範囲に使われている。

5. 그 호수는 위험하고 유독한 물질로 오염되어 있다.

   那个湖泊被危险和有毒物质污染。

   その湖は危険で有毒な物質で汚染されている。

6. 영어는 현재완료 시제가 있다.

   英语有现在完成时态。

   英語には現在完了形がある。

영어는 후치수식, 한중일어는 전치수식

01

관계 대명사 (Relative Pronoun)

1. **The car is running at full speed.**

   The car which is running at full speed.
   The car that is running at full speed.
   The car running at full speed.

2. **The shoes don't fit my feet properly.**

   The shoes which don't fit my feet properly.
   The shoes that don't fit my feet properly.

3. **Abundant natural resources lie off our coast.**

   Abundant natural resources which lie off our coast.
   Abundant natural resources that lie off our coast.
   Abundant natural resources lying off our coast.

4. **English is more widely spoken than any other language.**

   English which is more widely spoken than any other language.
   English that is more widely spoken than any other language.
   English more widely spoken than any other language.

5. **The lake is polluted by dangerous and toxic substances.**

   The lake which is polluted by dangerous and toxic substances.
   The lake that is polluted by dangerous and toxic substances.
   The lake polluted by dangerous and toxic substances.

6. **The English language has the present perfect tense.**

   The English language which has the present perfect tense.
   The English language that has the present perfect tense.
   The English language having the present perfect tense.

7. 그 손실은 내가 견뎌내기에는 너무 버겁다.

   那些损失对我来说很难承受。

   その損失は私が耐えるにはとても手強い。

8. 그 자백은 강압과 고문에 의해서 이루어졌다.

   那口供是在强迫和酷刑下承认的。

   その自白は強圧と拷問によって行なわれた。

9. 열차가 승강대로 접근하고 있다.

   火车正在接近站台。

   列車がプラットフォームに接近している。

10. 어떤 인공 화학물질들은 오존층을 파괴한다.

    某些人造化学品破坏臭氧层。

    ある人工化学物質はオゾン層を破壊する。

11. 호주는 유대류 동물로 유명하다.

    澳大利亚以有袋类动物而闻名。

    オーストラリアは有袋類動物で有名だ。

12. 영어 능력은 오직 꾸준한 연습으로만 얻어질 수 있다.

    只有不断练习才能达到英语水准。

    英語能力はひとえに堅実な練習だけで得られる。

7. **The loss is too heavy for me to bear.**

   The loss which is too heavy for me to bear.
   The loss that is too heavy for me to bear.
   The loss too heavy for me to bear.

8. **The confession was made under coercion and torture.**

   The confession which was made under coercion and torture.
   The confession that was made under coercion and torture.
   The confession made under coercion and torture.

9. **A train is approaching the platform.**

   A train which is approaching the platform.
   A train that is approaching the platform.
   A train approaching the platform.

10. **Certain man-made chemicals destroy the ozone layer.**

    Certain man-made chemicals which destroy the ozone layer.
    Certain man-made chemicals that destroy the ozone layer.
    Certain man-made chemicals destroying the ozone layer.

11. **Australia is famous for its marsupial mammals.**

    Australia which is famous for its marsupial mammals.
    Australia that is famous for its marsupial mammals.
    Australia famous for its marsupial mammals.

12. **English proficiency can be attained only by constant practice.**

    English proficiency which can be attained only by constant practice.
    English proficiency that can be attained only by constant practice.
    English proficiency able to be attained only by constant practice.

13. 병에 담긴 물이 비싼 가격에 식료품점에서 팔리고 있다.

瓶装水在杂货店以高的价格出售。

食料品店でペットボトルの水が割高な価格で売られている。

14. 유전자가 우리의 모든 특징을 결정한다.

遗传基因决定我们所有的特征。

遺伝子が我々のすべての特徴を決定する。

15. 민물 양식은 지금까지 수 세기 동안 이루어져 왔다.

淡水养殖至今已经进行了几个世纪。

淡水養殖は今まで数世紀の間行われてきた。

16. 지구가 서서히 오염으로 죽어가고 있다.

地球由于逐渐污染而正走向灭亡。

地球は徐々に汚染で死にかけている。

17. 방부제는 곰팡이가 피는 것을 막아준다.

防腐剂防止霉菌形成。

防腐剤はカビが生えるのを食い止める。

18. 중국어는 세계에서 가장 많은 사람들에 의해서 사용되고 있다.

中文在世界上被最多人使用。

中国語は世界で最も多くの人たちによって使用されている。

영어는 후치수식, 한중일어는 전치수식

01 관계 대명사 (Relative Pronoun)

13. **Bottled water is sold at the grocery store at a high price.**

Bottled water which is sold at the grocery store at a high price.
Bottled water that is sold at the grocery store at a high price.
Bottled water sold at the grocery store at a high price.

14. **Genes determine all of our characteristics.**

Genes which determine all of our characteristics.
Genes that determine all of our characteristics.
Genes determining all of our characteristics.

15. **Freshwater fish farming has been carried out for centuries.**

Freshwater fish farming which has been carried out for centuries.
Freshwater fish farming that has been carried out for centuries.
Freshwater fish farming carried out for centuries.

16. **The earth is slowly dying from pollution.**

The earth which is slowly dying from pollution.
The earth that is slowly dying from pollution.
The earth slowly dying from pollution.

17. **Preservatives stop molds from forming.**

Preservatives which stop molds from forming.
Preservatives that stop molds from forming.
Preservatives stopping molds from forming.

18. **Chinese is spoken by the largest number of people in the world.**

Chinese which is spoken by the largest number of people in the world.
Chinese that is spoken by the largest number of people in the world.
Chinese spoken by the largest number of people in the world.

19. 그 다리는 견고함과 아름다움을 결합하고 있다.

那座桥梁结合坚固与美丽。

その橋は堅固さと美しさを結合している。

20. 북극곰 한 마리가 우리를 향해 다가오고 있다.

一只北极熊正在接近我们。

一匹のホツキヨクグマが私たちに近づいている。

21. 경쟁은 우리에게 우리의 최선을 다하게 한다.

竞争促使我们尽最大努力。

競争は我々に最善を尽くせるようにする。

22. 그 나라는 급속한 기술 발전을 이루고 있다.

那个国家正在急速实现技术发展。

その国は急速な技術発展を遂げている。

23. 그 결정은 다수결에 의해서 이루어진다.

那个决定是由大多数人通过的。

その決定は多数決によって行われる。

24. 몇 마리의 까치가 서로 싸우느라 많은 소음을 내고 있다.

有些喜鹊互相对抗发出了很多噪音。

いくつかのカササギが互いに戦いながら大騒音を出している。

19. **The bridge combines solidity with beauty.**

   The bridge which combines solidity with beauty.
   The bridge that combines solidity with beauty.
   The bridge combining solidity with beauty.

20. **A polar bear is coming towards us.**

   A polar bear which is coming towards us.
   A polar bear that is coming towards us.
   A polar bear coming towards us.

21. **Competition makes us do our best.**

   Competition which makes us do our best.
   Competition that makes us do our best.
   Competition making us do our best.

22. **The country is making rapid technological advances.**

   The country which is making rapid technological advances.
   The country that is making rapid technological advances.
   The country making rapid technological advances.

23. **The decision is made by the majority.**

   The decision which is made by the majority.
   The decision that is made by the majority.
   The decision made by the majority.

24. **Some magpies are making a lot of noise fighting each other.**

   Some magpies which are making a lot of noise fighting each other.
   Some magpies that are making a lot of noise fighting each other.
   Some magpies making a lot of noise fighting each other.

25. 그 직장은 몇 년간의 경력을 요구한다.

    那项工作需要有几年的经验。

    その職場は数年間の経歴を要求する。

26. 안전 의식은 우리가 사고를 예방하도록 도와준다.

    安全意识有助于我们预防事故。

    安全意識は私たちが事故を予防できるようにしてくれる。

27. 그 질문들은 복잡하지도 않고 사적이지도 않다.

    那些问题既不复杂也不隐私。

    それらの質問は複雑でもなく、私的でもない。

28. 자선단체가 가난한 사람과 궁핍한 사람을 도와주고 있다.

    慈善组织帮助穷人和有需要的人。

    慈善団体が貧しい人と窮乏した人を援助している。

29. 담배 연기 속에 들어있는 검은 물질이 암을 유발한다.

    香烟烟雾中的黑色物质导致癌症。

    タバコの煙の中に含まれる黒い物質がガンを誘発する。

30. 단서는 어떤 사람이 범죄에 대해서 유죄라는 것을 입증해준다.

    一条线索能证明一个人犯了罪。

    手がかりはある人が犯罪に対して有罪かということを立証している。

25. **The job requires a few years of experience.**

   The job which requires a few years of experience.
   The job that requires a few years of experience.
   The job requiring a few years of experience.

26. **A sense of safety helps us prevent accidents.**

   A sense of safety which helps us prevent accidents.
   A sense of safety that helps us prevent accidents.
   A sense of safety helping us prevent accidents.

27. **The questions are neither complicated nor personal.**

   The questions which are neither complicated nor personal.
   The questions that are neither complicated nor personal.
   The questions neither complicated nor personal.

28. **Charitable organizations help the poor and the needy.**

   Charitable organizations which help the poor and the needy.
   Charitable organizations that help the poor and the needy.
   Charitable organizations helping the poor and the needy.

29. **A black substance in cigarette smoke causes cancer.**

   A black substance in cigarette smoke which causes cancer.
   A black substance in cigarette smoke that causes cancer.
   A black substance in cigarette smoke causing cancer.

30. **A clue proves that a certain person is guilty of the crime.**

   A clue which proves that a certain person is guilty of the crime.
   A clue that proves that a certain person is guilty of the crime.
   A clue proving that a certain person is guilty of the crime.

31. 인체는 약 75%의 물로 구성되어 있다.

人体由约75%的水组成。

人体は約75パーセントの水で構成されている。

32. 핵폭탄은 수많은 사람을 죽이고 불구로 만든다.

核炸弹杀了很多人并且使人伤残。

核爆弾は多くの人を殺し、不自由な体にする。

33. 많은 걸작이 현재 미술관에서 전시 중이다.

很多杰作目前在美术馆展出。

多くの傑作が現在美術館で展示中だ。

34. 영화는 우리를 대단한 흥분 상태 속에 유지시켜 준다.

电影让我们处于极度兴奋的状态。

映画は私たちを大変な興奮状態の中に維持させる。

35. 월드컵은 4년에 한 번씩 열린다.

世界杯每四年举行一次。

ワールドカップは4年に一度開かれる。

36. 몇몇 광고는 소비자를 상당히 오도하고 있다.

一些广告在相当误导消费者。

いくつかの広告は消費者らを相当誤った方に導いている。

31. **A human body consists of about 75 precent water.**

   A human body which consists of about 75 precent water.
   A human body that consists of about 75 precent water.
   A human body consisting of about 75 precent water.

32. **A nuclear bomb leaves numerous people dead and crippled.**

   A nuclear bomb which leaves numerous people dead and crippled.
   A nuclear bomb that leaves numerous people dead and crippled.
   A nuclear bomb leaving numerous people dead and crippled.

33. **Many masterpieces are currently on display in the art museum.**

   Many masterpieces which are currently on display in the art museum.
   Many masterpieces that are currently on display in the art museum.
   Many masterpieces currently on display in the art museum.

34. **A movie keeps us in a state of great excitement.**

   A movie which keeps us in a state of great excitement.
   A movie that keeps us in a state of great excitement.
   A movie keeping us in a state of great excitement.

35. **The World Cup is held once every four years.**

   The World Cup which is held once every four years.
   The World Cup that is held once every four years.
   The World Cup held once every four years.

36. **Some advertisements are quite misleading consumers.**

   Some advertisements which are quite misleading consumers.
   Some advertisements that are quite misleading consumers.
   Some advertisements quite misleading consumers.

37. 썰매는 한 팀 네 마리의 개에 의해서 이끌린다.

    雪橇由四只狗组成一个队拉。

    そりは1チーム四匹の犬によって引かれる。

38. 민담은 구전으로 후세에 전해진다.

    民间故事通过口传传递给后代。

    民話は口伝えで後世に伝わる。

39. 일부 물질은 어떠한 환경문제도 일으키지 않는다.

    有些材料不引起任何环境问题。

    一部の物質は如何なる環境問題も起こさない。

40. 애국가는 국민의 가슴에 애국심을 불러일으킨다.

    爱国歌激发人民的爱国心。

    愛国歌は国民の胸に愛国心を呼び起こす。

41. 생명공학은 생물학과 기술의 결합을 일컫는다.

    生物技术是指生物学和技术的结合。

    生命工学は生物学と技術の結合を指す。

42. 소나무 한 그루가 도로 한가운데에 위엄 있게 서 있다.

    一棵松树高大威严地站立在路中间。

    一本の松が道路の真ん中に威厳ありげに立っている。

37. Sledges are pulled by a team of four dogs.

Sledges which are pulled by a team of four dogs.
Sledges that are pulled by a team of four dogs.
Sledges pulled by a team of four dogs.

38. Folk tales are passed on to posterity by word of mouth.

Folk tales which are passed on to posterit by word of mouth.
Folk tales that are passed on to posterity by word of mouth.
Folk tales passed on to posterity by word of mouth.

39. Some materials do not cause any environmental problems.

Some materials which do not cause any environmental problems.
Some materials that do not cause any environmental problems.
Some materials not causing any environmental problems.

40. A national anthem stirs up patriotism in the hearts of the people.

A national anthem which stirs up patriotism in the hearts of the people.
A national anthem that stirs up patriotism in the hearts of the people.
A national anthem stirring up patriotism in the hearts of the people.

41. Biotechnology refers to a combination of biology and technology.

Biotechnology which refers to a combination of biology and technology.
Biotechnology that refers to a combination of biology and technology.
Biotechnology referring to a combination of biology and technology.

42. A pine tree stands majestically in the middle of the road.

A pine tree which stands majestically in the middle of the road.
A pine tree that stands majestically in the middle of the road.
A pine tree standing majestically in the middle of the road.

43. 그 책들은 나의 초등학교 시절에 읽은 것이다.

那些书在我的小学时代读过。

それらの本は私が小学校時代に読んだものだ。

44. 그 영화는 내가 예상했던 것보다 훨씬 더 재미있다.

那部电影比我预想的更有趣。

その映画は私が予想していたより、はるかにおもしろい。

45. 핵무기는 세계를 파괴할 수 있는 잠재력을 가지고 있다.

核武器有破坏世界的潜力。

核兵器は世界を破壊できる潜在能力を持っている。

46. 의학 서적은 사람들이 이해하기에 아주 어렵다.

医学书很难让人理解。

医学書籍は人々が理解するのにはとても難しい。

47. 영어의 알파벳은 26개의 글자로 구성되어 있다.

英语字母由26个字母组成。

英語のアルファベットは26個の文字で構成されている。

48. 그 수업은 영어로 토론식으로 이루어진다.

该课程用英语讨论的形式进行。

その授業は英語で討論式で行われる。

43. The books were read during my elementary school days.

The books which were read during my elementary school days.
The books that were read during my elementary school days.
The books read during my elementary school days.

44. The movie is a lot more interesting than I expected.

The movie which is a lot more interesting than I expected.
The movie that is a lot more interesting than I expected.
The movie a lot more interesting than I expected.

45. Nuclear weapons have the potential of destroying the world.

Nuclear weapons which have the potential of destroying the world.
Nuclear weapons that have the potential of destroying the world.
Nuclear weapons having the potential of destroying the world.

46. Medical books are very difficult for people to understand.

Medical books which are very difficult for people to understand.
Medical books that are very difficult for people to understand.
Medical books very difficult for people to understand.

47. The English alphabet consists of 26 letters.

The English alphabet which consists of 26 letters.
The English alphabet that consists of 26 letters.
The English alphabet consisting of 26 letters.

48. The class is conducted in English on a discussion basis.

The class which is conducted in English on a discussion basis.
The class that is conducted in English on a discussion basis.
The class conducted in English on a discussion basis.

49. 보편적인 속성이 인간의 언어에 고유하게 존재한다.

普遍的属性存在于人类语言中。

普遍的な属性が人間の言語に固有に存在する。

50. 피부암은 태양에 너무 많이 노출되어서 유발된다.

皮肤癌是由于常时间将皮肤暴露在太阳光下引起的。

皮膚がんは太陽に多くさらされたことで誘発される。

49. **Universal properties are unique to the language of man.**

Universal properties which are unique to the language of man.
Universal properties that are unique to the language of man.
Universal properties unique to the language of man.

50. **Skin cancer is caused by too much exposure to the sun.**

Skin cancer which is caused by too much exposure to the sun.
Skin cancer that is caused by too much exposure to the sun.
Skin cancer caused by too much exposure to the sun.

5. 관계 대명사 Whose / Of Which
(소유격/Genitive)

   관계 대명사 whose 또는 of which는 선행사가 사람이 아닌 동물이나 사물인 경우에 사용하는 소유격 관계 대명사이다. 구조는 '선행사 + whose + 명사' 또는 '선행사 + of which + the + 명사'로 되어 있다. 물론, 관계 대명사 whose는 선행사가 사람인 경우에도 사용할 수 있다는 것은 이미 앞에서 설명한 바와 같다.

   여기서 한 가지 주의할 것은 관계 대명사 of which를 사용할 경우 그다음 명사에 정관사 the를 붙여야 한다는 것이다. 왜냐하면 명사가 뒷말에 의해서 수식을 받을 때는 한정되었다는 의미가 강하기 때문에 일반적으로 정관사 the를 쓰는 것이 보통이다. 그리고 이것과 관련하여 'of which + the + 명사'를 뒤바꾸어서 'the + 명사 + of which'를 쓸 수도 있다.

   또 한 가지 기억해야 할 것은 관계 대명사 whose나 of which는 관계 대명사 that으로 대체할 수 없다는 것이다. 관계 대명사 that이 선행사가 사람이든 동물이든 사물이든 가리지 않고 모든 명사를 수식할 수 있는 수식 범위가 가장 넓은 관계 대명사이지만 that의 소유격이 없기 때문에 이것은 불가능하다.

   단순히 명사를 수식하는 것을 어렵다고 생각할 사람은 아무도 없겠지만, 영어의 경우에는 명사 수식 구조가 우리말의 전치수식 구조와는 다른 후치수식 구조이기 때문에 우리에게는 영어의 명사 후치수식 구조가 극복해야 할 난관이자 핵심과제라 하지 않을 수 없다.

   본 교재에서는, 이런 명사 후치수식 구조가 영어 정복의 난관이자 핵심과제이면서 동시에 첩경이자 열쇠라는 것을 깊이 인식하고, 보통의 일반 문장을 명사 후치수식 구조의 구문으로 전환시키는 연습을 통해서 학습자들의 영어 구사력을 쉽고 빠르고, 그리고 폭발적으로 향상시킬 수 있도록 노력했다.

영어는 **후치수식**, 한중일어는 **전치수식**

01

관계 대명사 (Relative Pronoun)

여기서 "그것의 발전은 지금까지 빠르고 괄목할만했다."와 "컴퓨터 기술의 발전은 지금까지 빠르고 괄목할만했다."라는 문장을 '그것의 발전이 지금까지 빠르고 괄목할 만했던 컴퓨터 기술'이라는 명사 후치수식 구문으로 전환시켜보면 다음과 같이 할 수 있겠다.

Its development has been rapid and remarkable.

The development of computer technology has been rapid and remarkable.

1. Computer technology whose development has been rapid and remarkable.
2. Computer technology of which the development has been rapid and remarkable.
3. Computer technology the development of which has been rapid and remarkable.

1. 관계 대명사 whose
2. 관계 대명사 of which
3. 관계 대명사 of which

1. 그 책의 표지는 빨간색이다.

    那本书的封面是红色的。
    その本の表紙は赤だ。

2. 그 고속도로의 길이는 약 5,000km이다.

    那条高速公路的长度约为5,000公里。
    その高速道路の長さは約5,000kmだ。

3. 그 개들의 일은 마약을 탐지하는 것이다.

    那些狗的工作是检测药物。
    その犬らの仕事は麻薬を探知することだ。

4. 이 고양이의 이름은 나리이다.

    这只猫的名字是纳里。
    この猫の名前はナリだ。

1. **The cover of the book is red.**

   Its cover is red.

   The book whose cover is red.
   The book of which the cover is red.
   The book the cover of which is red.

2. **The length of the expressway is about 5,000 kilometers.**

   Its length is about 5,000 kilometers.

   The expressway whose length is about 5,000 kilometers.
   The expressway of which the length is about 5,000 kilometers.
   The expressway the length of which is about 5,000 kilometers.

3. **The dogs' job is to detect drugs.**

   The job of the dogs is to detect drugs.

   The dogs whose job is to detect drugs.
   The dogs of which the job is to detect drugs.
   The dogs the job of which is to detect drugs.

4. **The cat's name is Nary.**

   The name of the cat is Nary.

   The cat whose name is Nary.
   The cat of which the name is Nary.
   The cat the name of which is Nary.

5. 그 집의 지붕은 하얗다.

   那房子的屋顶是白色的。

   その家の屋根は白い。

6. 부동산 시장의 가치는 올해 급등했다.

   房地产市场的价值在今年暴涨。

   不動産市場の価値は今年急騰した。

7. 그 책의 이야기는 우리에게 잘 알려져 있다.

   那本书的故事是我们所熟知的。

   その本の話は我々によく知られている。

8. 이 개의 다리는 너무너무 짧다.

   这只狗的腿很短。

   この犬の脚はとても短い。

5. **The roof of the house is white.**

   Its roof is white.

   The house whose roof is white.
   The house of which the roof is white.
   The house the roof of which is white.

6. **The value of the real estate market has skyrocketed this year.**

   Its value has skyrocketed this year.

   The real estate market whose value has skyrocketed this year.
   The real estate market of which the value has skyrocketed this year.
   The real estate market the value of which has skyrocketed this year.

7. **The story of the book is well known to us.**

   Its story is well known to us.

   The book whose story is well known to us.
   The book of which the story is well known to us.
   The book the story of which is well known to us.

8. **The legs of the dog are too short.**

   Its legs are too short.

   The dog whose legs are too short.
   The dog of which the legs are too short.
   The dog the legs of which are too short.

9. 그 제품의 미래가격은 불확실하다.

那个产品的未来价格不确定。

その製品の未来の価格は不確かだ。

10. 우리는 그것의 손실을 영원히 애통해한다.

我们永远哀痛它的损失。

私たちはそれの損失を永遠に悲しむ。

11. 그 앵무새의 주인은 영어를 한다.

那只鹦鹉的主人说英语。

そのオウムの飼い主は英語を話す。

12. 코끼리의 상아가 밀렵되고 있다.

大象的象牙被偷猎。

象牙が密猟されている。

9. **The future price of the product is uncertain.**

   Its future price is uncertain.

   The product whose future price is uncertain.
   The product of which the future price is uncertain.
   The product the future price of which is uncertain.

10. **We lament the loss of the thing forever.**

    We lament its loss forever.

    The thing whose loss we lament forever.
    The thing of which the loss we lament forever.
    The thing the loss of which we lament forever.

11. **The parrot's master speaks English.**

    The master of the parrot speaks English.

    The parrot whose master speaks English.
    The parrot of which the master speaks English.
    The parrot the master of which speaks English.

12. **The elephants' ivory is poached.**

    The ivory of the elephants is poached.

    The elephants whose ivory is poached.
    The elephants of which the ivory is poached.
    The elephants the ivory of which is poached.

13. 그 산의 정상은 눈으로 덮여있다.

那座山的顶部被雪覆盖着。

その山の頂上は雪で覆われている。

14. 그 집의 지붕이 날아가 버렸다.

那房子的屋顶飞走了。

その家の屋根が吹っ飛んでしまった。

15. 나는 그 전문용어의 의미를 이해할 수 없다.

我不明白那个专业术语的含义。

私はその専門用語の意味を理解できない。

16. 그 건물의 벽은 하얀색으로 칠해져 있다.

那座建筑物的墙壁被漆成了白色。

その建物の壁は白色で塗られている。

13. The top of the mountain is covered with snow.

Its top is covered with snow.

The mountain whose top is covered with snow.
The mountain of which the top is covered with snow.
The mountain the top of which is covered with snow.

14. The roof of the house is blown off.

Its roof is blown off.

The house whose roof is blown off.
The house of which the roof is blown off.
The house the roof of which is blown off.

15. I can't understand the meaning of the buzz word.

I can't understand its meaning.

The buzz word whose meaning I can't understand.
The buzz word of which the meaning I can't understand.
The buzz word the meaning of which I can't understand.

16. The wall of the building is painted white.

Its wall is painted white.

The building whose wall is painted white.
The building of which the wall is painted white.
The building the wall of which is painted white.

17. 토끼의 꼬리는 짧다.

兔子的尾巴很短。
ウサギの尾は短い。

18. 그 집의 창문은 모두 열려있다.

那房子的窗户都是开着的。
その家の窓は全部開いている。

19. 우리는 지금 그 산의 꼭대기를 보고 있다.

我们正在看那座山的山顶。
私たちは今その山の頂上を見ている。

20. 나는 그 속담의 의미를 이해할 수 없다.

我不明白那句谚语的意思。
私はそのことわざの意味を理解できない。

17. A rabbit's tail is short.

The tail of a rabbit is short.

A rabbit whose tail is short.
A rabbit of which the tail is short.
A rabbit the tail of which is short.

18. The windows of the house are all open.

Its windows are all open.

The house whose windows are all open.
The house of which the windows are all open.
The house the windows of which are all open.

19. We see the top of the mountain now.

We see its top now.

The mountain whose top we see now.
The mountain of which the top we see now.
The mountain the top of which we see now.

20. I can't understand the meaning of the proverb.

I can't understand its meaning.

The proverb whose meaning I can't understand.
The proverb of which the meaning I can't understand.
The proverb the meaning of which I can't understand.

21. 기린의 다리는 너무너무 길다.

长颈鹿的腿很长。

キリンの脚はとても長い。

22. 한 사회의 미래는 예측 불가능하다.

一个社会的未来是不可预测的。

ある社会の未来は予測不可能だ。

23. 그 대학의 학장은 미국인이다.

那所大学的校长是美国人。

その大学の学長はアメリカ人だ。

24. 그 제품들의 포장재는 재활용될 수 없다.

那些产品的包装不能再利用。

それらの製品の包装材はリサイクルできない。

21. The giraffe's legs are too long.

The legs of the giraffe are too long.

The giraffe whose legs are too long.
The giraffe of which the legs are too long.
The giraffe the legs of which are too long.

22. The future of a society is unpredictable.

Its future is unpredictable.

A society whose future is unpredictable.
A society of which the future is unpredictable.
A society the future of which is unpredictable.

23. The dean of the college is American.

Its dean is American.

The college whose dean is American.
The college of which the dean is American.
The college the dean of which is American.

24. The packaging of the products can not be recycled.

Their packaging can not be recycled.

The products whose packaging can not be recycled.
The products of which the packaging can not be recycled.
The products the packaging of which can not be recycled.

25. 정부의 권력은 국민의 손에 놓여 있다.

政府的权力在人民的手中。

政府の権力は国民の手に置かれている。

26. 그 나무들의 결은 재미있게 문양이 되어 있다.

那些树木的纹理形成很有趣的图案。

その木々の紋は面白い模様になっている。

27. 코끼리의 코는 물건을 잡기 위해서 사용된다.

大象的鼻子是用来抓东西的。

象の鼻は物をつかむために使用される。

28. 그 나라들의 음악적 취향은 아주 다르다.

那些国家的音乐上的取向很不同。

それらの国々の音楽の好みはとても異なる。

25. The government's power lies in the hands of the people.

The power of the government lies in the hands of the people.

The government whose power lies in the hands of the people.
The government of which the power lies in the hands of the people.
The government the power of which lies in the hands of the people.

26. The grains of the woods are interestingly patterned.

Its grains are interestingly patterned.

The woods whose grains are interestingly patterned.
The woods of which the grains are interestingly patterned.
The woods the grains of which are interestingly patterned.

27. An elephant's trunk is used for grabbing things.

The trunk of an elephant is used for grabbing things.

An elephant whose trunk is used for grabbing things.
An elephant of which the trunk is used for grabbing things.
An elephant the trunk of which is used for grabbing things.

28. The countries' musical tastes are very different.

The musical tastes of the countries are very different.

The countries whose musical tastes are very different.
The countries of which the musical tastes are very different.
The countries the musical tastes of which are very different.

29. 그 뱀의 독은 치명적이다.

   那条蛇的毒是致命的。
   その蛇の毒は致命的だ。

30. 멸종위기에 처한 종의 수명은 얼마 남지 않았다.

   濒危物种的寿命所剩不多了。
   絶滅の危機に瀕した種の寿命は僅かしか残っていない。

31. 우리는 청춘이 지나가는 것을 슬픔과 후회로 지켜본다.

   我们带着悲伤和遗憾看着青春流逝。
   私たちは青春が通過することを悲しみと後悔で見守る。

32. 그 클럽의 회원은 영어에 관심이 있다.

   那个俱乐部的成员对英语感兴趣。
   そのクラブの会員は英語に関心がある。

29. **The snake's poison is deadly.**

   The poison of the snake is deadly.

   The snake whose poison is deadly.
   The snake of which the poison is deadly.
   The snake the poison of which is deadly.

30. **The days of endangered species are numbered.**

   Their days are numbered.

   Endangered species whose days are numbered.
   Endangered species of which the days are numbered.
   Endangered species the days of which are numbered.

31. **We watch the passing of youth with sorrow and regret.**

   We watch its passing with sorrow and regret.

   Youth whose passing we watch with sorrow and regret.
   Youth of which the passing we watch with sorrow and regret.
   Youth the passing of which we watch with sorrow and regret.

32. **The members of the club are interested in English.**

   Its members are interested in English.

   The club whose members are interested in English.
   The club of which the members are interested in English.
   The club the members of which are interested in English.

33. 그 나라들의 인구는 1억이 넘는다.

那些国家的人口超过一亿。

それらの国々の人口は1億を超える。

34. 그 책들의 글은 읽기에 너무너무 어렵다.

那些书的文章太难阅读。

それらの本の文章を読むのはとても難しい。

35. 무지개의 색깔은 100가지도 될 수 있을 것이다.

彩虹的颜色可以有一百种。

虹の色は100種類の色がなることもできるだろう。

36. 덜 익은 석류의 맛은 지독하게 시다.

未成熟的石榴味道极酸。

未完熟の石榴の味はひどくすっぱい。

33. **The countries' population is over one hundred million.**

    The population of the countries is over one hundred million.

    The countries whose population is over one hundred million.
    The countries of which the population is over one hundred million.
    The countries the population of which is over one hundred million.

34. **The writings of the books are too hard to read.**

    Their writings are too hard to read.

    The books whose writings are too hard to read.
    The books of which the writings are too hard to read.
    The books the writings of which are too hard to read.

35. **The colors of the rainbow could be a hundred.**

    Its colors could be a hundred.

    The rainbow whose colors could be a hundred.
    The rainbow of which the colors could be a hundred.
    The rainbow the colors of which could be a hundred.

36. **The taste of an unripe pomegranate is extremely sour.**

    Its taste is extremely sour.

    An unripe pomegranate whose taste is extremely sour.
    An unripe pomegranate of which the taste is extremely sour.
    An unripe pomegranate the taste of which is extremely sour.

37. 그 식당의 분위기는 새롭고 이국적이다.

   那家餐厅的气氛有新的异国情调。

   そのレストランの雰囲気は新しくて異国的だ。

38. 그 책의 내용은 철학적인 글로 가득 차 있다.

   那本书的内容充满了哲学性的文章。

   その本の内容は哲学的な文章でいっぱいだ。

39. 이 컴퓨터의 용량은 내 프로그램을 작동시킬 만큼 충분히 크다.

   这台电脑的容量足够可以操作我的程序。

   このコンピューターの容量は私のプログラムを作動させるくらい十分大きい。

40. 4대 강국의 이해관계가 이 나라에 모여 있다.

   四个超级大国的利益集中在这个国家。

   4大強国の利害関係がこの国に集まっている。

37. **The restaurant's ambience is new and exotic.**

   The ambience of the restaurant is new and exotic.

   The restaurant whose ambience is new and exotic.
   The restaurant of which the ambience is new and exotic.
   The restaurant the ambience of which is new and exotic.

38. **The book's content is full of philosophical writings.**

   The content of the book is full of philosophical writings.

   The book whose content is full of philosophical writings.
   The book of which the content is full of philosophical writings.
   The book the content of which is full of philosophical writings.

39. **The computer's capacity is big enough to run my programs.**

   The capacity of the computer is big enough to run my programs.

   The computer whose capacity is big enough to run my programs.
   The computer of which the capacity is big enough to run my programs.
   The computer the capacity of which is big enough to run my programs.

40. **The four superpowers' interests converge on the country.**

   The interests of the four superpowers converge on the country.

   The four superpowers whose interests converge on the country.
   The four superpowers of which the interests converge on the country.
   The four superpowers the interests of which converge on the country.

41. 폭력영화의 희생자는 십 대가 될 가능성이 대단히 크다.

    10几岁的青少年成为暴力电影的受害者的可能性非常高。

    暴力映画の犠牲者は十代になる可能性が非常に高い。

42. 그 강의 어귀는 바다만큼 넓다.

    那条河的河口和海一样宽。

    その川の川口は海ほど広い。

43. 그 문의 경첩이 지금 새것으로 교체되었다.

    那扇门的铰链已被新的所取代。

    その戸の蝶番が今新しいものに交替された。

44. 그 회사의 명성이 지금 일련의 예상치 못한 사건들로 손상을 입었다.

    该公司的名誉现在被一系列的意外事件玷污了。

    その会社の名声が今一連の予想できなかった事件で損傷を負った。

41. **The victims of violent movies are most likely to be teenagers.**

   Their victims are most likely to be teenagers.

   Violent movies whose victims are most likely to be teenagers.
   Violent movies of which the victims are most likely to be teenagers.
   Violent movies the victims of which are most likely to be teenagers.

42. **The mouth of the river is as wide as the sea.**

   Its mouth is as wide as the sea.

   The river whose mouth is as wide as the sea.
   The river of which the mouth is as wide as the sea.
   The river the mouth of which is as wide as the sea.

43. **The hinges of the door have been replaced by new ones.**

   Its hinges have been replaced by new ones.

   The door whose hinges have been replaced by new ones.
   The door of which the hinges have been replaced by new ones.
   The door the hinges of which have been replaced by new ones.

44. **The reputation of the company has been tarnished by a series of unexpected events.**

   Its reputation has been tarnished by a series of unexpected events.

   The company whose reputation has been tarnished by a series of unexpected events.
   The company of which the reputation has been tarnished by a series of unexpected events.
   The company the reputation of which has been tarnished by a series of unexpected events.

45. 그 교재의 내용은 대학생이 파악하기에는 너무 어렵다.

那本教科书的内容对大学生太难掌握。

その教材の内容は大学生が把握するにはとても難しい。

46. 대형 여객기의 엔진은 특정한 순서로 걸린다.

大型飞机的发动机以特定的顺序启动。

大型旅客機のエンジンは特定の手順でかかる。

47. 그 건물의 엘리베이터는 이번 주에 벌써 두 번씩이나 수리되었다.

那个建筑的电梯在本周已经修复了两次。

その建物のエレベーターは今週にもう二度も修理された。

48. 나는 그의 흘려 쓴 글씨 때문에 그 보고서의 글자를 읽을 수가 없다.

我不能读那份报告的字体，因为他的笔迹太潦草。

私は彼が崩し書きした字のせいでその報告書の文字を読むことができない。

45. The content of the textbook is too difficult for college students to grasp.

Its content is too difficult for college students to grasp.

The textbook whose content is too difficult for college students to grasp.
The textbook of which the content is too difficult for college students to grasp.
The textbook the content of which is too difficult for college students to grasp.

46. The engines of jumbo air-crafts are started in a specific order.

Their engines are started in a specific order.

Jumbo air-crafts whose engines are started in a specific order.
Jumbo air-crafts of which the engines are started in a specific order.
Jumbo air-crafts the engines of which are started in a specific order.

47. The elevator of the building was already repaired even twice this week.

Its elevator was already repaired even twice this week.

The building whose elevator was already repaired even twice this week.
The building of which the elevator was already repaired even twice this week.
The building the elevator of which was already repaired even twice this week.

48. I cannot read the letters of the report because of his sloppy handwriting.

I cannot read its letters because of his sloppy handwriting.

The report whose letters I cannot read because of his sloppy handwriting.
The report of which the letters I cannot read because of his sloppy handwriting.
The report the letters of which I cannot read because of his sloppy handwriting.

49. 그 박물관의 미술품은 세계적으로 유명한 화가들에 의해서 그려졌다.

那个博物馆的艺术品是由世界著名的画家画的。

その博物館の美術品は世界的に有名な画家たちによって描かれた。

50. 미국의 수도는 초대 대통령의 이름을 본떠서 명명되었다.

美国的首都是以第一任总统的名字命名的。

米国の首都は初代大統領の名前に倣って命名された。

49. **The artworks of the museum were painted by world-renowned artists.**

Its artworks were painted by world-renowned artists.

The museum whose artworks were painted by world-renowned artists.
The museum of which the artworks were painted by world-renowned artists.
The museum the artworks of which were painted by world-renowned artists.

50. **The capital city of the United States is named after its first president.**

Its capital city is named after its first president.

The United States whose capital city is named after its first president.
The United States of which the capital city is named after its first president.
The United States the capital city of which is named after its first president.

6. 관계 대명사 Which
(목적격/Objective)

목적격 관계 대명사 which는 선행사가 사람이 아닌 동물이나 사물인 경우에 사용하는 관계 대명사이다. 구조는 '선행사 + which + 주어' 또는 '선행사 + 전치사 + which + 주어'로 되어 있고 동사의 목적어나 전치사의 목적어로 사용된다. 해석은 '주어가 ~한 동물/사물'로 하면 되겠다. 문법적으로 관계 대명사 which도 접속사와 대명사의 역할을 하며 선행사인 명사를 후치수식하는 형용사절의 기능을 갖고 있다.

여기서 몇 가지 주의할 점이 있는데 하나는 목적격 관계 대명사 which도 주격 관계 대명사 which처럼 관계 대명사 that으로 바꿔 쓸 수 있다는 것이다. 이것은 관계 대명사 that은 선행사가 사람이든 동물이든 사물이든 명사는 모두 다 수식할 수 있기 때문이다.

또 하나 주의할 점은 목적격 관계 대명사 which는 생략할 수 있다는 점이다. 그 이유 중 하나는 선행사와 목적격 관계 대명사가 이끄는 형용사절이 매우 밀접한 관계에 있어서 관계 대명사를 생략하여도 의미의 혼란이 일어나지 않기 때문이다. 그리고 또 하나의 이유는 같은 말을 두 번 반복하고 싶어 하지 않는 경향 때문이다.

마지막 세 번째로 주의할 점은 관계 대명사 which가 전치사의 목적어일 경우에는 전치사와 관계 대명사 which가 붙어 있는 경우도 있고 전치사가 관계 대명사와 떨어져서 뒤에 올 수도 있다는 것이다. 전치사와 관계 대명사가 붙어 있는 경우에는 관계 대명사를 바로 생략할 수 없다. 만약 전치사와 관계 대명사가 붙어 있는 경우에 관계 대명사를 생략하고 싶다면 전치사를 뒤로 돌려놓아야 한다. 전치사와 관계 대명사가 떨어져 있는 경우에는 관계 대명사를 바로 생략할 수 있다. 그리고 관계 대명사 that 앞에는 전치사를 쓰지 못한다는 것은 주지의 사실이다.

참고로, 전치사와 관계 대명사가 붙어 있는 경우와 전치사와 관계 대명사가 떨어져 있는 경우를 비교해보면, 전치사와 관계 대명사가 붙어 있는 경우가 떨어져 있는 경우보다 더 격식을 갖춘 표현이라는 것과 앞에서도 언급한 것처럼 관계 대명사 who, whom, which는 문어체에서 더 자주 사용되고 관계 대명사 that과 관계 대명사 생략은 구어체에서 훨씬 더 자주 사용된다는 것도 알아두면 좋겠다.

여기서 "우리는 날씨를 전혀 제어할 수 없다."라는 문장을 '우리가 전혀 제어할 수 없는 날씨'라는 명사 후치수식 구문으로 전환시켜보면 다음과 같이 할 수 있겠다.

We have no control over the weather.

1. The weather which we have no control over.
2. The weather over which we have no control.
3. The weather that we have no control over.
4. The weather we have no control over.

1. 관계 대명사 which
2. 전치사 + 관계 대명사 which
3. 관계 대명사 that
4. 관계 대명사 생략

위의 예문들을 사용 빈도에서 비교해본다면 4번, 3번, 1번, 2번 순서로 많이 사용된다고 할 수 있겠다. 하지만 어느 예문이든 거리낌 없이 자유자재로 사용할 수 있도록 충분한 연습을 해주기 바란다.

1. 그들은 그 제품을 대량으로 생산한다.

   他们大量生产那种产品。

   彼らはその製品を大量に生産する。

2. 우리는 그 활동들을 일 년 내내 즐긴다.

   我们常年喜欢那些活动。

   私たちはそれらの活動を一年中楽しむ。

3. 나는 지금까지 그 원칙들을 존중해왔다.

   我至今一向尊重那些原则。

   私は今までそれらの原則を尊重してきた。

4. 우리는 모두 깨우침의 경지를 추구한다.

   我们都追求启发的境地。

   私たちは皆悟りの境地を追求する。

5. 우리는 우리의 미래를 준비하기 위해서 몇 가지 것들을 해야만 한다.

   为了准备我们的未来我们应该做一些事情。

   私たちは未来を準備するために、いくつかのことをしなければならない。

6. 그녀가 지금 그의 방에 장문의 편지를 남겨놓았다.

   她在他的房间里留了一封长信。

   彼女が今彼の部屋に長文の手紙を残した。

1. **They produce the product in bulk.**

    The product which they produce in bulk.
    The product that they produce in bulk.
    The product they produce in bulk.

2. **We enjoy the activities throughout the year.**

    The activities which we enjoy throughout the year.
    The activities that we enjoy throughout the year.
    The activities we enjoy throughout the year.

3. **I have honored the principles.**

    The principles which I have honored.
    The principles that I have honored.
    The principles I have honored.

4. **We all seek a state of enlightenment.**

    A state of enlightenment which we all seek.
    A state of enlightenment that we all seek.
    A state of enlightenment we all seek.

5. **We should do some things to get ready for our future.**

    Some things which we should do to get ready for our future.
    Some things that we should do to get ready for our future.
    Some things we should do to get ready for our future.

6. **She has left a long letter in his room.**

    A long letter which she has left in his room.
    A long letter that she has left in his room.
    A long letter she has left in his room.

7. 우리 인간은 그런 능력을 갖고 있지 않다.

我们人类没有那种能力。

我々人間はそのような能力を持っていない。

8. 한 세대는 또 다른 세대에게 유전형질을 전해준다.

一代传给另一代遗传基因。

世代は他の世代に遺伝形質を伝えている。

9. 그들은 지금까지 돈을 의심스럽거나 부적절한 방식으로 취득했다.

他们一向以可疑或不正当的方式取得钱。

彼らはこれまで金を疑わしい方法や不適切な方法で取得した。

10. 우리는 이 일을 하기 위해서는 의지와 인내가 필요하다.

我们为了做这项工作需要意志和耐力。

私たちがこの仕事をするためには意志と忍耐が必要だ。

11. 우리는 영어를 성공적으로 배우기 위해서 몇 가지 것을 알아야 한다.

为了能成功地学习英语我们必须知道几点。

私たちは英語を成功的に学ぶために、いくつかのことを知らなければならない。

12. 지구는 매일 태양으로부터 엄청난 에너지를 받고 있다.

地球每天从太阳那儿接收巨大的能量。

地球は毎日太陽から莫大なエネルギーを受けている。

7. **We human beings do not have the abilities.**

The abilities which we human beings do not have.
The abilities that we human beings do not have.
The abilities we human beings do not have.

8. **One generation passes on genetic traits to another.**

Genetic traits which one generation passes on to another.
Genetic traits that one generation passes on to another.
Genetic traits one generation passes on to another.

9. **They have acquired money in questionable or improper ways.**

Money which they have acquired in questionable or improper ways.
Money that they have acquired in questionable or improper ways.
Money they have acquired in questionable or improper ways.

10. **We bring the will and endurance to this work.**

The will and endurance which we bring to this work.
The will and endurance that we bring to this work.
The will and endurance we bring to this work.

11. **We have to know a few things to learn English successfully.**

A few things which we have to know to learn English successfully.
A few things that we have to know to learn English successfully.
A few things we have to know to learn English successfully.

12. **The earth receives the enormous energy from the sun every day.**

The enormous energy which the earth receives from the sun every day.
The enormous energy that the earth receives from the sun every day.
The enormous energy the earth receives from the sun every day.

13. 우리는 혹독한 세계에서 살아남기 위해서 어떤 기술이 필요하다.

我们为了在严酷的世界中生存下来需要某种技术。

私たちは厳しい世界で生き残るためにある技術が必要である。

14. 우리는 언어학습을 고도로 복잡한 과정이라고 여긴다.

我们认为语言学习是一个非常复杂的过程。

私たちは言語学習を高度で複雑な過程だと思っている。

15. 우리는 사적인 감정을 자유롭게 표현할 수 없다.

我们不能自由地表达私人感情。

私たちは私的な感情を自由に表現できない。

16. 우리는 지금까지 책을 통해서 지식과 지혜를 축적했다.

我们至今通过书籍积累知识和智慧。

私たちは今まで本を通して知識と知恵を蓄積した。

17. 모든 사람은 삶의 질을 향상시키려고 열심히 노력하고 있다.

所有人在为了提高自己的生活质量而坚苦努力着。

すべての人は暮らしの質を向上させようと一生懸命に努力している。

18. 우리는 공동체에 속해 있다.

我们属于共同体。

我々は共同体に属している。

13. **We need some skill in order to survive in a harsh world.**

Some skill which we need in order to survive in a harsh world.
Some skill that we need in order to survive in a harsh world.
Some skill we need in order to survive in a harsh world.

14. **We regard language learning as a highly sophisticated process.**

Language learning which we regard as a highly sophisticated process.
Language learning that we regard as a highly sophisticated process.
Language learning we regard as a highly sophisticated process.

15. **We cannot express our personal feelings freely.**

Our personal feelings which we cannot express freely.
Our personal feelings that we cannot express freely.
Our personal feelings we cannot express freely.

16. **We have accumulated knowledge and wisdom through books.**

Knowledge and wisdom which we have accumulated through books.
Knowledge and wisdom that we have accumulated through books.
Knowledge and wisdom we have accumulated through books.

17. **Everyone is working hard to improve the quality of life.**

The quality of life which everyone is working hard to improve.
The quality of life that everyone is working hard to improve.
The quality of life everyone is working hard to improve.

18. **We belong to the community.**

The community which we belong to.
The community to which we belong.
The community that we belong to.
The community we belong to.

19. 우리는 많은 다른 방식으로 존재한다.

我们存在于很多不同的方式。

私たちは多くの他の方式として存在している。

20. 우리는 자유 민주주의 국가에서 살고 있다.

我们生活在一个自由和民主的国家里。

我々は自由民主主義国家に住んでいる。

21. 나는 지금까지 그 신조를 지키며 살아왔다.

我一直守着那个信条生活着。

私は今までその信条を守りながら生きて来た。

22. 그는 지금까지 그 주제에 대해서 얘기했다.

他到目前为止谈到了那个话题。

彼は今までそのテーマについて話をした。

23. 그 기념비는 이런 정신에서 세워졌다.

那座纪念碑是以这种精神建立的。

その記念碑はこのような精神で建てられた。

19. We exist in many different ways.

Many different ways which we exist in.
Many different ways in which we exist.
Many different ways that we exist in.
Many different ways we exist in.

20. We live in a free and democratic country.

A free and democratic country which we live in.
A free and democratic country in which we live.
A free and democratic country that we live in.
A free and democratic country we live in.

21. I have lived by the creed.

The creed which I have lived by.
The creed by which I have lived.
The creed that I have lived by.
The creed I have lived by.

22. He has talked about the topic.

The topic which he has talked about.
The topic about which he has talked.
The topic that he has talked about.
The topic he has talked about.

23. The monument was erected in the spirit.

The spirit which the monument was erected in.
The spirit in which the monument was erected.
The spirit that the monument was erected in.
The spirit the monument was erected in.

24. 그는 그 문제를 이런 방법으로 해결했다.

他以这种方式解决了那个问题。

彼はその問題をこのような方法で解決した。

25. 지원서는 그 순서로 접수되었다.

申请表按此顺序接受。

志願書はその順序で受け付けられた。

26. 우리는 그곳에서 정숙을 유지해야만 할 것이다.

我们在那里应该保持肃静。

我々はそこで静粛を維持しなければならないだろう。

27. 유엔 회원국들은 그 도시에서 모인다.

联合国成员国聚集在那座城市。

国連加盟国はその都市に集まる。

28. 독일은 그해에 통일되었다.

德国是在那一年统一的。

ドイツはその年に統一された。

24. He solved the problem in the way.

The way which he solved the problem in.
The way in which he solved the problem.
The way that he solved the problem in.
The way he solved the problem in.

25. The application forms were received in the order.

The order which the application forms were received in.
The order in which the application forms were received.
The order that the application forms were received in.
The order the application forms were received in.

26. We should keep silent in the place.

The place which we should keep silent in.
The place in which we should keep silent.
The place that we should keep silent in.
The place we should keep silent in.

27. The UN member states meet in the city.

The city which the UN member states meet in.
The city in which the UN member states meet.
The city that the UN member states meet in.
The city the UN member states meet in.

28. Germany was unified in the year.

The year which Germany was unified in.
The year in which Germany was unified.
The year that Germany was unified in.
The year Germany was unified in.

29. 우리는 그런 활동들에서 많은 즐거움을 얻는다.

我们从那些活动中获得了很多的乐趣。

私たちはそれらのような活動から多くの楽しみを得る。

30. 그 유명한 철학자는 예전에 그 벤치에 앉곤 했었다.

那位著名的哲学家曾经经常坐在那条长椅上。

その有名な哲学者は以前にそのベンチに座っていた。

31. 우리 민족의 삶이 그 영화에서 묘사되어 있다.

我们的民族生活描绘在那部电影中。

私たち民族の生活がその映画で描かれている。

32. 우리는 그런 방식으로 핵폐기물을 처리한다.

我们以那种方式处置核废料。

私たちはそのような方式で核廃棄物を処理する。

33. 우리는 그 지도가 없었더라면 길을 잃어버렸을 것이다.

如果我们没有那张地图可能会迷路。

私たちはその地図がなかったら道に迷っただろう。

29. We get a lot of pleasure from the activities.

The activities which we get a lot of pleasure from.
The activities from which we get a lot of pleasure.
The activities that we get a lot of pleasure from.
The activities we get a lot of pleasure from.

30. The famous philosopher used to sit on the bench.

The bench which the famous philosopher used to sit on.
The bench on which the famous philosopher used to sit.
The bench that the famous philosopher used to sit on.
The bench the famous philosopher used to sit on.

31. Our people's life is depicted in the film.

The film which our people's life is depicted in.
The film in which our people's life is depicted.
The film that our people's life is depicted in.
The film our people's life is depicted in.

32. We dispose of nuclear waste in the way.

The way which we dispose of nuclear waste in.
The way in which we dispose of nuclear waste.
The way that we dispose of nuclear waste in.
The way we dispose of nuclear waste in.

33. We would have been lost without the map.

The map which we would have been lost without.
The map without which we would have been lost.
The map that we would have been lost without.
The map we would have been lost without.

34. 우리는 이 시대에 컴퓨터 없이는 지낼 수 없다.

我们这个时代没有电脑无法生活。

私たちは今の時代コンピュータなしでは過ごせない。

35. 식물과 동물이 그 대륙에서는 거의 살 수 없다.

植物和动物几乎不能在那个大陆上生活。

植物や動物はその大陸ではほとんど生きていけない。

36. 우리는 이런 아름다운 곳에서 주말을 지낼 수 있다.

我们可以在这个美丽的地方度过周末。

私たちはこのような美しいところで週末を過ごすことができる。

37. 환경을 구하는 것이 이 시대에는 생과 사의 문제이다.

拯救环境是这个时代的生死问题。

環境を救うことがこの時代には生と死の問題だ。

38. 우리는 친밀한 우정 속에서 깊은 생각과 감정을 공유한다.

我们在密切的友谊中分享深刻的思想和感情。

私たちは親密な友情の中で深い考えや感情を共有する。

34. We cannot do without computers in the age.

The age which we cannot do without computers in.
The age in which we cannot do without computers.
The age that we cannot do without computers in.
The age we cannot do without computers in.

35. Few plants and animals can live on the continent.

The continent which few plants and animals can live on.
The continent on which few plants and animals can live.
The continent that few plants and animals can live on.
The continent few plants and animals can live on.

36. We can spend a weekend in the beautiful place.

The beautiful place which we can spend a weekend in.
The beautiful place in which we can spend a weekend.
The beautiful place that we can spend a weekend in.
The beautiful place we can spend a weekend in.

37. Saving the environment is a matter of life and death in the age.

The age which saving the environment is a matter of life and death in.
The age in which saving the environment is a matter of life and death.
The age that saving the environment is a matter of life and death in.
The age saving the environment is a matter of life and death in.

38. We share deep thoughts and feelings in a close friendship.

A close friendship which we share deep thoughts and feelings in.
A close friendship in which we share deep thoughts and feelings.
A close friendship that we share deep thoughts and feelings in.
A close friendship we share deep thoughts and feelings in.

39. 모든 사람은 어떤 특별한 분야에서 전문가가 될 수 있다.

每个人都能成为任何特殊领域的专家。

すべての人はある特別な分野で専門家になることができる。

40. 우리는 이날에 지난해를 보내고 새해를 맞이한다.

我们在这一天辞旧岁迎新年。

私たちはこの日に過ぎた年を送り、新年を迎える。

41. 우리는 이 지구를 다른 피조물들과 함께 공유하고 있다.

我们与其他生物共享这个地球。

私たちはこの地球を他の生き物らと共に共有している。

42. 그 세계에서는 전쟁도, 범죄도, 질병도 전혀 없다.

在那个世界上完全没有战争,没有犯罪,没有疾病。

その世界では戦争も、犯罪も、疾病も全くない。

43. 너와 같은 사람들은 이런 직업들에서 성공을 발견하는 경향이 있다.

像你这样的人在这些职业中有成功的倾向。

あなたのような人たちはこれらのような職業で成功を発見する傾向がある。

39. Everyone can be an expert in a special field.

A special field which everyone can be an expert in.
A special field in which everyone can be an expert.
A special field that everyone can be an expert in.
A special field everyone can be an expert in.

40. We ring out the old year and ring in the new year on the day.

The day which we ring out the old year and ring in the new year on.
The day on which we ring out the old year and ring in the new year.
The day that we ring out the old year and ring in the new year on.
The day we ring out the old year and ring in the new year on.

41. We share this earth with other creatures.

Other creatures which we share this earth with.
Other creatures with which we share this earth.
Other creatures that we share this earth with.
Other creatures we share this earth with.

42. There is no war, no crime, and no disease in the world.

The world which there is no war, no crime, and no disease in.
The world in which there is no war, no crime, and no disease.
The world that there is no war, no crime, and no disease in.
The world there is no war, no crime, and no disease in.

43. People like you tend to find success in the occupations.

The occupations which people like you tend to find success in.
The occupations in which people like you tend to find success.
The occupations that people like you tend to find success in.
The occupations people like you tend to find success in.

44. 우리나라의 미래가 그 문제에 달려있다.

我们国家的未来取决于那一问题。

我が国の未来がその問題にかかっている。

45. 우리는 지금까지 그 문제에 대한 해결책을 찾을 수 없었다.

我们到现在还没有找到解决那个问题的办法。

私たちは今までその問題に対する解決策を見いだせなかった。

46. 그는 오늘날 이런 덕행들로 찬사를 받고 있다.

他今天以这些美德受到赞赏。

彼は今日、このような徳行で賛辞を受けている。

47. 우리의 태양과 같은 수십 억 개의 별들이 은하계에 위치하고 있다.

与我们的太阳相同的数十亿的星星位于银河系。

我々の太陽と同じ数十億個の星が銀河系に位置している。

48. 사람은 잠수함을 타고 물속에서 살 수 있다.

人可以乘坐潜水艇在水下生活。

人は潜水艦に乗って水の中で生活できる。

44. **The future of our country depends on the issue.**

   The issue which the future of our country depends on.
   The issue on which the future of our country depends.
   The issue that the future of our country depends on.
   The issue the future of our country depends on.

45. **We have not been able to find the solution to the problem.**

   The problem which we have not been able to find the solution to.
   The problem to which we have not been able to find the solution.
   The problem that we have not been able to find the solution to.
   The problem we have not been able to find the solution to.

46. **He is admired for the virtues today.**

   The virtues which he is admired for today.
   The virtues for which he is admired today.
   The virtues that he is admired for today.
   The virtues he is admired for today.

47. **Billions of stars like our sun are located in the galaxy.**

   The galaxy which billions of stars like our sun are located in.
   The galaxy in which billions of stars like our sun are located.
   The galaxy that billions of stars like our sun are located in.
   The galaxy billions of stars like our sun are located in.

48. **Man can live under water in a submarine.**

   A submarine which man can live under water in.
   A submarine in which man can live under water.
   A submarine that man can live under water in.
   A submarine man can live under water in.

49. 당연하게 생각되는 것이 경우에 따라서는 적절하다고 생각되지 않는다.

被认为理所当然的某种东西在某些情况下被认为是不合适的。

当然のことと思われるものが場合によっては適切と思われない。

50. 우리는 흉금을 터놓고 하는 대화를 통해서 서로를 더 잘 이해할 수 있게 되었다.

我们能够通过开诚布公的对话更好地理解彼此。

私たちは胸襟を開いてする対話を通して互いをもっとよく理解できるようになった。

49. What is taken for granted is not considered proper in a case.

A case which what is taken for granted is not considered proper in.
A case in which what is taken for granted is not considered proper.
A case that what is taken for granted is not considered proper in.
A case what is taken for granted is not considered proper in.

50. We came to understand each other better through a heart-to-heart talk.

A heart-to-heart talk which we came to understand each other better through.
A heart-to-heart talk through which we came to understand each other better.
A heart-to-heart talk that we came to understand each other better through.
A heart-to-heart talk we came to understand each other better through.

7. 관계 대명사 What
(주격/Nominative)

주격 관계 대명사 what은 선행사가 자신 속에 포함된 관계 대명사이다. 형식은 주로 'what + 동사'로 되어 있고 해석은 '~하는 것'으로 하면 되겠다. 다른 관계 대명사들, 즉 who, which, that이 선행사인 명사를 수식하는 형용사절을 이끄는 것과는 달리, 관계 대명사 what은 선행사가 자신 속에 포함되어 있기 때문에 명사절의 기능을 담당한다. 따라서 관계 대명사 what은 독자적으로 주어, 보어, 목적어로 쓰일 수 있다.

주격 관계 대명사 what은 명사 수식 구조인 형용사절이 아니라 명사절을 이끌기 때문에 선행사인 명사를 후치수식하는 관계절을 다루고 있는 본 교재와는 약간 거리가 있어 보이지만, 본 교재에서 관계 대명사 what을 다루고 있는 이유는, 먼저 다른 관계 대명사들과 본질적으로 같은 기능과 구조를 갖고 있기 때문이며, 또 하나는 우리가 너무도 많이 사용하고 있고 또한 쉬운 구조로 된 이 표현에 학습자들이 익숙해 있지 않다는 점을 감안한 것이라는 점을 참고해주기 바란다.

여기서 "그것은 정말로 나를 기쁘게 해 준다."라는 문장을 관계 대명사 what과 관계 대명사 which와 that을 사용해서 '나를 정말로 기쁘게 해주는 것'이라는 구문으로 전환시켜보면 다음과 같이 할 수 있겠다.

It really pleases me.

1. What really pleases me.
2. The thing which really pleases me.
3. The thing that really pleases me.

1. 관계 대명사 what
2. 관계 대명사 which
3. 관계 대명사 that

물론 이 세 예문 가운데서 관계 대명사 what을 사용한 1번 예문이 가장 많이 사용된다는 것은 모두 알고 있을 것이다. 하지만 2번과 3번 예문도 거리끼지 말고 많이 사용할 수 있도록 연습해주기 바란다.

우리말의 명사 수식 구조인 전치수식 구조와는 완전히 정반대인 후치수식 구조를 갖고 있는 영어를 우리가 학습하는 데 있어서, 본 교재에서 다루고 있는 보통의 단문(simple sentence)을 명사 후치수식 구문으로 전환시킬 수 있는 능력을 기르는 것은 영어를 포함한 모든 언어를 학습하고 구사하는 데 있어서 첩경이자 열쇠이며 핵심과제라는 것을 깊이 인식하고 충분한 연습을 해주기 바란다.

1. 그것은 옳다.

    那是正确的。

    それは正しい。

2. 그것은 언제든지 일어날 수 있다.

    那随时都可能发生。

    それはいつでも起こり得る。

3. 그것은 괜찮아 보인다.

    那个看起来不错。

    それは大丈夫そうだ。

4. 그것은 보고서에 언급되어 있지 않다.

    那个没有在报告中提及。

    それは報告書で言及されていない。

5. 그것은 유감스럽다.

    那是令人遗憾的。

    それは残念だ。

6. 그것은 되돌릴 수 없다.

    那个不可以挽回。

    それは後戻りできない。

1. **It is right.**

   What is right.
   The thing which is right.
   The thing that is right.

2. **It can happen anytime.**

   What can happen anytime.
   The thing which can happen anytime.
   The thing that can happen anytime.

3. **It looks OK.**

   What looks OK.
   The thing which looks OK.
   The thing that looks OK.

4. **It is not stated in the report.**

   What is not stated in the report.
   The thing which is not stated in the report.
   The thing that is not stated in the report.

5. **It is regrettable.**

   What is regrettable.
   The thing which is regrettable.
   The thing that is regrettable.

6. **It cannot be undone.**

   What cannot be undone.
   The thing which cannot be undone.
   The thing that cannot be undone.

7. 나는 그것이 옳다고 생각한다.

   我认为那是正确的。

   私はそれが正しいと思う。

8. 그것이 그를 부자로 만들어주었다.

   那使他成为富翁。

   それが彼を金持ちにしてくれた。

9. 그것이 나를 직장에 지각하게 만들었다.

   它让我上班迟到了。

   それが私を職場に遅刻させた。

10. 그것은 반드시 이루어져야만 한다.

    那是必须要实现的。

    それは必ず行われなければならない。

11. 그것이 지금까지 나를 무척 슬프게 만들었다.

    它一直让我非常伤心。

    それが今まで私をとても悲しくした。

12. 그것이 민주주의가 작동되도록 만든다.

    它促使民主主义运作。

    それが民主主義を作動させている。

7. **I think it is correct.**

   What I think is correct.
   The thing which I think is correct.
   The thing that I think is correct.

8. **It made him rich.**

   What made him rich.
   The thing which made him rich.
   The thing that made him rich.

9. **It made me late for work.**

   What made me late for work.
   The thing which made me late for work.
   The thing that made me late for work.

10. **It must be done.**

    What must be done.
    The thing which must be done.
    The thing that must be done.

11. **It has made me so sad.**

    What has made me so sad.
    The thing which has made me so sad.
    The thing that has made me so sad.

12. **It makes democracy work.**

    What makes democracy work.
    The thing which makes democracy work.
    The thing that makes democracy work.

13. 그것은 이해할 수 없다.

    它无法理解。

    それは理解できない。

14. 그것이 지금까지 나를 괴롭히고 있다.

    它一直在困扰着我。

    それが今まで私を苦しめている。

15. 그것은 훨씬 더 나쁘다.

    那个更糟。

    それははるかに悪い。

16. 그것은 상황을 더욱 악화시킨다.

    它使情况更加恶化。

    それは状況をさらに悪化させる。

17. 그것은 나에게 좋다.

    那对我有好处。

    それは私にとって良い。

18. 그것은 나의 기분을 북돋아 준다.

    它鼓励着我的情绪。

    それは私を奮い立たせてくれる。

13. It is incomprehensible.

What is incomprehensible.
The thing which is incomprehensible.
The thing that is incomprehensible.

14. It has been torturing me.

What has been torturing me.
The thing which has been torturing me.
The thing that has been torturing me.

15. It is much worse.

What is much worse.
The thing which is much worse.
The thing that is much worse.

16. It makes things much worse.

What makes things much worse.
The thing which makes things much worse.
The thing that makes things much worse.

17. It is good for me.

What is good for me.
The thing which is good for me.
The thing that is good for me.

18. It cheers me up.

What cheers me up.
The thing which cheers me up.
The thing that cheers me up.

19. 그것은 너의 건강에 해롭다.

它对你的健康有害。

それはあなたの健康に有害だ。

20. 나는 그것이 정당하다고 생각한다.

我认为那是正当的。

私はそれが正当だと思う。

21. 그것은 몇 해 전에 일어났다.

那个发生在几年前。

それは数年前に起きた。

22. 그것은 할 만한 가치가 있다.

那个值得做的。

それは行うほどの価値がある。

23. 그것은 이용 가능하다, 그것은 구입 가능하다.

它是可用的。它是可购买的。

それは利用可能だ。それは購入可能だ。

24. 그것이 나에게 바람직스럽다.

那个对我很可取。

それが僕には好ましい。

19. **It is harmful to your health.**

   What is harmful to your health.
   The thing which is harmful to your health.
   The thing that is harmful to your health.

20. **I think it is just.**

   What I think is just.
   The thing which I think is just.
   The thing that I think is just.

21. **It happened several years ago.**

   What happened several years ago.
   The thing which happened several years ago.
   The thing that happened several years ago.

22. **It is worth doing.**

   What is worth doing.
   The thing which is worth doing.
   The thing that is worth doing.

23. **It is available.**

   What is available.
   The thing which is available.
   The thing that is available.

24. **It is desirable to me.**

   What is desirable to me.
   The thing which is desirable to me.
   The thing that is desirable to me.

25. 그것은 인생을 즐겁게 만들어준다.

它使人生变得快乐。

それは人生を楽しくしてくれる。

26. 그것은 훨씬 더 재미있다.

它更有趣。

それははるかに面白い。

27. 그것은 이 세상을 살 만한 가치가 있는 곳으로 만들어준다.

它使这个世界成为值得生活的地方。

それはこの世を生きる価値がある所にしてくれる。

28. 그것이 지금까지 나에게 가장 많은 영향을 주었다.

到目前为止它给了我非常大的影响。

それが今まで私に最も多くの影響を与えた。

29. 그것은 사람을 동물과 다르게 만들어준다.

它使人与动物不同。

それは人を動物と違うものにしている。

30. 그것은 잊어서는 안 될 것이다.

它不应该被忘记。

それは忘れてはならないだろう。

25. **It makes life enjoyable.**

What makes life enjoyable.
The thing which makes life enjoyable.
The thing that makes life enjoyable.

26. **It is a lot more interesting.**

What is a lot more interesting.
The thing which is a lot more interesting.
The thing that is a lot more interesting.

27. **It makes this world a place worth living in.**

What makes this world a place worth living in.
The thing which makes this world a place worth living in.
The thing that makes this world a place worth living in.

28. **It has influenced me the most.**

What has influenced me the most.
The thing which has influenced me the most.
The thing that has influenced me the most.

29. **It makes men different from animals.**

What makes men different from animals.
The thing which makes men different from animals.
The thing that makes men different from animals.

30. **It should not be forgotten.**

What should not be forgotten.
The thing which should not be forgotten.
The thing that should not be forgotten.

31. 그것은 훨씬 더 당혹스럽다.

那更令人尷尬。

それははるかに当惑的だ。

32. 그것은 내가 퇴근길에 일어났다.

那发生在我下班回家的路上。

それは私の仕事帰りに起きた。

33. 그것이 그를 가출하게 만들었다.

那使他离家出走。

それが彼を家出させた。

34. 그것이 나로 하여금 마음을 바꾸게 만들었다.

那个使我改变了主意。

それが私の心を変えさせた。

35. 그것이 한때는 불가능하다고 생각되었었다.

它曾经被认为是不可能的。

それは一時は不可能だと思われていた。

36. 그것은 상황을 훨씬 더 복잡하게 만든다.

它使情况变得更复杂。

それは状況をさらに複雑にさせる。

31. It is still more embarrassing.

What is still more embarrassing.
The thing which is still more embarrassing.
The thing that is still more embarrassing.

32. It happened on my way home from work.

What happened on my way home from work.
The thing which happened on my way home from work.
The thing that happened on my way home from work.

33. It made him leave home.

What made him leave home.
The thing which made him leave home.
The thing that made him leave home.

34. It made me change my mind.

What made me change my mind.
The thing which made me change my mind.
The thing that made me change my mind.

35. It was once thought impossible.

What was once thought impossible.
The thing which was once thought impossible.
The thing that was once thought impossible.

36. It makes the situation far more complicated.

What makes the situation far more complicated.
The thing which makes the situation far more complicated.
The thing that makes the situation far more complicated.

37. 그것은 지금까지 대대로 전해져 왔다.

到目前为止那是一代代传下来的。

それは今まで代々伝わってきた。

38. 그것이 수업 중에 나를 가장 졸리게 한다.

那个让我在上课时很困倦。

それが授業中に私を一番眠くさせる。

39. 그것은 많은 10대들 사이에서 유행하고 있다.

那个在很多十几岁青少年之间流行。

それは多くの10代の間で流行している。

40. 그것은 한 사람을 행복하게 만들어준다.

那使一个人快乐。

それは一人の人間を幸せにしてくれる。

41. 그것은 비도덕적이다.

那是不道德的。

それは非道徳的だ。

42. 나는 그것이 불가능하다고 생각한다.

我认为那是不可能的。

私はそれが不可能だと思う。

37. It has been handed down from generation to generation.

What has been handed down from generation to generation.
The thing which has been handed down from generation to generation.
The thing that has been handed down from generation to generation.

38. It makes me sleepy the most during the class.

What makes me sleepy the most during the class.
The thing which makes me sleepy the most during the class.
The thing that makes me sleepy the most during the class.

39. It is fashionable among many teenagers.

What is fashionable among many teenagers.
The thing which is fashionable among many teenagers.
The thing that is fashionable among many teenagers.

40. It makes a human being happy.

What makes a human being happy.
The thing which makes a human being happy.
The thing that makes a human being happy.

41. It is immoral.

What is immoral.
The thing which is immoral.
The thing that is immoral.

42. I think it is impossible.

What I think is impossible.
The thing which I think is impossible.
The thing that I think is impossible.

43. 그것이 그녀를 아주 특별하게 만들어준다.

那使她非常特别。

それが彼女をとても特別にしてくれる。

44. 그것이 그를 다른 가수들과 다르게 만들어준다.

那使他不同于其他歌手。

それが彼を別の歌手たちと違うものにしている。

45. 그것이 한때에는 건강을 유지하는 최고의 방법이라고 여겨졌었다.

它曾经被认为是保持健康的最好的方法。

それがかつては健康を維持する最高の方法だとされていた。

46. 그것이 나에게는 분명한 상식처럼 보인다.

那对我来说是很明显的常识。

それが私には明確な常識のように見える。

47. 그것은 매일 세상에서 일어나고 있다.

那每天都在世界各地发生。

それは毎日世界で起きている。

48. 그것은 학교에서 가르치지 않는다.

那不是在学校教的。

それは学校で教えていない。

43. It makes her so special.

What makes her so special.
The thing which makes her so special.
The thing that makes her so special.

44. It makes him different from other singers.

What makes him different from other singers.
The thing which makes him different from other singers.
The thing that makes him different from other singers.

45. It was once regarded as the best way of staying healthy.

What was once regarded as the best way of staying healthy.
The thing which was once regarded as the best way of staying healthy.
The thing that was once regarded as the best way of staying healthy.

46. It seems clear common sense to me.

What seems clear common sense to me.
The thing which seems clear common sense to me.
The thing that seems clear common sense to me.

47. It is taking place in the world every day.

What is taking place in the world every day.
The thing which is taking place in the world every day.
The thing that is taking place in the world every day.

48. It is not taught at school.

What is not taught at school.
The thing which is not taught at school.
The thing that is not taught at school.

49. 그것은 그밖에 어떤 것보다도 나를 더 많이 슬프게 한다.

它比其它任何东西都让我伤心。

それはその他のどんなことよりも私を悲しくさせる。

50. 그것이 예전에는 재미있고 즐거웠었다.

那个在以前是有趣和愉快的。

それが以前は面白く、楽しかった。

49. **It makes me sad more than anything else.**

What makes me sad more than anything else.
The thing which makes me sad more than anything else.
The thing that makes me sad more than anything else.

50. **It used to be fun and enjoyable.**

What used to be fun and enjoyable.
The thing which used to be fun and enjoyable.
The thing that used to be fun and enjoyable.

8. 관계 대명사 What
(목적격/Objective)

　목적격 관계 대명사 what도 주격 관계 대명사 what과 마찬가지로 선행사가 자신 속에 포함된 관계 대명사이다. 형식은 'what + 주어 + 동사'로 되어 있고 해석은 '주어가 ~하는 것'으로 하면 되겠다. 관계 대명사 what은 선행사가 포함되어 있기 때문에 다른 관계 대명사인 who, which, that이 앞에 있는 선행사를 수식하는 형용사절을 이끄는 것과는 달리 명사절을 이끌기 때문에 독자적으로 주어, 보어, 목적어로 쓰일 수 있다.

　목적격 관계 대명사 what은 명사 수식 구조인 형용사절이 아니라 명사절을 이끌기 때문에 선행사인 명사를 후치수식하는 관계절을 다루고 있는 본 교재와는 약간 거리가 있어 보이지만, 본 교재에서 관계 대명사 what을 다루고 있는 이유는, 먼저 다른 관계 대명사들과 본질적으로 같은 기능과 구조를 갖고 있기 때문이며, 또 하나는 우리가 너무도 많이 사용하고 있고 또한 쉬운 구조로 된 이 표현에 학습자들이 익숙해 있지 않다는 점을 감안한 것이라는 점을 참고해주기 바란다.

관계 대명사 (Relative Pronoun)

여기서 "나는 지금까지 그것을 간절히 바라고 있었다."라는 문장을 관계 대명사 what과 관계 대명사 which와 that을 사용해서 '내가 지금까지 간절히 바라고 있었던 것'이라는 후치수식 구문으로 전환시켜보면 다음과 같이 할 수 있겠다.

I have been looking forward to it.

1. What I have been looking forward to.
2. The thing which I have been looking forward to.
3. The thing to which I have been looking forward.
4. The thing that I have been looking forward to.
5. The thing I have been looking forward to.

1. 관계 대명사 what
2. 관계 대명사 which
3. 전치사 + 관계 대명사 which
4. 관계 대명사 that
5. 관계 대명사 생략

본 교재에서 문법적인 용어를 사용해서 문장들을 설명하고 있지만, 이것은 학습자들의 학습 편의를 위해서 분류한 것에 불과하고 실제로 학습자들이 신경을 써야 할 부분은 문법이라는 생각 없이 일반 문장을 명사 후치수식 구문으로 자유롭게 전환시킬 수 있는 능력을 기르는 것이다. 일반 문장을 명사 후치수식 구문으로 자유롭게 전환시킬 수 있어야만 비로소 영어를 자유롭게 구사할 수 있다는 것을 인식해주기 바란다.

1. 나는 그것을 의미한다. 내 말은 그 뜻이다.

   那就是我的意思。 我是说那个意思。

   私はそれを意味する。 私の話はそういう意味だ。

2. 나는 그것을 하지 않았다.

   我没有做那件事。

   私はそれをしなかった。

3. 나는 그녀에게 그것을 제안했다.

   我向她提出了那个建议。

   私は彼女にそれを提案した。

4. 그녀는 지금 당장 그것이 필요하다.

   她现在需要它。

   彼女は今すぐそれが必要である。

5. 나는 그것이 두렵다.

   我害怕它。

   私はそれが怖い。

1. **I mean it.**

   What I mean.
   The thing which I mean.
   The thing that I mean.
   The thing I mean.

2. **I didn't do it.**

   What I didn't do.
   The thing which I didn't do.
   The thing that I didn't do.
   The thing I didn't do.

3. **I suggested it to her.**

   What I suggested to her.
   The thing which I suggested to her.
   The thing that I suggested to her.
   The thing I suggested to her.

4. **She needs it right now.**

   What she needs right now.
   The thing which she needs right now.
   The thing that she needs right now.
   The thing she needs right now.

5. **I'm afraid of it.**

   What I'm afraid of.
   The thing which I'm afraid of.
   The thing of which I'm afraid.
   The thing that I'm afraid of.
   The thing I'm afraid of.

6. 나는 그것에 익숙해 있다.

    我对它已经习惯了。

    私はそれに慣れている。

7. 이 이야기는 그것을 함축하고 있다.

    这个故事暗示着那个。

    この話はそれを含蓄している。

8. 나는 그것을 말로 표현하고 싶다.

    我想用语言来表达它。

    私はそれを言葉で表現したい。

9. 그녀는 그때 그것을 하고 있었다.

    她那时正在做那个。

    彼女はその時それをしていた。

10. 그는 생계를 위해서 그것을 하고 있다.

    他为了生计在做那个。

    彼は生計を立てるためにそれをしている。

6. **I am used to it.**

   What I am used to.
   The thing which I am used to.
   The thing to which I am used.
   The thing that I am used to.
   The thing I am used to.

7. **The story implies it.**

   What the story implies.
   The thing which the story implies.
   The thing that the story implies.
   The thing the story implies.

8. **I want to put it into words.**

   What I want to put into words.
   The thing which I want to put into words.
   The thing that I want to put into words.
   The thing I want to put into words.

9. **She was doing it at the moment.**

   What she was doing at the moment.
   The thing which she was doing at the moment.
   The thing that she was doing at the moment.
   The thing she was doing at the moment.

10. **He does it for a living.**

    What he does for a living.
    The thing which he does for a living.
    The thing that he does for a living.
    The thing he does for a living.

11. 나는 그것을 말할 의도가 아니었다.

我不是故意说它。

私はそれを言う意図がなかった。

12. 우리는 그것을 하기 위해 갹출을 해야만 했다.

我们为它不得不捐了一些钱。

私たちはそれをするため拠出しなければならなかった。

13. 나는 그것을 가장 잘할 수 있다.

我能把它做得最好。

私はそれを最も上手くできる。

14. 그는 나에게 그것을 기대했었다.

他对我期待着那个。

彼は私にそれを期待していた。

15. 나는 그것을 학교에서 배웠다.

我在学校学到了它。

私はそれを学校で学んだ。

11. **I didn't mean to say it.**

What I didn't mean to say.
The thing which I didn't mean to say.
The thing that I didn't mean to say.
The thing I didn't mean to say.

12. **We had to chip in for it.**

What we had to chip in for.
The thing which we had to chip in for.
The thing for which we had to chip in.
The thing that we had to chip in for.
The thing we had to chip in for.

13. **I can do it best.**

What I can do best.
The thing which I can do best.
The thing that I can do best.
The thing I can do best.

14. **He expected it of me.**

What he expected of me.
The thing which he expected of me.
The thing that he expected of me.
The thing he expected of me.

15. **I learned it at school.**

What I learned at school.
The thing which I learned at school.
The thing that I learned at school.
The thing I learned at school.

16. 나는 그것을 잘 알지 못한다.

我不熟悉它。

私はそれをよく知らない。

17. 나는 그것을 인터넷으로 한다.

我在互联网上做那个。

私はそれをインターネットでしている。

18. 나는 요즘 그것을 많이 듣는다.

最近我经常听到它。

私は最近それをたくさん聞く。

19. 너는 손에 그것을 갖고 있구나.

你手里拿着那个啊。

あなたは手にそれを持っているんだな。

20. 그는 그것을 받을 자격이 없다.

他不配得到它。

彼はそれを受ける資格がない。

16. I'm not familiar with it.

What I'm not familiar with.
The thing which I'm not familiar with.
The thing with which I'm not familiar.
The thing that I'm not familiar with.
The thing I'm not familiar with.

17. I do it on the Internet.

What I do on the Internet.
The thing which I do on the Internet.
The thing that I do on the Internet.
The thing I do on the Internet.

18. I hear it a lot these days.

What I hear a lot these days.
The thing which I hear a lot these days.
The thing that I hear a lot these days.
The thing I hear a lot these days.

19. You have it in your hand.

What you have in your hand.
The thing which you have in your hand.
The thing that you have in your hand.
The thing you have in your hand.

20. He doesn't deserve it.

What he doesn't deserve.
The thing which he doesn't deserve.
The thing that he doesn't deserve.
The thing he doesn't deserve.

21. 나는 그것에 대해서 궁금하다.

我对那件事很好奇。

私はそれについて知りたい。

22. 나는 일요일마다 그것을 한다.

我每个星期天做那个。

私は日曜日ごとにそれをする。

23. 나는 너에게 그것에 관하여 묻고 싶었다.

关于那件事我想问你。

私はあなたにそれに関して質問したかった。

24. 그녀는 그것을 성취하려고 노력하고 있다.

她正在努力实现它。

彼女はそれを成就させようと努力している。

25. 많은 사람들이 그것을 모르고 있다.

很多人不知道它。

多くの人たちがそれを知らずにいる。

21. I'm curious about it.

What I'm curious about.
The thing which I'm curious about.
The thing about which I'm curious.
The thing that I'm curious about.
The thing I'm curious about.

22. I do it on Sundays.

What I do on Sundays.
The thing which I do on Sundays.
The thing that I do on Sundays.
The thing I do on Sundays.

23. I wanted to ask you about it.

What I wanted to ask you about.
The thing which I wanted to ask you about.
The thing about which I wanted to ask you.
The thing that I wanted to ask you about.
The thing I wanted to ask you about.

24. She is trying to achieve it.

What she is trying to achieve.
The thing which she is trying to achieve.
The thing that she is trying to achieve.
The thing she is trying to achieve.

25. Many people don't know it.

What many people don't know.
The thing which many people don't know.
The thing that many people don't know.
The thing many people don't know.

26. 사람들은 그것을 가장 귀중하게 여긴다.

    人们把它看做是最宝贵的。

    人々はそれを最も貴重に思っている。

27. 많은 사람들이 그것을 멀리하고 있다.

    很多人远离它。

    多くの人がそれを遠ざけている。

28. 모든 사람은 그것에 관심이 있다.

    每个人都对它感兴趣。

    すべての人はそれに関心がある。

29. 나는 이번 다가오는 휴일에 그것을 하고 싶다.

    我想在这个即将到来的假期做那件事。

    私は今週の休日にそれをしたい。

30. 나는 지금 그것을 하지 말라고 들었다.

    我被告知不要做那件事。

    私はそれをするなと聞いた。

26. **People value it most.**

   What people value most.
   The thing which people value most.
   The thing that people value most.
   The thing people value most.

27. **Many people keep away from it.**

   What many people keep away from.
   The thing which many people keep away from.
   The thing from which many people keep away.
   The thing that many people keep away from.
   The thing many people keep away from.

28. **Everyone is interested in it.**

   What everyone is interested in.
   The thing which everyone is interested in.
   The thing in which everyone is interested.
   The thing that everyone is interested in.
   The thing everyone is interested in.

29. **I feel like doing it on this coming holiday.**

   What I feel like doing on this coming holiday.
   The thing which I feel like doing on this coming holiday.
   The thing that I feel like doing on this coming holiday.
   The thing I feel like doing on this coming holiday.

30. **I have been told not to do it.**

   What I have been told not to do.
   The thing which I have been told not to do.
   The thing that I have been told not to do.
   The thing I have been told not to do.

31. 너는 그것을 책임져야 한다.

你必须对它承担责任。

あなたはその責任を負わなければならない。

32. 우리는 지금까지 그것을 처음부터 알고 있었다.

我们从开始到现在都知道它。

私たちは今までそれを最初から知っていた。

33. 그녀는 매번 자신의 남편에게 그 말을 한다.

她每次都对她的丈夫说那句话。

彼女は毎回自分の夫にその言葉を言う。

34. 그는 휴식으로 그것을 한다.

他利用休息做那个。

彼は休息としてそれをする。

35. 나는 다른 사람들과 그것을 공유하고 싶다.

我想和别人分享它。

私はほかの人たちとそれを共有したい。

31. You are responsible for it.

What you are responsible for.
The thing which you are responsible for.
The thing for which you are responsible.
The thing that you are responsible for.
The thing you are responsible for.

32. We have known it all along.

What we have known all along.
The thing which we have known all along.
The thing that we have known all along.
The thing we have known all along.

33. She says it to her husband each time.

What she says to her husband each time.
The thing which she says to her husband each time.
The thing that she says to her husband each time.
The thing she says to her husband each time.

34. He does it for relaxation.

What he does for relaxation.
The thing which he does for relaxation.
The thing that he does for relaxation.
The thing he does for relaxation.

35. I want to share it with others.

What I want to share with others.
The thing which I want to share with others.
The thing that I want to share with others.
The thing I want to share with others.

36. 그녀는 그것을 피하려고 노력한다.

她努力避开它。

彼女はそれを避けようと努力する。

37. 나는 지금까지 그것을 오랫동안 마음속에 품고 있었다.

我一直把它藏在我心里很长时间。

私は今までそれを長い間心の中に秘めていた。

38. 나는 나의 영어 실력 향상을 위해서 그것이 필요하다.

为了提高我的英语能力我需要它。

私は私の英語の実力向上のためにそれが必要である。

39. 나는 그것을 참을 수 없다.

我不能忍受它。

私はそれを我慢できない。

40. 우리는 현재 그것이 몹시 필요하다.

我们现在非常需要它。

私たちは現在それが非常に必要である。

36. **She tries to avoid it.**

   What she tries to avoid.
   The thing which she tries to avoid.
   The thing that she tries to avoid.
   The thing she tries to avoid.

37. **I've had it in mind for a long time.**

   What I've had in mind for a long time.
   The thing which I've had in mind for a long time.
   The thing that I've had in mind for a long time.
   The thing I've had in mind for a long time.

38. **I need it for the improvement of my English ability.**

   What I need for the improvement of my English ability.
   The thing which I need for the improvement of my English ability.
   The thing that I need for the improvement of my English ability.
   The thing I need for the improvement of my English ability.

39. **I can't put up with it.**

   What I can't put up with.
   The thing which I can't put up with.
   The thing with which I can't put up.
   The thing that I can't put up with.
   The thing I can't put up with.

40. **We need it badly at the moment.**

   What we need badly at the moment.
   The thing which we need badly at the moment.
   The thing that we need badly at the moment.
   The thing we need badly at the moment.

41. 그는 지금까지 그것을 그밖에 어느 누구에게도 결코 말한 적이 없다.

他从来没有对任何人说过它。

彼は今までそれをその他の誰にも決して言ったことはない。

42. 내가 뉴욕에 체재하는 동안 그녀는 나를 위해서 그것을 해주었다.

我逗留在纽约时她为我做了那个。

私がニューヨークに滞在している間彼女は私のためにそれをしてくれた。

43. 나는 그것에 대해서 지금 무척 감사하게 여기고 있다.

我对它非常感激。

私はそれについて今すごくありがたく思っている。

44. 나는 그것을 잊고 싶지 않다.

我不想忘记它。

私はそれを忘れたくない。

45. 나는 내 여행에서 그것을 배웠다.

我在我的旅行中学到了它。

私は旅行でそれを学んだ。

41. **He has never said it to anyone else.**

What he has never said to anyone else.
The thing which he has never said to anyone else.
The thing that he has never said to anyone else.
The thing he has never said to anyone else.

42. **She did it for me during my stay in New York.**

What she did for me during my stay in New York.
The thing which she did for me during my stay in New York.
The thing that she did for me during my stay in New York.
The thing she did for me during my stay in New York.

43. **I am very grateful for it now.**

What I am very grateful for now.
The thing which I am very grateful for now.
The thing for which I am very grateful now.
The thing that I am very grateful for now.
The thing I am very grateful for now.

44. **I don't want to forget it.**

What I don't want to forget.
The thing which I don't want to forget.
The thing that I don't want to forget.
The thing I don't want to forget.

45. **I learned it on my journey.**

What I learned on my journey.
The thing which I learned on my journey.
The thing that I learned on my journey.
The thing I learned on my journey.

46. 이 소설은 그것에 기반을 두고 있다.

这部小说以它为基础。

この小説はそれに基盤を置いている。

47. 나는 그때 그것을 깨닫지 못했다.

我当时并没有意识到它。

私はその時それを気づけなかった。

48. 모든 TV 시청자들은 그것을 갖고 있어야만 할 것이다.

每个电视观众都应该拥有它。

すべてのTV視聴者たちはそれを持っていなければならないだろう。

49. 많은 사람들이 보통 그것이 사실이라고 믿고 있다.

很多人通常相信那是真的。

多くの人たちが普通それが事実だと信じている。

50. 그는 지금까지 그것을 단 일 년 만에 이루었다.

他到现在为止只用一年就完成了那个东西。

彼は今までそれをたった一年で成し遂げた。

46. This story is based on it.

What this story is based on.
The thing which this story is based on.
The thing on which this story is based.
The thing that this story is based on.
The thing this story is based on.

47. I failed to realize it at that time.

What I failed to realize at that time.
The thing which I failed to realize at that time.
The thing that I failed to realize at that time.
The thing I failed to realize at that time.

48. Every TV viewer should have it.

What every TV viewer should have.
The thing which every TV viewer should have.
The thing that every TV viewer should have.
The thing every TV viewer should have.

49. Many people commonly believe it to be true.

What many people commonly believe to be true.
The thing which many people commonly believe to be true.
The thing that many people commonly believe to be true.
The thing many people commonly believe to be true.

50. He has accomplished it in just a year.

What he has accomplished in just a year.
The thing which he has accomplished in just a year.
The thing that he has accomplished in just a year.
The thing he has accomplished in just a year.

9. 관계 대명사 That
(주격/Nominative)

주격 관계 대명사 that은 선행사가 사람이든 동물이든 사물이든 가리지 않고 어떤 명사든 모두 다 수식할 수 있는 관계 대명사이다. 따라서 사용 빈도가 가장 높은 관계 대명사라고 할 수 있겠다. 구조는 '선행사 + that + 동사'의 구조로 되어있고 해석은 '~하는 명사'로 하면 되겠다. 주격 관계 대명사 that도 문법적으로 접속사와 대명사의 역할을 하면서 어떤 명사든 모두 다 수식할 수 있는 형용사절의 기능을 갖고 있다고 보면 되겠다.

관계 대명사 that은 몇 가지 주의할 점이 있는데, 첫째로 관계 대명사 that은 소유격 관계 대명사가 없다는 것이고, 둘째로 관계 대명사 that은 제한적 용법(restrictive use 또는 defining relative clause)으로만 사용되고 계속적 용법(non-restrictive use 또는 non-defining relative clause)으로는 사용되지 않는다는 점이다. 셋째, 주격 관계 대명사 that과 다음에 있는 be 동사는 동시에 생략할 수 있다. 이것은 주격 관계 대명사 who, which에서도 언급한 것처럼 주격 관계 대명사 that과 be 동사 다음에 동격의 의미가 있는 명사가 오는 경우에는 명사의 앞과 뒤에 콤마를 찍어서 관계 대명사와 be 동사를 생략할 수 있고, 이 경우를 제외하면 주격 관계 대명사 that과 be 동사 다음에는 형용사구나 현재분사나 아니면 과거분사가 위치하므로 이것들은 관계 대명사를 사용하는 것보다 더 간단한 명사 후치수식 구조이기 때문이다. 넷째로, 관계 대명사 that 앞에는 전치사를 쓸 수 없다. 마지막 다섯 번째로 관계 대명사 that은 모든 명사를 다 수식할 수 있는 기능을 갖고 있지만, 다음의 세 가지의 경우에는 관계 대명사 who나 which를 쓰지 않고 that을 쓴다는 것이다.

첫째, 의문사로 시작하는 특수 의문문일 경우에 관계 대명사 who나 which를 쓰면 잘못해서 의문문을 두 개로 알아들을 수 있기 때문에 이런 애매모호성을 없애기 위해

01 관계 대명사 (Relative Pronoun)

서 관계 대명사 who나 which보다 that을 사용하게 되고, 둘째, 사람을 의미하지 않는 선행사 앞에서 최상급, 서수, the only, the very, the same 등이 선행사를 수식할 때와 all, none, nothing, everything, something, anything, many, much, few, little 과 같은 단어들이 선행사로 올 때도 관계 대명사 who나 which보다는 that을 사용하게 된다. 그리고 셋째, 선행사가 '사람 + 동물'이나 '사람 + 사물' 두 개로 되어 있을 경우에도 관계 대명사 that을 사용하게 된다.

선행사가 사람일 경우에 관계 대명사 who나 whom을 쓰는 경우와 that을 쓰는 경우를 비교해보면 that보다는 who나 whom을 쓰는 경우가 훨씬 더 많다. 하지만 북미 영어권의 구어에서는 that도 많이 사용한다. 그리고 선행사가 동물이나 사물일 경우에는 which보다 that을 사용하는 경우가 더 많다는 사실도 참고로 알아두면 좋겠다.

> 여기서 "돈이 우리에게 모든 것을 다 사줄 수는 없다."라는 문장을 '우리에게 모든 것을 다 사줄 수는 없는 돈'이라는 명사 후치수식 구문으로 전환시켜보면 다음과 같이 할 수 있겠다.
>
> Money cannot buy everything for us.
>
> 1. Money that cannot buy everything for us.
> 2. Money which cannot buy everything for us.
> 3. Money unable to buy everything for us.
> 4. Money not able to buy everything for us.
> 5. Money not to buy everything for us.
>
> 1. 관계 대명사 that
> 2. 관계 대명사 which
> 3. 관계 대명사 + be 동사 생략
> 4. 관계 대명사 + be 동사 생략
> 5. 관계 대명사 + be 동사 생략, 또는 to-부정사

1. 그것들은 많은 설탕을 함유하고 있다.

   那些东西含有大量的糖。

   それらは多くの砂糖を含有している。

2. 갖가지 사연들이 그 사건과 연루되어 있다.

   那一事件中涉及各种情况。

   さまざまな事情がその事件とかかわっている。

3. 몇몇 동물이 예상보다 더 빠르게 사라져 가고 있다.

   有些动物比预期灭亡得快。

   いくつかの動物が予想より早く絶滅していっている。

4. 벌어지고 있는 경제력의 차이가 그 나라 국민을 갈라놓고 있다.

   不断扩大的经济差距使那个国家人民分裂。

   拡大している経済力の差がその国の国民を分断している。

5. 청바지는 결코 유행을 타지 않는다.

   蓝色牛仔裤从永不过时。

   ジーンズは決して流行に乗らない。

6. 많은 물건이 거의 사용되지 않는다.

   很多东西都几乎不用。

   多くの物がほとんど使用されていない。

영어는 후치수식, 한중일어는 전치수식

01 관계 대명사 (Relative Pronoun)

1. **They contain a lot of sugar.**

   The things that contain a lot of sugar.
   The things which contain a lot of sugar.
   The things containing a lot of sugar.

2. **Various circumstances are involved in the incident.**

   Various circumstances that are involved in the incident.
   Various circumstances which are involved in the incident.
   Various circumstances involved in the incident.

3. **Some animals are disappearing faster than expected.**

   Some animals that are disappearing faster than expected.
   Some animals which are disappearing faster than expected.
   Some animals disappearing faster than expected.

4. **A widening economic gap divides the people of the country.**

   A widening economic gap that divides the people of the country.
   A widening economic gap which divides the people of the country.
   A widening economic gap dividing the people of the country.

5. **Blue jeans never go out of fashion.**

   Blue jeans that never go out of fashion.
   Blue jeans which never go out of fashion.
   Blue jeans never going out of fashion.

6. **A lot of things are rarely used.**

   A lot of things that are rarely used.
   A lot of things which are rarely used.
   A lot of things rarely used.

7. 그것들은 학교에서 가르치지 않는다.

   学校不教那些东西。

   それらは学校で教えていない。

8. 그 지역은 매년 여름마다 정기적으로 홍수가 난다.

   那个地区每年夏天定期发生洪水。

   その地域は毎年夏ごとに定期的に洪水が起こる。

9. 건설 회사는 많은 고용을 창출한다.

   建筑公司创造了很多就业岗位。

   建設会社は多くの雇用を創出する。

10. 그들은 컴퓨터 시스템에 나쁜 짓을 한다.

    他们做计算机系统的恶作剧。

    彼らはコンピューターシステムに悪さをする。

11. 그런 질문들은 대화를 진전시켜준다.

    那些问题促进了谈话。

    それらのような質問は対話を進展させてくれる。

12. 이 음료들은 우리의 원기를 북돋아 줄 수 있다.

    这些饮料可以增强我们的活力。

    これらの飲み物は私たちの元気を増強することができる。

7. **They are not taught in school.**

   The things that are not taught in school.
   The things which are not taught in school.
   The things not taught in school.

8. **The area is flooded regularly every summer.**

   The area that is flooded regularly every summer.
   The area which is flooded regularly every summer.
   The area flooded regularly every summer.

9. **Construction companies create a lot of employment.**

   Construction companies that create a lot of employment.
   Construction companies which create a lot of employment.
   Construction companies creating a lot of employment.

10. **They do mischief to computer systems.**

    People that do mischief to computer systems.
    People who do mischief to computer systems.
    People doing mischief to computer systems.

11. **The questions advance the conversation.**

    The questions that advance the conversation.
    The questions which advance the conversation.
    The questions advancing the conversation.

12. **The drinks can boost our energy.**

    The drinks that can boost our energy.
    The drinks which can boost our energy.
    The drinks able to boost our energy.

13. 강한 공동체 의식이 우리를 함께 묶어주고 있다.

强烈的共同体意识将我们联系在一起。

強い共同体意識が私たちを一つにしてくれている。

14. 오랜 습관은 정말로 깨기 힘들다.

老习惯真的很难打破。

長年の習慣は本当に破るのが難しい。

15. 그 멜로디는 밤낮으로 나의 뇌리를 떠나지 않는다.

那个旋律日夜都不离我的脑海。

そのメロディは昼も夜も私の脳裏から離れない。

16. 신발이 스카프와 잘 어울린다.

鞋子跟围巾很般配。

靴がスカーフによく似合う。

17. 부동액은 추운 날씨에 물이 얼지 않게 막아준다.

防冻液在寒冷的天气里防止水冻结。

不凍液は寒い天気に水が凍らないように防いでくれる。

18. 소박한 일상 활동이 우리에게 즐거움을 가져다준다.

简单的日常活动给我们带来欢乐。

素朴な日常活動が私たちに楽しみをもたらす。

13. **A strong sense of community binds us together.**

A strong sense of community that binds us together.
A strong sense of community which binds us together.
A strong sense of community binding us together.

14. **Old habits are really tough to break.**

Old habits that are really tough to break.
Old habits which are really tough to break.
Old habits really tough to break.

15. **The melody haunts me night and day.**

The melody that haunts me night and day.
The melody which haunts me night and day.
The melody haunting me night and day.

16. **The shoes go well with the scarf.**

The shoes that go well with the scarf.
The shoes which go well with the scarf.
The shoes going well with the scarf.

17. **Antifreeze prevents water from freezing in cold weather.**

Antifreeze that prevents water from freezing in cold weather.
Antifreeze which prevents water from freezing in cold weather.
Antifreeze preventing water from freezing in cold weather.

18. **Simple daily activities bring us delight.**

Simple daily activities that bring us delight.
Simple daily activities which bring us delight.
Simple daily activities bringing us delight.

19. 그것은 내가 지금 방금 말한 것과 모순된다.

那个与我刚才说的是矛盾的。

それは私が今さっき話したことと矛盾する。

20. 매가 토끼를 덮치려고 급강하할 태세를 갖추고 있다.

鹰正准备俯冲袭击兔子。

鷹がウサギを襲うために急降下する態勢を整えている。

21. 강한 정신 자세가 큰 차이를 만들어낸다.

强烈的精神态度产生了巨大的区别。

強い精神姿勢が大きな違いを作り出す。

22. 음식 냄새가 내 입에 군침이 돌게 한다.

食物的味道让我流口水。

食べ物の匂いが私の口によだれをたらさせる。

23. 모든 생명체는 반드시 죽게 되어 있다.

所有的生命体都必然死亡。

すべての生命体は必ず死ぬことになっている。

24. 식당에서 이따금 성가신 일이 일어난다.

食堂里偶尔会发生一些烦人的事。

食堂で時折厄介な事が起こる。

19. **It contradicts what I have just said.**

   The thing that contradicts what I have just said.
   The thing which contradicts what I have just said.
   The thing contradicting what I have just said.

20. **The hawk is poised to swoop down on the rabbit.**

   The hawk that is poised to swoop down on the rabbit.
   The hawk which is poised to swoop down on the rabbit.
   The hawk poised to swoop down on the rabbit.

21. **A strong mental attitude makes a big difference.**

   A strong mental attitude that makes a big difference.
   A strong mental attitude which makes a big difference.
   A strong mental attitude making a big difference.

22. **The smell of food makes my mouth water.**

   The smell of food that makes my mouth water.
   The smell of food which makes my mouth water.
   The smell of food making my mouth water.

23. **All the living things are bound to die.**

   All the living things that are bound to die.
   All the living things which are bound to die.
   All the living things bound to die.

24. **Annoying things sometimes happen in restaurants.**

   Annoying things that sometimes happen in restaurants.
   Annoying things which sometimes happen in restaurants.
   Annoying things sometimes happening in restaurants.

25. 진실한 사과는 네가 큰 곤경에 처하는 것을 막아준다.

真诚的道歉阻止你陷入大的困境。

真実の謝罪はあなたが苦境に直面するのを防止する。

26. 행운은 보통 우리가 몹시 필요할 때 오지 않는다.

好运一般不在我们最需要它的时候到来。

幸運は普通私たちが非常に必要な時に来ない。

27. 그 문제는 아직도 미해결 상태로 남아 있다.

那个问题仍然处于未解决的状态。

その問題はまだ未解決の状態で残っている。

28. 얼음물은 우리의 갈증을 해소하는 데 도움을 준다.

冰水有助于解渴。

氷水は私たちの喉の渇きを解消するのに役立つ。

29. 밤하늘은 수백만 개의 작은 반짝이는 별로 가득 차있다.

夜空充满了数百万的微小闪烁的星星。

夜空は数百万個の小さなきらきら光る星でいっぱいだ。

30. 지폐 계수기는 다량의 지폐를 정확하게 세어준다.

纸币计数机准确地计数纸币的数量。

紙幣計数機は多量の紙幣を正確に数える。

25. A sincere apology keeps you from getting into big trouble.

A sincere apology that keeps you from getting into big trouble.
A sincere apology which keeps you from getting into big trouble.
A sincere apology keeping you from getting into big trouble.

26. Good fortune doesn't usually come when we need it badly.

Good fortune that doesn't usually come when we need it badly.
Good fortune which doesn't usually come when we need it badly.
Good fortune not usually coming when we need it badly.

27. The problem still remains unresolved.

The problem that still remains unresolved.
The problem which still remains unresolved.
The problem still remaining unresolved.

28. Iced water helps quench our thirst.

Iced water that helps quench our thirst.
Iced water which helps quench our thirst.
Iced water helping quench our thirst.

29. The night sky is filled with millions of tiny twinkling stars.

The night sky that is filled with millions of tiny twinkling stars.
The night sky which is filled with millions of tiny twinkling stars.
The night sky filled with millions of tiny twinkling stars.

30. A bank-note counter counts a quantity of bills accurately.

A bank-note counter that counts a quantity of bills accurately.
A bank-note counter which counts a quantity of bills accurately.
A bank-note counter counting a quantity of bills accurately.

31. 미세먼지가 우리의 도시를 덮고 있다.

微尘覆盖着我们的城市。
PM2.5が私たちの都市を覆っている。

32. 엄청나게 많은 세균이 컴퓨터 키보드에 숨어 있다.

大量的细菌隐藏在电脑键盘上。
非常に多くの細菌がコンピュータのキーボードに潜んでいる。

33. 대도시는 매일 많은 양의 쓰레기를 배출하고 있다.

大城市每天都会产生大量的垃圾。
大都市は毎日大量のゴミを排出している。

34. 어떤 별들은 우리 지구와 같은 행성을 갖고 있을 가능성이 있다.

有的星星可能有类似地球的行星。
どこかの星にも私たちの地球のような惑星が存在する可能性がある。

35. 일련의 송년회가 이번 달에 다가오고 있다.

一连串年终聚会即将在这个月来临。
一連の忘年会が今月に迫っている。

36. 그것은 나에게 나의 고등학교 시절을 생각나게 한다.

那个让我想起我高中时的日子。
それは私に高校時代を思い出させる。

31. Fine dust covers our cities.

Fine dust that covers our cities.
Fine dust which covers our cities.
Fine dust covering our cities.

32. A huge number of germs lurk on the computer keyboards.

A huge number of germs that lurk on the computer keyboards.
A huge number of germs which lurk on the computer keyboards.
A huge number of germs lurking on the computer keyboards.

33. Big cities produce large amounts of waste every day.

Big cities that produce large amounts of waste every day.
Big cities which produce large amounts of waste every day.
Big cities producing large amounts of waste every day.

34. Some stars are likely to have planets like our earth.

Some stars that are likely to have planets like our earth.
Some stars which are likely to have planets like our earth.
Some stars likely to have planets like our earth.

35. A series of year-end parties are coming up this month.

A series of year-end parties that are coming up this month.
A series of year-end parties which are coming up this month.
A series of year-end parties coming up this month.

36. It reminds me of my high school days.

The thing that reminds me of my high school days.
The thing which reminds me of my high school days.
The thing reminding me of my high school days.

37. 그들은 설득이 무력보다 더 낫다는 것을 알고 있다.

他们知道说服力比武力更好。

彼らは説得が武力よりましだということを知っている。

38. 많은 문제가 문화적 차이에서 비롯된다.

很多问题来自文化差异。

多くの問題が文化的違いから始まる。

39. 등산은 너의 건강과 지구력을 향상시키는 데 도움을 준다.

爬山有助于提高你的健康和耐力。

登山はあなたの健康と持久力を向上させるのに役立つ。

40. 고전은 우리에게 많은 지적인 즐거움을 준다.

经典给我们很多理性的快乐。

古典は私たちに多くの知的な楽しみを与える。

41. 그 작업은 아주 많은 끊임없는 노력을 필요로 한다.

那项工作需要坚持不懈的努力。

その作業は非常に多くの絶え間ない努力を必要とする。

42. 공정한 사회는 열심히 일하는 사람들을 보상해준다.

公平的社会补偿那些努力工作的人。

公正な社会は熱心に働く人たちを補償している。

37. They know persuasion is better than force.

People that know persuasion is better than force.
People who know persuasion is better than force.
People knowing persuasion is better than force.

38. A lot of problems come from cultural differences.

A lot of problems that come from cultural differences.
A lot of problems which come from cultural differences.
A lot of problems coming from cultural differences.

39. Hiking helps improve your health and endurance.

Hiking that helps improve your health and endurance.
Hiking which helps improve your health and endurance.
Hiking helping improve your health and endurance.

40. The classics give us a lot of intellectual pleasure.

The classics that give us a lot of intellectual pleasure.
The classics which give us a lot of intellectual pleasure.
The classics giving us a lot of intellectual pleasure.

41. The task takes a great deal of constant effort.

The task that takes a great deal of constant effort.
The task which takes a great deal of constant effort.
The task taking a great deal of constant effort.

42. A fair society rewards the people who work hard.

A fair society that rewards the people who work hard.
A fair society which rewards the people who work hard.
A fair society rewarding the people who work hard.

43. 성공은 노력이나 재수나 팔자에 달렸다.

成功取决于努力或运气或命运。

成功は努力や幸運や運命にかかった。

44. 어느 고등학교는 학생들을 위한 수면실이 있다.

一个高中为学生们提供了睡眠室。

ある高校には生徒たちのための睡眠室がある。

45. 백혈구는 우리의 몸을 건강하게 유지시키기 위해서 병균을 공격한다.

白细胞为了保持我们的身体健康攻击细菌。

白血球は私たちの体の健康を維持させるために病原菌を攻撃する。

46. 그것들은 과학과 기술과 많은 관련이 있다.

那些东西与科学和技术有很多关系。

それらは科学や技術と多くの関連がある。

47. 백신은 우리 몸이 질병을 물리치는 항체를 만드는 데 도움을 준다.

疫苗帮助我们的身体制造排除疾病的抗体。

ワクチンは私たちの体が疾病を退ける抗体を作るのに役立つ。

48. 항생제는 병균을 죽이거나 아니면 약화시킨다.

抗生素杀死病菌或削弱它们。

抗生物質は病菌を殺したり弱めたりする。

43. Success depends on endeavor or luck or fate.

Success that depends on endeavor or luck or fate.
Success which depends on endeavor or luck or fate.
Success depending on endeavor or luck or fate.

44. A high school has nap rooms for students.

A high school that has nap rooms for students.
A high school which has nap rooms for students.
A high school having nap rooms for students.
A high school with nap rooms for students.

45. White blood cells attack germs to keep our body healthy.

White blood cells that attack germs to keep our body healthy.
White blood cells which attack germs to keep our body healthy.
White blood cells attacking germs to keep our body healthy.

46. They have a lot to do with science and technology.

The things that have a lot to do with science and technology.
The things which have a lot to do with science and technology.
The things having a lot to do with science and technology.

47. A vaccine helps our body make antibodies to fight off disease.

A vaccine that helps our body make antibodies to fight off disease.
A vaccine which helps our body make antibodies to fight off disease.
A vaccine helping our body make antibodies to fight off disease.

48. An antibiotic destroys or weakens germs.

An antibiotic that destroys or weakens germs.
An antibiotic which destroys or weakens germs.
An antibiotic destroying or weakening germs.

49. 그 사람은 세계 평화에 크게 기여한 것으로 찬사를 받고 있다.

那个人因对世界和平做出的巨大贡献而受到敬佩。

その人は世界平和に大きく貢献したことで賛辞を受けている。

50. 고양이는 호기심이 있고 자존심이 있고 그리고 독립적이라고 생각된다.

猫被认为是好奇，自豪，和独立的动物。

猫は好奇心があり、自尊心があり、そして独立的であると考えられる。

49. **The man is admired for his great contribution to world peace.**

The man that is admired for his great contribution to world peace.
The man who is admired for his great contribution to world peace.
The man admired for his great contribution to world peace.

50. **Cats are thought to be curious, proud, and independent.**

Cats that are thought to be curious, proud, and independent.
Cats which are thought to be curious, proud, and independent.
Cats thought to be curious, proud, and independent.

10. 관계 대명사 That
(목적격/Objective)

    목적격 관계 대명사 that은 선행사가 사람이든 동물이든 사물이든 가리지 않고 어떤 명사든 모두 다 수식할 수 있는 관계 대명사이다. 따라서 사용 빈도가 가장 높은 관계 대명사라고 할 수 있다. 구조는 '선행사 + that + 주어 + 동사'의 구조로 되어 있고, 해석은 '주어가 ~하는 명사'로 하면 되겠다. 목적격 관계 대명사 that도 문법적으로 접속사와 대명사의 역할을 하면서 어떤 명사든 모두 다 수식할 수 있는 형용사절을 이끄는 기능을 갖고 있다고 보면 되겠다.

    여기서 몇 가지 주의할 점이 있는데, 첫째, 목적격 관계 대명사 that은 생략할 수 있다는 것이고, 둘째, 목적격 관계 대명사 that 앞에는 전치사를 쓸 수 없다는 점, 셋째, 목적격 관계 대명사 that은 제한적 용법(restrictive use 또는 defining relative clause)으로만 사용되고 계속적 용법(non-restrictive use 또는 non-defining relative clause)으로는 사용되지 않는다는 점이며, 마지막 네 번째로 목적격 관계 대명사 that은 모든 명사를 다 수식할 수 있는 기능을 갖고 있지만, 다음의 세 가지의 경우에는 관계 대명사 that을 쓴다는 것이다.

    첫째, 의문사로 시작하는 특수 의문문일 경우에 관계 대명사 who나 which를 쓰면 잘못해서 의문문을 두 개로 알아들을 수 있기 때문에 이런 애매모호성을 없애기 위해서 관계 대명사 who나 which보다 that을 사용하게 되고, 둘째, 사람을 의미하지 않는 선행사 앞에서 최상급, 서수, the only, the very, the same 등이 선행사를 수식할 때와 all, none, nothing, everything, something, anything, many, much, few, little과 같은 단어들이 선행사로 올 때에도 관계 대명사 who나 which보다는 that을 사용하게 된다. 그리고 셋째, 선행사가 '사람 + 동물'이나 '사람 + 사물' 두 개로 되어 있을 경우에도 관계 대명사 that을 사용하게 된다.

관계 대명사 (Relative Pronoun)

목적격 관계 대명사 whom, who, which, that의 사용 빈도를 비교해보면 물론 that이 압도적으로 많이 사용되고, 이렇게 압도적으로 많이 사용되는 목적격 관계 대명사 that을 쓸 경우와 생략했을 경우를 비교해보면, 둘 다 많이 사용되지만, 조금이라도 더 짧고, 간단하게 말하고 쓰려는 속성 때문인지 관계 대명사 that을 생략하는 경우가 좀 더 많다는 사실과 특히 선행사가 사람일 경우 관계 대명사 whom이나 who를 쓰는 경우와 that을 쓰는 경우를 비교해보면 that보다는 whom이나 who를 쓰는 경우가 훨씬 더 많다. 하지만 구어에서는 that도 많이 사용한다. 그리고 선행사가 동물이나 사물일 경우에는 which보다 that을 사용하는 경우가 더 많다는 사실도 참고로 알아두면 좋겠다.

여기서 "각국은 항공 안전에 각별한 신경을 쓰고 있다."라는 문장을 '각국이 각별한 신경을 쓰고 있는 항공 안전'이라는 명사 후치수식 구문으로 전환시켜보면 다음과 같이 할 수 있겠다.

Each country pays special attention to aviation security.

1. Aviation security that each country pays special attention to.
2. Aviation security which each country pays special attention to.
3. Aviation security to which each country pays special attention.
4. Aviation security each country pays special attention to.

1. 관계 대명사 that
2. 관계 대명사 which
3. 전치사 + 관계 대명사 which
4. 관계 대명사 생략

1. 그는 배움의 즐거움을 알고 있다.

    他知道学习的乐趣。

    彼は学びの楽しさを知っている。

2. 나는 그것을 내 힘닿는 데까지 할 것이다.

    我会尽我所能去做的。

    私はそれを自分の能力を最大限発揮できるところまでやるだろう。

3. 우리는 많은 공통된 가치관을 공유하고 있다.

    我们有许多共同的价值观。

    私たちは多くの共通の価値観を共有している。

4. 나는 인터넷으로 그 책을 주문했다.

    我在互联网上订了那本书。

    わたしはインターネットでその本を注文した。

5. 그는 지금까지 부모님의 터무니없는 기대에 부응하려고 노력해왔다.

    他努力满足父母的妄想。

    彼は今まで親のばかげた期待に応えるように努力してきた。

6. 그는 박사학위를 취득하려고 노력하고 있다.

    他为获得博士学位正在努力当中。

    彼は博士学位を取得しようと努力している。

1. **He knows the pleasure of learning.**

   The pleasure of learning that he knows.
   The pleasure of learning which he knows.
   The pleasure of learning he knows.

2. **I will do it to the best of my ability.**

   The thing that I will do to the best of my ability.
   The thing which I will do to the best of my ability.
   The thing I will do to the best of my ability.

3. **We share many common values.**

   Many common values that we share.
   Many common values which we share.
   Many common values we share.

4. **I ordered the book on the internet.**

   The book that I ordered on the internet.
   The book which I ordered on the internet.
   The book I ordered on the internet.

5. **He has tried to meet the ridiculous expectations of parents.**

   The ridiculous expectations of parents that he has tried to meet.
   The ridiculous expectations of parents which he has tried to meet.
   The ridiculous expectations of parents he has tried to meet.

6. **He is trying to get a doctor's degree.**

   A doctor's degree that he is trying to get.
   A doctor's degree which he is trying to get.
   A doctor's degree he is trying to get.

7. 우리는 지금까지 그것들을 당연한 것으로 여겨왔다.

   我们认为那些是理所当然的。

   私たちは今までそれらを当然のことと考えてきた。

8. 나는 이번 달 말까지 이 요금청구서들을 납부해야만 한다.

   我到本月底止必须支付交费通知单。

   私は今月末までにこの料金請求書を納付しなければならない。

9. 나는 그의 파렴치한 태도를 더 이상 용납할 수 없다.

   我再也不能接受他无耻的态度了。

   私は彼の破廉恥な態度をこれ以上容認できない。

10. 그는 현재 대안을 고려하고 있다.

    他正在考虑一个替代方案。

    彼は現在代案を考慮している。

11. 우리는 우글거리는 뱀을 보기 싫어한다.

    我们讨厌看到一群蛇。

    私たちは一群の蛇を見るのが嫌いだ。

12. 그녀는 중요한 스케줄을 달력에 표시해둔다.

    她在日历上标出重要的行程。

    彼女は重要なスケジュールをカレンダーに表示しておく。

7. **We have taken them for granted.**

   The things that we have taken for granted.
   The things which we have taken for granted.
   The things we have taken for granted.

8. **I have to pay the bills by the end of this month.**

   The bills that I have to pay by the end of this month.
   The bills which I have to pay by the end of this month.
   The bills I have to pay by the end of this month.

9. **I can't allow his shameless attitude any more.**

   His shameless attitude that I can't allow any more.
   His shameless attitude which I can't allow any more.
   His shameless attitude I can't allow any more.

10. **He is considering an alternative at the moment.**

    An alternative that he is considering at the moment.
    An alternative which he is considering at the moment.
    An alternative he is considering at the moment.

11. **We hate to see a swarm of snakes.**

    A swarm of snakes that we hate to see.
    A swarm of snakes which we hate to see.
    A swarm of snakes we hate to see.

12. **She marks down important schedules on the calendar.**

    Important schedules that she marks down on the calendar.
    Important schedules which she marks down on the calendar.
    Important schedules she marks down on the calendar.

13. 그녀는 지금 아주 멋진 제안을 하나 했다.

她提出了一个很好的建议。

彼女は今とても素敵な提案を一つした。

14. 나는 그 차 산 것을 지금 후회하고 있다.

我买了那辆车现在后悔了。

私はその車を買ったことを今後悔している。

15. 그녀는 우주비행사처럼 무중력상태를 경험하고 싶어 한다.

她想像宇航员一样体验失重状态。

彼女は宇宙飛行士のように無重力状態を経験することを望んでいる。

16. 내가 다양한 감정을 영어로 잘 표현할 수 있다면 좋을 텐데.

如果我能用英语表达各种感情该多好啊。

私がいろんな感情を英語でうまく表現できたら良いのに。

17. 그는 지금까지 30년 이상 동안 이 사무실에서 근무해왔다.

他在这个办公室工作30多年了。

彼は今まで30年以上の間このオフィスで勤務してきた。

18. 나는 그 꿈을 내 마음속에 품고 있다.

我在我的心里怀惴着那个梦想。

私はその夢を心の中に抱いている。

13. She has made a wonderful suggestion.

The wonderful suggestion that she has made.
The wonderful suggestion which she has made.
The wonderful suggestion she has made.

14. I regret buying the car now.

The car that I regret buying now.
The car which I regret buying now.
The car I regret buying now.

15. She wants to experience weightlessness like astronauts.

Weightlessness that she wants to experience like astronauts.
Weightlessness which she wants to experience like astronauts.
Weightlessness she wants to experience like astronauts.

16. I wish I could express various feelings very well in English.

Various feelings that I wish I could express very well in English.
Various feelings which I wish I could express very well in English.
Various feelings I wish I could express very well in English.

17. He has worked in this office for more than 30 years.

The office that he has worked in for more than 30 years.
The office which he has worked in for more than 30 years.
The office in which he has worked for more than 30 years.
The office he has worked in for more than 30 years.

18. I hold the dream in my heart.

The dream that I hold in my heart.
The dream which I hold in my heart.
The dream I hold in my heart.

19. 그는 비행기를 하마터면 놓칠 뻔했다.

他差点了错过了飞机。

彼は飛行機に危うく乗り遅れるところだった。

20. 나는 그 일을 가능한 한 빨리 끝내고 싶다.

我想尽快完成那件事。

私はその仕事を可能な限り早く終えりたい。

21. 우리는 몇 가지 흔한 실수를 저지른다.

我们犯了一些常见的错误。

私たちはいくつかのありふれた失敗を犯している。

22. 우리는 지금 아주 어려운 상황을 겪고 있다.

我们正在经历一个非常艰难的局面。

私たちは今とても困難な状況を経験している。

23. 많은 젊은이들은 건강의 중요성을 잊어버리기 쉽다.

很多年轻人很容易忘记健康的重要性。

多くの若者たちは健康の重要性を忘れがちだ。

24. 나는 그것을 하고 싶어 기다릴 수가 없다.

我迫不及待地想做那个。

私はそれをしたくて待つことができない。

19. He nearly missed the plane.

The plane that he nearly missed.
The plane which he nearly missed.
The plane he nearly missed.

20. I want to get the job done as soon as possible.

The job that I want to get done as soon as possible.
The job which I want to get done as soon as possible.
The job I want to get done as soon as possible.

21. We make some common mistakes.

Some common mistakes that we make.
Some common mistakes which we make.
Some common mistakes we make.

22. We are going through a very tough situation.

A very tough situation that we are going through.
A very tough situation which we are going through.
A very tough situation through which we are going.
A very tough situation we are going through.

23. Many young people are apt to forget the importance of health.

The importance of health that many young people are apt to forget.
The importance of health which many young people are apt to forget.
The importance of health many young people are apt to forget.

24. I can't wait to do it.

The thing that I can't wait to do.
The thing which I can't wait to do.
The thing I can't wait to do.

25. 그는 매일 점심식사로 패스트푸드를 먹는다.

    他每天午饭吃快餐。

    彼は毎日昼食にファーストフードを食べる。

26. 우리는 요즈음 항생제를 남용하고 있다.

    我们最近滥用抗生素。

    私たちは近頃抗生物質を乱用している。

27. 우리는 눈에 대해서 이 의성어를 사용한다.

    我们对雪使用该拟声词。

    我々は雪に対してこの擬声語を使っている。

28. 나는 이 차를 마지못해 팔아야만 한다.

    我不得不不情愿地卖车。

    私はこの車をやむを得ず売らなければならない。

29. 나는 예전에 영어를 공부하면서 많은 답답했던 순간이 있었다.

    我以前学习英语的同时有过郁闷的瞬间。

    私は昔英語を勉強しながら挫折の瞬間が多くあった。

30. 모든 운전자는 안전규칙을 명심해야만 할 것이다.

    每个驾驶员都应该铭记安全规则。

    全ての運転者は安全規則を肝に銘じなければならないだろう。

25. He eats fast food for lunch every day.

Fast food that he eats for lunch every day.
Fast food which he eats for lunch every day.
Fast food he eats for lunch every day.

26. We abuse antibiotics these days.

Antibiotics that we abuse these days.
Antibiotics which we abuse these days.
Antibiotics we abuse these days.

27. We use the onomatopoeia for snow.

The onomatopoeia that we use for snow.
The onomatopoeia which we use for snow.
The onomatopoeia we use for snow.

28. I will have to sell the car with reluctance.

The car that I will have to sell with reluctance.
The car which I will have to sell with reluctance.
The car I will have to sell with reluctance.

29. I used to have many frustrating moments studying English.

Many frustrating moments that I used to have studying English.
Many frustrating moments which I used to have studying English.
Many frustrating moments I used to have studying English.

30. Every driver should keep the safety rules in mind.

The safety rules that every driver should keep in mind.
The safety rules which every driver should keep in mind.
The safety rules every driver should keep in mind.

31. 나는 그 책들을 읽어서 정신적으로 더 부유해졌다고 느낀다.

我读了那些书感觉在精神上更富有。

私はその本を読んで精神的にさらに富かになったと感じる。

32. 그녀는 지금까지 나에게 그런 슬픈 소식을 숨기고 있었다.

她一直对我隐藏着悲伤消息。

彼女は今まで私にそんな悲しい知らせを隠していた。

33. 우리는 문화 초월적인 행동에 익숙하지 않다.

我们不习惯文化超越行为。

私たちは文化超越的な行動に慣れていない。

34. 우리는 서로에 대해서 편견을 가질 수도 있다.

我们对彼此可能有偏见。

私たちはお互いについて偏見を持つこともある。

35. 많은 대학생이 재정적인 어려움으로 고통받고 있다.

很多大学生面临经济困难。

多くの大学生が財政的困難に苦しんでいる。

36. 나는 청소년들에게 이런 메시지를 전달해주고 싶다.

我想向青少年传递这样的信息。

私は青少年らにこのようなメッセージを伝えてあげたい。

31. **I feel the richer mentally for having read the books.**

   The books that I feel the richer mentally for having read.
   The books which I feel the richer mentally for having read.
   The books I feel the richer mentally for having read.

32. **She has been hiding the sad news from me.**

   The sad news that she has been hiding from me.
   The sad news which she has been hiding from me.
   The sad news she has been hiding from me.

33. **We are not accustomed to cross-cultural behaviors.**

   Cross-cultural behaviors that we are not accustomed to.
   Cross-cultural behaviors which we are not accustomed to.
   Cross-cultural behaviors to which we are not accustomed.
   Cross-cultural behaviors we are not accustomed to.

34. **We may have prejudices against one another.**

   Prejudices that we may have against one another.
   Prejudices which we may have against one another.
   Prejudices we may have against one another.

35. **Many college students are suffering from financial difficulties.**

   Financial difficulties that many college students are suffering from.
   Financial difficulties which many college students are suffering from.
   Financial difficulties from which many college students are suffering.
   Financial difficulties many college students are suffering from.

36. **I want to get across the message to adolescents.**

   The message that I want to get across to adolescents.
   The message which I want to get across to adolescents.
   The message I want to get across to adolescents.

37. 나는 지금까지 여러 해에 걸쳐서 그것들에 관심이 있었다.

我多年来对它们很感兴趣。

私は今まで長年にわたってそれらに関心があった。

38. 우리는 어려움에 처한 사람들을 돕기 위해서 많은 것을 할 수 있다.

我们可以做很多事情来帮助困难的人们。

私たちは困難に直面した人たちを助けるために多くのことができる。

39. 그녀는 지금까지 훌륭한 명분을 위해서 적지 않은 돈을 기부했다.

到目前为止她为一个好的名义捐赠了不少的钱。

彼女は今までに立派な名分のために少なくないお金を寄付した。

40. 우리는 우리의 목표를 달성하기 위해서 그것들을 해야 한다.

为了达成目标我们必须做那些。

私たちは目標を達成するためにそれらをしなければならない。

41. 우리는 그 주제를 좀 더 자세하게 토론하는 게 더 좋겠다.

我们最好能够更详细地讨论那个主题。

私たちはその主題をより詳しく討論する方がいい。

42. 나의 어머니가 나에게 털실로 그 스웨터를 떠주셨다.

我的母亲用毛线给我织了那件毛衣。

母が私に毛糸でそのセーターを編んだくれた。

37. I have been interested in them over the years.

The things that I have been interested in over the years.
The things which I have been interested in over the years.
The things in which I have been interested over the years.
The things I have been interested in over the years.

38. We can do a lot of things to help people in need.

A lot of things that we can do to help people in need.
A lot of things which we can do to help people in need.
A lot of things we can do to help people in need.

39. She has donated not a little money for a good cause.

Not a little money that she has donated for a good cause.
Not a little money which she has donated for a good cause.
Not a little money she has donated for a good cause.

40. We should do the things to achieve our aims.

The things that we should do to achieve our aims.
The things which we should do to achieve our aims.
The things we should do to achieve our aims.

41. We had better discuss the subject in more detail.

The subject that we had better discuss in more detail.
The subject which we had better discuss in more detail.
The subject we had better discuss in more detail.

42. My mother knitted the sweater for me with the woolen yarn.

The sweater that my mother knitted for me with the woolen yarn.
The sweater which my mother knitted for me with the woolen yarn.
The sweater my mother knitted for me with the woolen yarn.

43. 우리는 사적인 질문을 하는 것을 피해야 한다.

我们应该避免提个人问题。

私たちは私的な質問を問うことを避けなければならない。

44. 너는 인생에서 성공하기 위해서 반드시 그 습관을 갖고 있어야만 한다.

在你人生中为了成功必须具备那一习惯。

あなたは人生で成功するために必ずその習慣を持っていなければならない。

45. 나는 지금 잠시동안 그 계획을 뒤로 미루어 놓았다.

我现在暂时推迟该计划。

私は少しの間その計画を先送りしておいた。

46. 적지 않은 사람들이 정말로 흡연에 중독되어 있다.

不少人的确是吸烟上瘾。

少なくない人々が本当に喫煙に中毒になっている。

47. 모든 사람은 상대적인 박탈감을 느낀다.

每个人都感觉到相对剥夺的感觉。

すべての人は相対的な剥奪感を感じる。

48. 그녀는 지금까지 어느 고아원을 위해서 자원봉사를 해오고 있다.

她一直在为孤儿院做志愿工作。

彼女は今まである孤児院のためにボランティア活動をしてきている。

43. We should avoid asking personal questions.

Personal questions that we should avoid asking.
Personal questions which we should avoid asking.
Personal questions we should avoid asking.

44. You must have the habit to be successful in life.

The habit that you must have to be successful in life.
The habit which you must have to be successful in life.
The habit you must have to be successful in life.

45. I have put the plan on the back burner for a while.

The plan that I have put on the back burner for a while.
The plan which I have put on the back burner for a while.
The plan I have put on the back burner for a while.

46. Not a few people are really addicted to smoking.

Smoking that not a few people are really addicted to.
Smoking which not a few people are really addicted to.
Smoking to which not a few people are really addicted.
Smoking not a few people are really addicted to.

47. Everyone feels the sense of relative deprivation.

The sense of relative deprivation that everyone feels.
The sense of relative deprivation which everyone feels.
The sense of relative deprivation everyone feels.

48. She has been doing volunteer work for an orphanage.

Volunteer work that she has been doing for an orphanage.
Volunteer work which she has been doing for an orphanage.
Volunteer work she has been doing for an orphanage.

49. 우리는 다른 문화에 대해서 고정관념이나 편견을 가질 수 있다.

我们对其他文化可能有固定规念或偏见。

私たちは他の文化について固定観念や偏見を持つこともある。

50. 우리는 영어를 배울 때 한 가지 중요한 점을 명심해야만 한다.

我们应该在学习英语时需要铭记一个重要的点。

私たちは英語を学ぶ時ひとつ重要な点を肝に銘じなければならない。

49. We may have stereotypes or prejudices against other cultures.

Stereotypes or prejudices that we may have against other cultures.
Stereotypes or prejudices which we may have against other cultures.
Stereotypes or prejudices we may have against other cultures.

50. We should bear one important thing in mind in learning English.

One important thing that we should bear in mind in learning English.
One important thing which we should bear in mind in learning English.
One important thing we should bear in mind in learning English.

11. 관계 대명사 생략
(주격/Nominative)

　먼저 주격 관계 대명사는 생략하지 않는 것이 일반 원칙이지만 다음 세 가지 경우에는 생략할 수 있다.
　첫째, 주격 관계 대명사 who, which, that 다음에 be 동사가 올 경우에는 주격 관계 대명사와 be 동사를 동시에 생략할 수 있다. 이것은 주격 관계 대명사 who, which, that 각각에서 설명한 바와 같다.
　둘째, 관계 대명사가 be 동사의 보어가 될 경우에도 주격 관계 대명사를 생략할 수 있다. 그런데 주의할 것은 관계 대명사가 be 동사의 보어가 될 때는 선행사가 사람일지라도 주격 관계 대명사 who를 사용하지 않고 which를 사용한다는 것이다. 이것은 선행사가 사람일지라도 사람의 정체를 나타내는 것이 아니라 사람의 속성, 특징, 자질, 역할, 성격을 나타내기 때문이다. 여기서 be 동사의 보어로 주격 관계 대명사 which를 사용할 경우, that을 사용할 경우, 생략할 경우 등 이 세 가지를 비교해보면 생략할 경우가 훨씬 더 일반적이고, 다음으로 which, 그리고 that을 사용한다는 점도 알아두면 좋겠다.
　셋째, 관계 대명사 다음에 'there is' 구문이 올 경우와 또는 'there is', 'here is', 'it is'로 시작하는 구문에서도 주격 관계 대명사를 생략할 수 있다. 그런데 관계 대명사 다음에 'there is'가 오는 구문에서는 문법적으로 문제가 없지만 'there is', 'here is', 'it is'로 시작하는 구문에서 주격 관계 대명사를 생략할 경우에는 문법적으로 올바르거나 자연스러운 표현이라고 할 수 없다. 그래서 실제로 주격 관계 대명사가 생략된 문장은 잘 보이지 않고 쓰기를 장려하는 표현이라고 할 수는 없지만, 간혹 쓰이는 이유는 이런 구문은 일종의 강조 구문으로서 그다지 중요하지 않은 말보다 상대적으로 중요한 의미를 가진 선행사와 관계 대명사절을 관계 대명사를 생략하여 직접적으로 긴밀하게 연결시키기 위한 의도라고 보면 되겠다.

01 관계 대명사 (Relative Pronoun)

영어를 외국어로 배우고 있는 우리로서는 관계 대명사를 생략하는 것 못지않게 관계 대명사를 사용하는 것이 중요하므로 먼저 사용할 줄 알고 난 뒤에야 생략하는 것이 가능하다는 것을 인식하고 정확하게 사용하도록 많은 연습을 해주기 바란다. 이번 장에서는 첫 번째의 경우, 즉 주격 관계 대명사와 be 동사의 생략은 다른 관계 대명사에서 많이 다루고 있으므로 생략하고 두 번째와 세 번째의 경우를 다루고 있다.

여기서 "그는 예전에 그런 버릇없는 아이였다."라는 문장을 '그는 예전에 그런 버릇없던 아이'라는 명사 후치수식 구문과 "이 세상에 가장 카리스마가 넘치는 동물이 있다."라는 문장을 '이 세상에 존재하는 가장 카리스마가 넘치는 동물'이라는 명사 후치수식 구문으로 전환시켜보면 각각 다음과 같이 할 수 있겠다.

He used to be the spoiled child.

1. The spoiled child he used to be.
2. The spoiled child which he used to be.
3. The spoiled child that he used to be.

1. 주격 관계 대명사 생략
2. 주격 관계 대명사 which
3. 주격 관계 대명사 that

There is the most charismatic animal in the world.

1. The most charismatic animal there is in the world.
2. The most charismatic animal that there is in the world.

1. 주격 관계 대명사 생략
2. 주격 관계 대명사 that

1. 나는 현재 이런 사람이다.

    我现在是这样的人。
    私は現在こういう人だ。

2. 그는 과거에 그런 사람이었다.

    他过去是那样的人。
    彼は過去そういう人だった。

3. 그녀는 예전에 그런 여자였다.

    她以前是那样的女人。
    彼女は昔そういう女性だった。

4. 그는 그런 부류의 남자이다.

    他是那种男人。
    彼はそういう部類の男だ。

5. 그녀는 그런 부류의 여자이다.

    她是那种女人。
    彼女はそういう部類の女だ。

6. 나는 10년 전 그런 아가씨였다.

    我10年前是那样的姑娘。
    私は10年前そういう女の子だった。

관계 대명사 (Relative Pronoun)

영어는 **후치수식**, 한중일어는 **전치수식**

1. **I am the man.**

    The man I am.
    The man which I am.
    The man that I am.

2. **He was the man in the past.**

    The man he was in the past.
    The man which he was in the past.
    The man that he was in the past.

3. **She used to be the woman.**

    The woman she used to be.
    The woman which she used to be.
    The woman that she used to be.

4. **He is the kind of man.**

    The kind of man he is.
    The kind of man which he is.
    The kind of man that he is.

5. **She is the kind of woman.**

    The kind of woman she is.
    The kind of woman which she is.
    The kind of woman that she is.

6. **I was the girl ten years ago.**

    The girl I was ten years ago.
    The girl which I was ten years ago.
    The girl that I was ten years ago.

7. 그는 코페르니쿠스와 같은 그런 사람이다.

    他是像哥白尼那样的人。

    彼はコペルニクスのような人だ。

8. 나는 그런 가장이 아니었다.

    我以前不是那样的家长。

    私はそういう家長ではなかった。

9. 그녀는 10년 전 그런 교사였다.

    她十年前是那样的老师。

    彼女は10年前そういう教師だった。

10. 그녀는 그런 현모양처이다.

    她是那样的贤妻良母。

    彼女はそういう良妻賢母だ。

11. 중국은 그런 전통적인 인종의 도가니이다.

    中国是那种传统人种的熔炉。

    中国はそういう伝統的な人種のるつぼだ。

12. 그녀는 그런 모범적인 교사가 될 것이다.

    她将成为那样的模范老师。

    彼女はそういう模範的な教師になるだろう。

7. **He is the man like Copernicus.**

   The man like Copernicus he is.
   The man like Copernicus which he is.
   The man like Copernicus that he is.

8. **I was not the head of the family.**

   The head of the family I was not.
   The head of the family which I was not.
   The head of the family that I was not.

9. **She was the teacher ten years ago.**

   The teacher she was ten years ago.
   The teacher which she was ten years ago.
   The teacher that she was ten years ago.

10. **She is the good wife and wise mother.**

    The good wife and wise mother she is.
    The good wife and wise mother which she is.
    The good wife and wise mother that she is.

11. **China is the traditional melting pot.**

    The traditional melting pot China is.
    The traditional melting pot which China is.
    The traditional melting pot that China is.

12. **She will be the model teacher.**

    The model teacher she will be.
    The model teacher which she will be.
    The model teacher that she will be.

13. 그는 한때 그런 모범적인 학생이었다.

他曾是那样的模范学生。

彼は一時そういう模範的な学生だった。

14. 너는 그런 최고의 농구 선수가 될 수 있다.

你可以成为那样的最好的篮球运动员。

あなたはそういう最高のバスケットボール選手になることができる。

15. 그는 한때 그런 군인이었다.

他曾是那样的军人。

彼は一時そういう軍人だった。

16. 그것은 예전에는 그런 북적거리는 항구도시였다.

那曾经是那种繁华的港口城市。

それは以前はそういうにぎわう港町だった。

17. 그것은 한때 그런 적막한 도시였다.

那曾经是那种荒凉的城市。

それは一時そういうひっそりとした都市だった。

18. 그녀는 한때 그런 순종적인 아내였다.

她一度是那样顺从的妻子。

彼女は一時そういう従順な妻だった。

13. He once was the exemplary student.

The exemplary student he once was.
The exemplary student which he once was.
The exemplary student that he once was.

14. You can be the best basketball player.

The best basketball player you can be.
The best basketball player which you can be.
The best basketball player that you can be.

15. He once was the soldier.

The soldier he once was.
The soldier which he once was.
The soldier that he once was.

16. It used to be the bustling harbor city.

The bustling harbor city it used to be.
The bustling harbor city which it used to be.
The bustling harbor city that it used to be.

17. It once was the desolate city.

The desolate city it once was.
The desolate city which it once was.
The desolate city that it once was.

18. She once was the obedient wife.

The obedient wife she once was.
The obedient wife which she once was.
The obedient wife that she once was.

19. 그는 예전에 그런 버릇없는 아이였다.

他曾经是那样的不懂规矩的孩子。

彼は昔そういう不行儀な子供だった。

20. 그녀는 결혼하기 전 정말로 뛰어난 그런 피겨 스케이팅 선수였다.

她结婚前是那样出色的花样滑冰运动员。

彼女は結婚前は本当に優れたそういうフィギュアスケート選手だった。

21. 그는 한때 그런 최고의 축구 선수였다.

他一度是那样最好的足球运动员。

彼は一時そういう最高のサッカー選手だった。

22. 그는 한때 그런 고집이 센 친구였다.

他一度是那样顽固的朋友。

彼は一時そういう意地っ張りな友達だった。

23. 그가 회복할 모든 가능성이 있다.

他有恢复的所有可能性。

彼が回復するすべての可能性がある。

24. 모든 도움이 있다.

有所有的帮助。

すべての助けがある。

19. He used to be the spoiled child.

The spoiled child he used to be.
The spoiled child which he used to be.
The spoiled child that he used to be.

20. She was the brilliant figure skater before she married.

The brilliant figure skater she was before she married.
The brilliant figure skater which she was before she married.
The brilliant figure skater that she was before she married.

21. He once was the best soccer player.

The best soccer player he once was.
The best soccer player which he once was.
The best soccer player that he once was.

22. He once was the stubborn fellow.

The stubborn fellow he once was.
The stubborn fellow which he once was.
The stubborn fellow that he once was.

23. There is all the possibility of his recovery.

All the possibility of his recovery there is.
All the possibility of his recovery that there is.

24. There is all the help.

All the help there is.
All the help that there is.

25. 집에서 해야 할 모든 일이 있다.

    在家里有所有要做的工作。

    家でしなければならないすべてのことがある。

26. 집에 모든 평화가 있다.

    家里有一切和平。

    家にすべての平和がある。

27. 알아야 할 모든 것이 있다.

    有要知道的一切东西。

    知るべきことがすべてある。

28. 너에 대해서 알아야 할 모든 것이 있다.

    关于你的一切都要知道。

    あなたについて知るべきことがすべてある。

29. 감사해야 할 모든 것이 있다.

    有要感谢的一切东西。

    感謝すべきことがすべてある。

30. 극복해야 할 모든 일이 있다.

    有要克服的所有事情。

    克服すべきことがすべてある。

31. 그 주제에 관해서 눈에 띄는 책이 전혀 없다.

    关于那个主题没有显眼的书。

    そのテーマについて目に留まる本が全くない。

25. **There is all the work to do at home.**

   All the work there is to do at home.
   All the work that there is to do at home.

26. **There is all the peace at home.**

   All the peace there is at home.
   All the peace that there is at home.

27. **There is everything to know.**

   Everything there is to know.
   Everything that there is to know.

28. **There is everything to know about you.**

   Everything there is to know about you.
   Everything that there is to know about you.

29. **There is everything to be thankful for.**

   Everything there is to be thankful for.
   Everything that there is to be thankful for.

30. **There are all the things to get over.**

   All the things there are to get over.
   All the things that there are to get over.

31. **There are no outstanding books on the subject.**

   No outstanding books there are on the subject.
   No outstanding books that there are on the subject.

32. 이 도시에는 구경할 만한 몇 군데 고궁이 있다.

    在这座城市有几个值得参观的故宫。
    この都市には見るべき故宮がいくつかある。

33. 추구해야 할 모든 행복이 있다.

    有追求所有的幸福。
    追求すべき幸せがすべてある。

34. 해야 할 가장 중요한 일이 있다.

    有最重要的事情要做。
    最も重要なやるべきことがある。

35. 구경할 만한 최고의 관광명소가 있다.

    有最好的旅游景点看。
    見る価値のある最高の観光名所がある。

36. 지구상에서 가장 추운 지역이 있다.

    在地球上有最冷的地区。
    地球上に最も寒い地域がある。

37. 세계에서 가장 빠른 기차가 있다.

    在世界上有最快的火车。
    世界で最も速い列車がある。

38. 이 세상에 가장 사기성이 강한 형태의 사랑이 있다.

    在这个世界上有最强欺骗形式的爱。
    この世の中に最も詐欺性の強い愛の形がある。

32. **There are some old palaces to see in the city.**

   Some old palaces there are to see in the city.
   Some old palaces that there are to see in the city.

33. **There is all the happiness to seek after.**

   All the happiness there is to seek after.
   All the happiness that there is to seek after.

34. **There is the most important thing to do.**

   The most important thing there is to do.
   The most important thing that there is to do.

35. **There is the best tourist attraction to see.**

   The best tourist attraction there is to see.
   The best tourist attraction that there is to see.

36. **There is the coldest region on earth.**

   The coldest region there is on earth.
   The coldest region that there is on earth.

37. **There is the fastest train in the world.**

   The fastest train there is in the world.
   The fastest train that there is in the world.

38. **There is the most deceptive form of love in the world.**

   The most deceptive form of love there is in the world.
   The most deceptive form of love that there is in the world.

39. 지금까지 가장 준비가 잘된 대통령이 있었다.

到现在有做好准备的总统。

これまで最も手回しが良い大統領がいた。

40. 지금까지 고객으로부터 최악의 항의가 있었다.

到现在有一个最严重的客户投诉。

今まで顧客から最悪の抗議があった。

41. 이 세상에서 가장 가슴 아픈 순간이 있다.

在这个世界上有最心痛的瞬间。

この世の中に最も胸の痛む瞬間がある。

42. 이 세상에서 가장 파괴적인 무기가 있다.

在这个世界上有最具破坏性的武器。

この世の中に最も破壊的な武器がある。

43. 이 세상에서 가장 오묘한 감정이 있다.

在这个世界上有最微妙的感情。

この世の中に最も奥深い感情がある。

44. 이 세상에서 가장 자신감 넘치는 사람이 있다.

在这个世界上有最自信的人。

この世の中に最も自信に満ちた人がいる。

45. 이 세상에서 가장 귀신이 나올 것 같은 무서운 영화가 있다.

在这个世界上有最幽灵的电影。

この世の中に最も幽霊が出てきそうなホラー映画がある。

39. **There has been the best prepared president.**

   The best prepared president there has been.
   The best prepared president that there has been.

40. **There has been the worst complaint from customers.**

   The worst complaint there has been from customers.
   The worst complaint that there has been from customers.

41. **There is the most poignant moment in the world.**

   The most poignant moment there is in the world.
   The most poignant moment that there is in the world.

42. **There is the most destructive weapon in the world.**

   The most destructive weapon there is in the world.
   The most destructive weapon that there is in the world.

43. **There is the most delicate feeling in the world.**

   The most delicate feeling there is in the world.
   The most delicate feeling that there is in the world.

44. **There is the most confident person in the world.**

   The most confident person there is in the world.
   The most confident person that there is in the world.

45. **There is the spookiest movie in the world.**

   The spookiest movie there is in the world.
   The spookiest movie that there is in the world.

46. 이 세상에서 가장 카리스마가 넘치는 동물이 있다.

在这个世界上有最有魅力的动物。

この世の中に最もカリスマ性あふれる動物がいる。

47. 이 세상에서 가장 사려 깊은 대답이 있다.

在这个世界上有最深思熟虑的答案。

この世の中に最も思慮深い返事がある。

48. 이 세상에서 가장 못생기고 가장 기이한 동물이 있다.

在这个世界上有最丑陋的和最奇怪的动物。

この世の中に最も醜く最も奇怪な動物がいる。

49. 이 세상에서 최고의 분위기가 있다.

在这个世界上有最好的气氛。

この世の中に最高の雰囲気がある。

50. 이 세상에서 가장 어려운 결정이 있다.

在这个世界上有最困难的决定。

この世の中に最も難しい決定がある。

46. There is the most charismatic animal in the world.

The most charismatic animal there is in the world.
The most charismatic animal that there is in the world.

47. There is the most considerate answer in the world.

The most considerate answer there is in the world.
The most considerate answer that there is in the world.

48. There is the ugliest and the strangest animal in the world.

The ugliest and the strangest animal there is in the world.
The ugliest and the strangest animal that there is in the world.

49. There is the best ambience in the world.

The best ambience there is in the world.
The best ambience that there is in the world.

50. There is the most difficult decision in the world.

The most difficult decision there is in the world.
The most difficult decision that there is in the world.

12. 관계 대명사 생략
(목적격/Objective)

　관계 대명사가 동사의 목적어나 전치사의 목적어일 경우, 즉 목적격 관계 대명사일 경우에는 생략할 수 있다. 다시 말해서 선행사가 사람인 경우에 사용하는 목적격 관계 대명사인 whom 또는 who와 선행사가 동물이나 사물인 경우에 사용하는 목적격 관계 대명사인 which와 선행사가 사람, 동물, 사물에 대해서 모두 다 사용할 수 있는 목적격 관계 대명사인 that은 생략할 수 있다.

　목적격 관계 대명사는 두 가지의 이유로 생략할 수 있는데 그중 하나의 이유는 선행사와 목적격 관계 대명사가 이끄는 형용사절이 매우 밀접한 관계에 있어서 관계 대명사를 생략하여도 의미의 혼란이 일어나지 않기 때문이다. 그리고 다른 하나의 이유는 선행사와 관계 대명사가 같은 말이라는 인식이 강해서 같은 말을 두 번 반복해서 말하고 싶지 않은 경향 때문이다. 그래서 관계 대명사의 생략은 격식을 갖춘 문어에서보다는 구어에서 압도적으로 많이 사용된다.

　여기서 우리가 주의할 것이 두 가지가 있는데, 그중 한 가지는 관계 대명사는 선행사인 명사를 수식하는 형용사절을 이끌지만 관계 대명사 중에서 명사절을 이끄는 관계 대명사인 what은 목적격일지라도 생략할 수 없다는 점이다. 이것은 만약 목적격 관계 대명사 what을 생략하면 관계 대명사가 없는 완전히 다른 별개의 문장이 되어버리기 때문이다.

　또 한 가지 특히 주의할 것은, 앞에서도 설명했지만 관계 대명사가 전치사의 목적어일 때, 즉 '선행사 + 전치사 + whom'이나 '선행사 + 전치사 + which'로 되어 있을 경우에는 관계 대명사를 바로 생략할 수 없다는 것이다. 다시 말해서, 전치사와 관계 대명사가 붙어 있는 경우에는 관계 대명사를 바로 생략할 수 없다. 만약 전치사와 관계 대명사가 붙어 있는 경우에 목적격 관계 대명사를 생략하고 싶다면 전치사를 뒤로 돌려

놓아야 한다. 전치사와 관계 대명사가 떨어져 있는 경우에는 관계 대명사를 바로 생략할 수 있다. 이와 관련하여 목적격 관계 대명사 that 앞과 목적격 관계 대명사 who 앞에는 전치사를 쓸 수 없다는 것도 알고 있어야 하겠다.

앞에서도 언급했듯이, 목적격 관계 대명사 whom 또는 who와 which에 비해서 압도적으로 많이 사용되는 목적격 관계 대명사 that을 쓸 경우와 목적격 관계 대명사 that을 생략했을 경우, 두 가지를 비교해보면 둘 다 많이 사용되고 있지만, 조금이라도 더 짧고, 더 간단하게 말하고 쓰려는 속성 때문인지 목적격 관계 대명사 that을 생략하는 경우가 좀 더 많다는 것도 참고로 알아두면 좋겠다.

여기서 "관련국들은 군비 축소 문제들에 대해서 의견의 일치를 보았다."라는 문장을 '관련국들이 의견의 일치를 본 군비 축소 문제들'이라는 명사 후치수식 구문으로 전환시켜보면 다음과 같이 할 수 있겠다.

The countries concerned agreed upon the disarmament issues.

1. The disarmament issues the countries concerned agreed upon.
2. The disarmament issues which the countries concerned agreed upon.
3. The disarmament issues upon which the countries concerned agreed.
4. The disarmament issues that the countries concerned agreed upon.

1. 관계 대명사 생략
2. 관계 대명사 which
3. 전치사 + 관계 대명사 which
4. 관계 대명사 that

1. 그녀는 지금 마음 내키지 않은 결정을 내렸다.

   她做出了不情愿的决定。

   彼女は今消極的な決定を下した。

2. 그는 지금까지 여러 번의 가벼운 수술을 받았다.

   到现在为止他经历了几次小手术。

   彼は今まで数回の軽い手術を受けた。

3. 이 건설회사는 지금까지 많은 고층건물을 지었다.

   这家建筑公司迄今为止建造了很多摩天大楼。

   この建設会社はこれまで多くの高層ビルを建てた。

4. 우리는 귀중한 시간을 낭비해서는 안 된다.

   我们不应该浪费宝贵的时间。

   私たちは貴重な時間を無駄にしてはならない。

5. 그들은 지금 파란 바다를 배경으로 사진을 몇 장 찍었다.

   他们以蔚蓝的大海为背景拍了几张照片。

   彼らは今青い海を背景に写真を何枚か撮った。

6. 흡연은 심장병에 걸릴 수 있는 위험을 증가시킨다.

   吸烟增加患心脏病的危险。

   喫煙は心臓病にかかるリスクを上昇させる。

1. **She has made a reluctant decision.**

   The reluctant decision she has made.
   The reluctant decision which she has made.
   The reluctant decision that she has made.

2. **He has underwent several minor surgeries.**

   Several minor surgeries he has underwent.
   Several minor surgeries which he has underwent.
   Several minor surgeries that he has underwent.

3. **The construction company has built many skyscrapers.**

   Many skyscrapers the construction company has built.
   Many skyscrapers which the construction company has built.
   Many skyscrapers that the construction company has built.

4. **We should not waste precious time.**

   Precious time we should not waste.
   Precious time which we should not waste.
   Precious time that we should not waste.

5. **They have taken a few pictures against the blue sea.**

   A few pictures they have taken against the blue sea.
   A few pictures which they have taken against the blue sea.
   A few pictures that they have taken against the blue sea.

6. **Smoking increases the risk of developing heart disease.**

   The risk of developing heart disease smoking increases.
   The risk of developing heart disease which smoking increases.
   The risk of developing heart disease that smoking increases.

7. 그들은 요즘 심각한 가뭄으로 고통받고 있다.

   他们近来遭受严重的干旱。

   彼らはこのごろ深刻な日照りで苦痛している。

8. 그들은 지금 대선 후보에 관해서 여론 조사를 실시했다.

   他们对总统候选人进行了舆论调查。

   彼らは今大統領選挙候補に関して世論調査を実施した。

9. 그녀는 비만과 맞붙어 싸울 각오가 되어 있다.

   她决心解决肥胖问题。

   彼女は肥満に向き合って戦う覚悟ができている。

10. 그가 흡연하는 것을 막기 위해서 내가 할 수 있는 일이 아무것도 없다.

    我不能为阻止他吸烟做任何事情。

    彼が喫煙するのをやめさせるために私ができることは何もない。

11. 그는 그 법적인 분쟁을 해결하려고 노력하고 있다.

    他正在努力解决那场法律纠纷。

    彼はその法的な紛争を解決しようと努力している。

12. 태풍이 지금까지 농작물에 큰 피해를 입혔다.

    台风使农作物造成了很大的伤害。

    台風が今まで農作物に大きな被害を与えた。

7. **They are suffering from a severe drought these days.**

   The severe drought they are suffering from these days.
   The severe drought which they are suffering from these days.
   The severe drought from which they are suffering these days.
   The severe drought that they are suffering from these days.

8. **They have conducted an opinion poll on presidential candidates.**

   An opinion poll they have conducted on presidential candidates.
   An opinion poll which they have conducted on presidential candidates.
   An opinion poll that they have conducted on presidential candidates.

9. **She is determined to tackle obesity.**

   Obesity she is determined to tackle.
   Obesity which she is determined to tackle.
   Obesity that she is determined to tackle.

10. **I can do nothing to stop him from smoking.**

    Nothing I can do to stop him from smoking.
    Nothing that I can do to stop him from smoking.

11. **He is trying to settle the legal dispute.**

    The legal dispute he is trying to settle.
    The legal dispute which he is trying to settle.
    The legal dispute that he is trying to settle.

12. **The typhoon has done a lot of damage to the crops.**

    A lot of damage the typhoon has done to the crops.
    A lot of damage which the typhoon has done to the crops.
    A lot of damage that the typhoon has done to the crops.

13. 우리는 자신의 은밀한 죄를 보지 못한다.

    我们看不到我们自己隐秘的罪过。

    私たちは自分の隠密な罪を見ることができない。

14. 그는 지금 아주 넓은 면적의 땅을 사기로 계약했다.

    他承诺要买一大片土地。

    彼は今とても広い面積の土地を買うことに契約した。

15. 그는 지금까지 나에게 많은 실망을 안겨주었다.

    他给我带来了很多失望。

    彼は今まで私に多くの失望を与えた。

16. 나는 그 영화의 마지막 장면을 잊을 수 없다.

    我不能忘记那部电影的最后场景。

    私はその映画の最後の場面を忘れられない。

17. 우리는 매일 많은 종류의 알약을 복용한다.

    我们每天服用多种药丸。

    私たちは毎日たくさんの種類の錠剤を服用する。

18. 그는 한 가지 중요한 것을 깜빡 잊고 언급하지 못했다.

    他忘了提一件重要的事情。

    彼は一つの重要なことをうっかり忘れて言及できなかった。

영어는 후치수식, 한중일어는 전치수식

01

관계 대명사 (Relative Pronoun)

13. **We are blind to our own secret sins.**

Our own secret sins we are blind to.
Our own secret sins which we are blind to.
Our own secret sins to which we are blind.
Our own secret sins that we are blind to.

14. **He has contracted to buy a large tract of land.**

A large tract of land he has contracted to buy.
A large tract of land which he has contracted to buy.
A large tract of land that he has contracted to buy.

15. **He has caused me a lot of disappointments.**

A lot of disappointments he has caused me.
A lot of disappointments which he has caused me.
A lot of disappointments that he has caused me.

16. **I can't forget the final scene of the movie.**

The final scene of the movie I can't forget.
The final scene of the movie which I can't forget.
The final scene of the movie that I can't forget.

17. **We take many kinds of pills on a daily basis.**

Many kinds of pills we take on a daily basis.
Many kinds of pills which we take on a daily basis.
Many kinds of pills that we take on a daily basis.

18. **He forgot to mention one important thing.**

One important thing he forgot to mention.
One important thing which he forgot to mention.
One important thing that he forgot to mention.

19. 너는 독감 예방 접종을 할 필요가 있다.

    你需要接种流感疫苗。

    あなたはインフルエンザの予防接種をする必要がある。

20. 나는 지금까지 결코 그런 아름다운 강설을 본 적이 없다.

    我从来没有见过这样美丽的降雪。

    私は今まで決してそのような美しい降雪を見たことがない。

21. 개는 보통 고양이와 사이좋게 지내지 않는다.

    狗通常不会与猫很好地相处。

    犬は普通猫と仲良くしない。

22. 우리는 비행기로 한 시간 만에 목적지에 도달할 수 있다.

    我们乘飞机在一个小时内可以到达目的地。

    私たちは飛行機で一時間で目的地に到達することができる。

23. 너는 그 목표를 달성하기 위해서 지금까지 열심히 노력했구나.

    你为了实现那个目标直到现在都很努力啊。

    あなたはその目標を達成するために今まで一生懸命努力したんだね。

24. 그는 내가 극동에서 살기 위해서는 한자를 알아야 한다고 말한다.

    他说我为了住在远东必须知道中国汉字。

    彼は私が極東で生きるためには漢字が分からなければならないと言う。

19. You need to get a flu vaccination.

A flu vaccination you need to get.
A flu vaccination which you need to get.
A flu vaccination that you need to get.

20. I have never seen such a beautiful snowfall.

Such a beautiful snowfall I have never seen.
Such a beautiful snowfall which I have never seen.
Such a beautiful snowfall that I have never seen.

21. Canines don't usually get along well with felines.

Felines canines don't usually get along well with.
Felines which canines don't usually get along well with.
Felines with which canines don't usually get along well.
Felines that canines don't usually get along well with.

22. We can reach the destination in an hour by plane.

The destination we can reach in an hour by plane.
The destination which we can reach in an hour by plane.
The destination that we can reach in an hour by plane.

23. You have worked hard to achieve the aim.

The aim you have worked hard to achieve.
The aim which you have worked hard to achieve.
The aim that you have worked hard to achieve.

24. He says I must know Chinese letters to live in the Far East.

Chinese letters he says I must know to live in the Far East.
Chinese letters which he says I must know to live in the Far East.
Chinese letters that he says I must know to live in the Far East.

25. 자동차는 많은 소음과 대기오염을 유발한다.

汽车产生大量的噪音和空气污染。
自動車は多くの騒音と大気汚染を誘発する。

26. 우리에게는 단지 몇 년간의 삶이 주어졌을 뿐이다.

只是给了我们几年的生活。
私たちにはただ数年間の人生が与えられただけだ。

27. 대부분의 사람은 대중 연설에 익숙해 있지 않다.

大多数人不习惯公开演讲。
ほとんどの人は大衆演説に慣れていない。

28. 나는 저 아름다운 아가씨한테서 결코 눈을 뗄 수가 없다.

我绝对不能从那位美丽的女孩那儿移开视线。
私はあの美しいお嬢さんから決して目を離せない。

29. 디젤 차량은 휘발유 차량보다 유해 오염물질을 더 많이 배출한다.

柴油车比汽油车排放更多的有害污染物。
ディーゼル車両はガソリン車より有害汚染物質をさらに多く排出する。

25. **Cars create a lot of noise and air pollution.**

   A lot of noise and air pollution cars create.
   A lot of noise and air pollution which cars create.
   A lot of noise and air pollution that cars create.

26. **We are just given a few years of life.**

   A few years of life we are just given.
   A few years of life which we are just given.
   A few years of life that we are just given.

27. **Most people are not used to public speaking.**

   Public speaking most people are not used to.
   Public speaking which most people are not used to.
   Public speaking to which most people are not used.
   Public speaking that most people are not used to.

28. **I can never take my eyes off the beautiful girl.**

   The beautiful girl I can never take my eyes off.
   The beautiful girl whom I can never take my eyes off.
   The beautiful girl who I can never take my eyes off.
   The beautiful girl off whom I can never take my eyes.
   The beautiful girl that I can never take my eyes off.

29. **Diesel cars emit hazardous pollutants more than gasoline cars.**

   Hazardous pollutants diesel cars emit more than gasoline cars.
   Hazardous pollutants which diesel cars emit more than gasoline cars.
   Hazardous pollutants that diesel cars emit more than gasoline cars.

30. 그녀는 지금 그렇게 멋진 스웨터의 앞뒤를 거꾸로 입고 있다.

她现在把那件精美的毛衣前后倒穿了。

彼女は今そんなにすてきなセーターを前後逆に着ている。

31. 나는 지난주에 그에게 전기면도기를 사주었다.

我上星期给他买了一台电动剃须刀。

私は先週彼に電気シェーバーを買ってあげた。

32. 나는 그것을 갖고 있지만 그밖에 어느 누구도 그것을 갖고 있지 않다.

那个东西除了我谁都没有。

私はそれを持っているがその他に誰もそれを持っていない。

33. 아이들은 어른들보다 독감에 더 쉽게 잘 걸린다.

儿童比成人更容易得重感冒。

子供は大人よりインフルエンザにかかりやすい。

34. 우리는 우리의 아버지와 어머니에게 적지 않은 빚을 지고 있다.

我们对我们的父亲和母亲都欠有不少债务。

私たちは親に少なからず借金を負っている。

35. 우리는 남들을 도와주는 것으로부터 많은 만족감과 즐거움을 얻는다.

我们从帮助别人得到很多的满足和快乐。

私たちは他の人を助けることから多くの満足感と楽しさを得る。

30. **She has put that fine sweater on back to front.**

That fine sweater she has put on back to front.
That fine sweater which she has put on back to front.
That fine sweater that she has put on back to front.

31. **I bought an electric shaver for him last week.**

An electric shaver I bought (for) him last week.
An electric shaver which I bought (for) him last week.
An electric shaver that I bought (for) him last week.

32. **I have the thing but no one else has it.**

The thing I have but no one else has.
The thing which I have but no one else has.
The thing that I have but no one else has.

33. **Children get the flu more easily than adults.**

The flu children get more easily than adults.
The flu which children get more easily than adults.
The flu that children get more easily than adults.

34. **We have not a little debt to our father and mother.**

Not a little debt we have to our father and mother.
Not a little debt which we have to our father and mother.
Not a little debt that we have to our father and mother.

35. **We get a lot of satisfaction and pleasure from helping others.**

A lot of satisfaction and pleasure we get from helping others.
A lot of satisfaction and pleasure which we get from helping others.
A lot of satisfaction and pleasure that we get from helping others.

36. 그녀는 지금까지 그에게 많은 정신적인 고통을 안겨주었다.

    她给他带来了很多精神痛苦。

    彼女は今まで彼に多くの精神的な苦痛を与えた。

37. 우리는 충분한 양의 비타민과 미네랄을 섭취할 필요가 있다.

    我们需要摄取足量的维生素和矿物质。

    我々は十分な量のビタミンとミネラルを摂取する必要がある。

38. 우리는 여기서 단지 몇 마일 떨어진 곳에 아름다운 해변이 있다.

    在我们这里只有几公里的地方有美丽的海边。

    ここからたった数マイル離れたところに美しい海辺がある。

39. 모든 의사는 특정한 자격요건을 갖고 있어야만 한다.

    每个医生都必须有一定的资格。

    すべての医者は特定の資格要件を持っていなければならない。

40. 그녀는 지금까지 유복한 가정에서 비교적 편안한 삶을 살아왔다.

    她现在在一个富裕的家庭里过着相对舒适的生活。

    彼女は今まで裕福な家庭で比較的楽な人生を送ってきた。

41. 그는 그 병으로 너무 많은 약을 복용하는 것을 꺼린다.

    他不愿为这种疾病服用太多的药物。

    彼はその病気によってあまりにも多くの薬を服用することを嫌がる。

36. **She has caused him a lot of mental pain.**

   A lot of mental pain she has caused him.
   A lot of mental pain which she has caused him.
   A lot of mental pain that she has caused him.

37. **We need to take in a sufficient amount of vitamins and minerals.**

   A sufficient amount of vitamins and minerals we need to take in.
   A sufficient amount of vitamins and minerals which we need to take in.
   A sufficient amount of vitamins and minerals that we need to take in.

38. **We have a beautiful beach only a few miles from here.**

   A beautiful beach we have only a few miles from here.
   A beautiful beach which we have only a few miles from here.
   A beautiful beach that we have only a few miles from here.

39. **Every doctor has to have a certain qualification.**

   A certain qualification every doctor has to have.
   A certain qualification which every doctor has to have.
   A certain qualification that every doctor has to have.

40. **She has lived a relatively comfortable life in a wealthy family.**

   A relatively comfortable life she has lived in a wealthy family.
   A relatively comfortable life which she has lived in a wealthy family.
   A relatively comfortable life that she has lived in a wealthy family.

41. **He is reluctant to take too much medicine for the disease.**

   Too much medicine he is reluctant to take for the disease.
   Too much medicine which he is reluctant to take for the disease.
   Too much medicine that he is reluctant to take for the disease.

42. 사람들은 밖에 나가서 봄의 전조를 보는 것을 좋아한다.

人们喜欢去外面看春天的先兆。

人々は外に出て春の兆しを見るのが好きだ。

43. 나는 진실로 햇빛, 공기, 물, 그리고 흙을 사랑하고 감사하게 생각한다.

我的确热爱和感谢阳光, 空气, 水和土壤。

私は本当に太陽、空気、水、そして土を愛し、ありがたく思う。

44. 우리는 인종과 문화에 상관없이 공통적인 인간성을 공유하고 있다.

我们共享一个共同的人性, 不论种族和文化。

私たちは人種と文化に関係なく共通的な人間性を共有している。

45. TV 폭력은 지금까지 어린이들에게 부정적인 영향을 끼쳤다.

至今电视暴力对儿童有负面影响。

TV暴力は今まで子どもたちに否定的な影響を及ぼした。

46. 그는 미국의 상하 양원 합동회의에서 유명한 연설을 했다.

他在美国参众两院联席会议前做了著名演讲。

彼は米国の上下両院合同会議で有名な演説をした。

47. 나는 시꺼먼 연기가 공장 굴뚝에서 쏟아져 나오는 것을 볼 수 있다.

我可以看到从工厂的烟囱里冒出黑色的浓烟。

私は真っ黒い煙が工場の煙突から出てくるのを見ることができる。

42. People like to go outside and watch the signs of spring.

The signs of spring people like to go outside and watch.
The signs of spring which people like to go outside and watch.
The signs of spring that people like to go outside and watch.

43. I truly love and appreciate sunlight, air, water and earth.

Sunlight, air, water and earth I truly love and appreciate.
Sunlight, air, water and earth which I truly love and appreciate.
Sunlight, air, water and earth that I truly love and appreciate.

44. We share a common humanity regardless of race and culture.

A common humanity we share regardless of race and culture.
A common humanity which we share regardless of race and culture.
A common humanity that we share regardless of race and culture.

45. TV violence has had a negative influence on children.

The negative influence TV violence has had on children.
The negative influence which TV violence has had on children.
The negative influence that TV violence has had on children.

46. He made the famous speech before a joint session of Congress.

The famous speech he made before a joint session of Congress.
The famous speech which he made before a joint session of Congress.
The famous speech that he made before a joint session of Congress.

47. I can see thick black smoke pouring out of the factory stacks.

Thick black smoke I can see pouring out of the factory stacks.
Thick black smoke which I can see pouring out of the factory stacks.
Thick black smoke that I can see pouring out of the factory stacks.

48. 외국어를 배우는 데에는 많은 시간과 노력이 필요하다.

学习外语需要很多时间和努力。

外国語を学ぶには多くの時間と努力が必要だ。

49. 우리 몸은 우리가 흥분했을 때 어떤 화학물질을 배출한다.

当我们兴奋时，我们的身体排放出某种化学物质。

私たちの体は興奮した時ある化学物質を排出する。

50. 우리는 북극곰의 미래에 대해서 깊이 걱정하지 않을 수 없다.

我们不得不对北极熊的未来感到担忧。

私たちはホツキヨクグマの未来について深く心配しない訳にはいかない。

48. It takes a lot of time and effort to learn a foreign language.

A lot of time and effort it takes to learn a foreign language.
A lot of time and effort which it takes to learn a foreign language.
A lot of time and effort that it takes to learn a foreign language.

49. Our bodies release a chemical when we are excited.

A chemical our bodies release when we are excited.
A chemical which our bodies release when we are excited.
A chemical that our bodies release when we are excited.

50. We cannot help worrying deeply about the future of polar bears.

The future of polar bears we cannot help worrying deeply about.
The future of polar bears which we cannot help worrying deeply about.
The future of polar bears about which we cannot help worrying deeply.
The future of polar bears that we cannot help worrying deeply about.

02

영어는 **후치수식**, 한중일어는 **전치수식**

관계 부사
Relative Adverb

1. 관계 부사 When

　관계 부사도 관계 대명사와 마찬가지로 선행사인 명사를 후치수식하는 형용사절을 이끈다. 관계 대명사는 접속사와 대명사의 역할을 하고, 관계 부사는 접속사와 부사 역할을 한다는 것이 문법적인 특징이며 차이점이라 할 수 있지만, 관계 대명사와 관계 부사가 둘 다 선행사인 명사를 후치수식하는 형용사절을 이끌고 있다는 점에서 본질적으로 같은 기능을 담당하고 있다고 할 수 있다.

　관계 부사 when은 선행사가 시간일 때 사용하는 관계 부사이다. 관계 부사는 격변화가 없기 때문에 모든 관계 부사 다음에는 항상 '주어 + 동사'가 온다. 그래서 모든 관계 부사들이 다 그렇듯이 관계 부사 when의 구조도 '선행사 + when + 주어 + 동사'의 구조로 되어 있다. 해석은 '주어가 ~하는 시간'으로 하면 되겠다. 또한 관계 부사 when은 '전치사 + 관계 대명사'로 바꾸어 쓸 수 있다는 것도 알아두어야 하겠다. 즉, 선행사에 따라서 in which, at which, on which 중 하나로 바꾸어 쓸 수 있다는 것이다. 관계 부사 when 대신에 관계 부사 that을 쓸 수 있다는 점과 관계 부사 when은 생략할 수 있다는 점도 또한 잊지 말아야겠다.

　관계 대명사와 비교해서 관계 부사는 격변화를 생각할 필요가 없는 단순한 구조이므로 이해하고 사용하기가 훨씬 더 쉽다. 관계 부사도 관계 대명사와 마찬가지로 제한적 용법(restrictive use 또는 defining relative clause)과 계속적 용법(non-restrictive use 또는 non-defining relative clause)이라는 두 가지 용법이 있다.

　관계 부사의 제한적 용법은 관계 부사 앞에 콤마가 없는 것으로 관계 부사절이 선행사를 직접 수식하는 형용사절의 기능을 담당하는 용법이고, 관계 부사의 계속적 용법은 관계 부사 when과 관계 부사 where에만 적용되는 것으로서, 관계 부사 앞에 콤마가 있으며 선행사에 대해서 부가적으로 기술적인(descriptive) 설명을 하는 용법이다. '콤마 when'은 '그런데 그때', '콤마 where'는 '그런데 거기서'라고 물 흐르듯이 계속해서 해석하면 되겠다.

> 여기서 "브렉시트(영국의 유럽연합 탈퇴)는 2016년 6월 23일에 국민투표로 결정되었다."라는 문장을 관계 부사 when을 사용해서 '브렉시트가 국민투표로 결정되던 날'이라는 명사 후치수식 구문으로 전환시켜보면 다음과 같이 할 수 있겠다.
>
> The Brexit was decided by referendum on June 23, 2016.
>
> 1. The day when the Brexit was decided by referendum.
> 2. The day that the Brexit was decided by referendum.
> 3. The day the Brexit was decided by referendum.
> 4. The day which the Brexit was decided by referendum on.
> 5. The day on which the Brexit was decided by referendum.
> 6. The day that the Brexit was decided by referendum on.
> 7. The day the Brexit was decided by referendum on.
>
> 1. 관계 부사 when
> 2. 관계 부사 that
> 3. 관계 부사 생략
> 4. 관계 대명사 which
> 5. 전치사 + 관계 대명사 which
> 6. 관계 대명사 that
> 7. 관계 대명사 생략

명사 후치수식 구문이 아니라서 여기에서는 언급하지 않았지만 선행사를 생략하고 관계 부사 when만을 사용하는 구문도 구어체에서 많이 쓴다는 것도 동시에 알아두면 좋겠다.

1. **그는 그날 태어났다.**

    他那天出生。

    彼はその日に生まれた。

2. **그들은 그날 결혼했다.**

    他们那天结婚了。

    彼らはその日に結婚した。

3. **제1차 세계대전은 1914년에 발발했다.**

    第一次世界大战在1914年爆发。

    第1次世界大戦は1914年に勃発した。

4. **그는 그 시간에 모임 장소에 도착할 것이다.**

    他将在那个时间到达聚会地点。

    彼はその時間に集会場所に着くだろう。

영어는 **후치수식**, 한중일어는 **전치수식**

1. **He was born on the day.**

   The day when he was born.
   The day that he was born.
   The day he was born.
   The day which he was born on.
   The day on which he was born.
   The day that he was born on.
   The day he was born on.

2. **They got married on the day.**

   The day when they got married.
   The day that they got married.
   The day they got married.
   The day which they got married on.
   The day on which they got married.
   The day that they got married on.
   The day they got married on.

3. **World War I broke out in 1914.**

   The year when World War I broke out.
   The year that World War I broke out.
   The year World War I broke out.
   The year which World War I broke out in.
   The year in which World War I broke out.
   The year that World War I broke out in.
   The year World War I broke out in.

4. **He will arrive at the meeting place at the time.**

   The time when he will arrive at the meeting place.
   The time that he will arrive at the meeting place.
   The time he will arrive at the meeting place.
   The time which he will arrive at the meeting place at.
   The time at which he will arrive at the meeting place.
   The time that he will arrive at the meeting place at.
   The time he will arrive at the meeting place at.

02

관계 부사 (Relative Adverb)

5. 우리는 그날 다시 만날 것이다.

   我们将在那天再见面。

   私たちはその日に再び会うだろう。

6. 나는 그날 쉴 수 있다.

   我那天可以休息。

   私はその日休むことができる。

7. 나는 그날 집에 홀로 남았다.

   我那天独自留在了家里。

   私はその日家に一人残された。

8. 일행은 그 시간에 올 것이다.

   一行人将在那个时间里来。

   一行はその時間に来るだろう。

5. **We will meet again on the day.**

The day when we will meet again.
The day that we will meet again.
The day we will meet again.
The day which we will meet again on.
The day on which we will meet again.
The day that we will meet again on.
The day we will meet again on.

6. **I can relax on the day.**

The day when I can relax.
The day that I can relax.
The day I can relax.
The day which I can relax on.
The day on which I can relax.
The day that I can relax on.
The day I can relax on.

7. **I was left home alone on the day.**

The day when I was left home alone.
The day that I was left home alone.
The day I was left home alone.
The day which I was left home alone on.
The day on which I was left home alone.
The day that I was left home alone on.
The day I was left home alone on.

8. **The party will come at the time.**

The time when the party will come.
The time that the party will come.
The time the party will come.
The time which the party will come at.
The time at which the party will come.
The time that the party will come at.
The time the party will come at.

9. 나는 그날 직장에 가지 않는다.

   我那天不去上班。
   私はその日職場に行かない。

10. 나는 그날 고등학교를 졸업했다.

    那天我高中毕业了。
    私はその日高校を卒業した。

11. 우리는 그날 밤에 파티를 열었다.

    我们在那天晚上举办了宴会。
    私たちはその日の夜にパーティーを開いた。

12. 그 철교는 그해에 건설되었다.

    那铁桥是在那一年建成的。
    その鉄橋はその年に建設された。

9. I don't go to work on the day.

The day when I don't go to work.
The day that I don't go to work.
The day I don't go to work.
The day which I don't go to work on.
The day on which I don't go to work.
The day that I don't go to work on.
The day I don't go to work on.

10. I graduated from high school on the day.

The day when I graduated from high school.
The day that I graduated from high school.
The day I graduated from high school.
The day which I graduated from high school on.
The day on which I graduated from high school.
The day that I graduated from high school on.
The day I graduated from high school on.

11. We had the party on that night.

The night when we had the party.
The night that we had the party.
The night we had the party.
The night which we had the party on.
The night on which we had the party.
The night that we had the party on.
The night we had the party on.

12. The iron bridge was built in that year.

The year when the iron bridge was built.
The year that the iron bridge was built.
The year the iron bridge was built.
The year which the iron bridge was built in.
The year in which the iron bridge was built.
The year that the iron bridge was built in.
The year the iron bridge was built in.

13. 우리는 그때 농작물을 수확하기 시작한다.

那时我们开始收获庄稼。

私たちはその時農作物を収穫し始める。

14. 나의 아들은 그날 군에 입대했다.

我的儿子那天加入军队。

私の息子はその日軍に入隊した。

15. 나의 꿈은 그때 실현될 것이다.

我的梦想那时将会成真。

私の夢はその時実現するだろう。

16. 나는 그 시절에 나 자신의 생활비를 벌어야만 했다.

我不得不在那个时期赚我自己的生活费。

私はその時代自分の生活費を稼がなければならなかった。

13. We begin to harvest crops at that time.

The time when we begin to harvest crops.
The time that we begin to harvest crops.
The time we begin to harvest crops.
The time which we begin to harvest crops at.
The time at which we begin to harvest crops.
The time that we begin to harvest crops at.
The time we begin to harvest crops at.

14. My son joined the army on the day.

The day when my son joined the army.
The day that my son joined the army.
The day my son joined the army.
The day which my son joined the army on.
The day on which my son joined the army.
The day that my son joined the army on.
The day my son joined the army on.

15. My dream will come true at the time.

The time when my dream will come true.
The time that my dream will come true.
The time my dream will come true.
The time which my dream will come true at.
The time at which my dream will come true.
The time that my dream will come true at.
The time my dream will come true at.

16. I had to earn my own living in those days.

Those days when I had to earn my own living.
Those days that I had to earn my own living.
Those days I had to earn my own living.
Those days which I had to earn my own living in.
Those days in which I had to earn my own living.
Those days that I had to earn my own living in.
Those days I had to earn my own living in.

17. 나는 그때 그녀가 비명 지르는 소리를 들었다.

我听到她在那时的尖叫。

私はその時彼女が悲鳴をあげたのを聞いた。

18. 그는 2016년에 박사학위를 받았다.

他在2016年获得了博士学位。

彼は2016年に博士学位を取得した。

19. 나는 그날 TV에 처음 나왔다.

我那天第一次出现在电视上。

私はその日テレビに初めて出た。

20. 그녀는 그시간에 앉아서 커피를 한잔 마실 수 있다.

她那时可以坐下来, 喝一杯咖啡。

彼女はその時間に座ってコーヒーを一杯飲むことができる。

17. I heard her screaming at that moment.

The moment when I heard her screaming.
The moment that I heard her screaming.
The moment I heard her screaming.
The moment which I heard her screaming at.
The moment at which I heard her screaming.
The moment that I heard her screaming at.
The moment I heard her screaming at.

18. He got the doctor's degree in 2016.

The year when he got the doctor's degree.
The year that he got the doctor's degree.
The year he got the doctor's degree.
The year which he got the doctor's degree in.
The year in which he got the doctor's degree.
The year that he got the doctor's degree in.
The year he got the doctor's degree in.

19. I first appeared on TV on the day.

The day when I first appeared on TV.
The day that I first appeared on TV.
The day I first appeared on TV.
The day which I first appeared on TV on.
The day on which I first appeared on TV.
The day that I first appeared on TV on.
The day I first appeared on TV on.

20. She can sit down and have a cup of coffee at the time.

The time when she can sit down and have a cup of coffee.
The time that she can sit down and have a cup of coffee.
The time she can sit down and have a cup of coffee.
The time which she can sit down and have a cup of coffee at.
The time at which she can sit down and have a cup of coffee.
The time that she can sit down and have a cup of coffee at.
The time she can sit down and have a cup of coffee at.

21. 대부분의 사람이 이 계절에 감기에 잘 걸린다.

大多数人在这个季节很容易感冒。

ほとんどの人がこの季節に風邪をひきやすい。

22. 그 시절에는 차가 전혀 없었다.

那个时期完全没有汽车。

その時代には車が全くなかった。

23. 그들은 그때 자신의 고국을 떠나야만 했다.

在那个时候他们不得不离开他们的祖国。

彼らはその時故国を離れなければならなかった。

24. 우리는 그 시절에 서로에게 의존했었다.

那个时候我们互相依靠。

私たちはその時代お互いに依存していた。

21. Most people are apt to catch cold in the season.

The season when most people are apt to catch cold.
The season that most people are apt to catch cold.
The season most people are apt to catch cold.
The season which most people are apt to catch cold in.
The season in which most people are apt to catch cold.
The season that most people are apt to catch cold in.
The season most people are apt to catch cold in.

22. There were no cars in those days.

Those days when there were no cars.
Those days that there were no cars.
Those days there were no cars.
Those days which there were no cars in.
Those days in which there were no cars.
Those days that there were no cars in.
Those days there were no cars in.

23. They had to leave their home country at that time.

The time when they had to leave their home country.
The time that they had to leave their home country.
The time they had to leave their home country.
The time which they had to leave their home country at.
The time at which they had to leave their home country.
The time that they had to leave their home country at.
The time they had to leave their home country at.

24. We leaned on each other in those days.

Those days when we leaned on each other.
Those days that we leaned on each other.
Those days we leaned on each other.
Those days which we leaned on each other in.
Those days in which we leaned on each other.
Those days that we leaned on each other in.
Those days we leaned on each other in.

25. 인간은 처음으로 1969년에 달 위를 걸었다.

　　1969年人类第一次在月球上行走。

　　人間は1969年に初めて月面を歩いた。

26. 나는 그날 초등학교에 입학했다.

　　那天我进入小学。

　　私はその日小学校に入学した。

27. 비행기는 그 시간에 착륙할 것이다.

　　飞机将在那时降落。

　　飛行機はその時間に着陸するだろう。

28. 나는 그 순간에 처음으로 그것을 깨달았다.

　　我在那一刻第一次认识到那个。

　　私はその瞬間に初めてそれに気づいた。

25. Man first walked on the moon in 1969.

The year when man first walked on the moon.
The year that man first walked on the moon.
The year man first walked on the moon.
The year which man first walked on the moon in.
The year in which man first walked on the moon.
The year that man first walked on the moon in.
The year man first walked on the moon in.

26. I entered the primary school on that day.

The day when I entered the primary school.
The day that I entered the primary school.
The day I entered the primary school.
The day which I entered the primary school on.
The day on which I entered the primary school.
The day that I entered the primary school on.
The day I entered the primary school on.

27. The plane will land at the time.

The time when the plane will land.
The time that the plane will land.
The time the plane will land.
The time which the plane will land at.
The time at which the plane will land.
The time that the plane will land at.
The time the plane will land at.

28. I first realized the thing at the moment.

The moment when I first realized the thing.
The moment that I first realized the thing.
The moment I first realized the thing.
The moment which I first realized the thing at.
The moment at which I first realized the thing.
The moment that I first realized the thing at.
The moment I first realized the thing at.

29. 우리는 그 당시에 엄격한 통행금지 시간이 있었다.

在那些日子里，我们有严格的宵禁时间。
その当時厳しい通行止の時間があった。

30. 농부는 가을에 벼를 수확하느라고 바쁘다.

农夫们在秋天收割大米很忙。
農夫は秋は稲の収穫で忙しい。

31. 너는 그때 영어를 잘 말할 수 있을 것이다.

你在那个时候能够说好英语的。
あなたはその時には英語をうまく話すことができるだろう。

32. 나무는 이 계절에 잎을 떨어뜨린다.

树木在这个季节落下叶子。
木々はこの季節に葉を落とす。

29. We had the strict curfew time in those days.

Those days when we had the strict curfew time.
Those days that we had the strict curfew time.
Those days we had the strict curfew time.
Those days which we had the strict curfew time in.
Those days in which we had the strict curfew time.
Those days that we had the strict curfew time in.
Those days we had the strict curfew time in.

30. Farmers are busy reaping the rice in the autumn.

The autumn when farmers are busy reaping the rice.
The autumn that farmers are busy reaping the rice.
The autumn farmers are busy reaping the rice.
The autumn which farmers are busy reaping the rice in.
The autumn in which farmers are busy reaping the rice.
The autumn that farmers are busy reaping the rice in.
The autumn farmers are busy reaping the rice in.

31. You will be able to speak English well at the time.

The time when you will be able to speak English well.
The time that you will be able to speak English well.
The time you will be able to speak English well.
The time which you will be able to speak English well at.
The time at which you will be able to speak English well.
The time that you will be able to speak English well at.
The time you will be able to speak English well at.

32. The trees shed their leaves in the season.

The season when the trees shed their leaves.
The season that the trees shed their leaves.
The season the trees shed their leaves.
The season which the trees shed their leaves in.
The season in which the trees shed their leaves.
The season that the trees shed their leaves in.
The season the trees shed their leaves in.

33. 너는 그날 열심히 공부하지 않은 것을 후회할 것이다.

你那天会后悔不努力学习的。

あなたはその日熱心に勉強しなかったことを後悔するだろう。

34. 그 시절에는 대기오염이 전혀 없었다.

那个时候完全没有空气污染。

その時代には大気汚染が全くなかった。

35. 너는 그때 만족스럽게 웃을 수 있을 것이다.

你在那个时候能够满意地笑。

あなたはその時満足げに笑うことができるだろう。

36. 그 영화는 그해에 미국에서 개봉되었다.

那部电影那年在美国公映。

その映画はその年に米国で公開された。

33. You will regret not studying hard on the day.

The day when you will regret not studying hard.
The day that you will regret not studying hard.
The day you will regret not studying hard.
The day which you will regret not studying hard on.
The day on which you will regret not studying hard.
The day that you will regret not studying hard on.
The day you will regret not studying hard on.

34. There was no air pollution in those days.

Those days when there was no air pollution.
Those days that there was no air pollution.
Those days there was no air pollution.
Those days which there was no air pollution in.
Those days in which there was no air pollution.
Those days that there was no air pollution in.
Those days there was no air pollution in.

35. You will be able to smile with contentment at the time.

The time when you will be able to smile with contentment.
The time that you will be able to smile with contentment.
The time you will be able to smile with contentment.
The time which you will be able to smile with contentment at.
The time at which you will be able to smile with contentment.
The time that you will be able to smile with contentment at.
The time you will be able to smile with contentment at.

36. The movie was released in the United States that year.

The year when the movie was released in the United States.
The year that the movie was released in the United States.
The year the movie was released in the United States.
The year which the movie was released in the United States in.
The year in which the movie was released in the United States.
The year that the movie was released in the United States in.
The year the movie was released in the United States in.

37. 회의는 그날 열릴 예정이다.

会议将在那一天举行。

会議はその日開かれる予定だ。

38. 나는 그 시간에 공항에 도착했다.

我在那个时间抵达了机场。

私はその時間に空港に到着した。

39. 동서독은 1990년에 통일되었다.

东德和西德在1990年统一了。

東西ドイツは1990年に統一された。

40. 비행기는 공항에서 예정된 시간에 이륙할 것이다.

飞机将在预定的时间从机场起飞。

飛行機は空港を予定された時間に離陸するだろう。

37. The conference is due to be held on the day.

The day when the conference is due to be held.
The day that the conference is due to be held.
The day the conference is due to be held.
The day which the conference is due to be held on.
The day on which the conference is due to be held.
The day that the conference is due to be held on.
The day the conference is due to be held on.

38. I arrived at the airport at the time.

The time when I arrived at the airport.
The time that I arrived at the airport.
The time I arrived at the airport.
The time which I arrived at the airport at.
The time at which I arrived at the airport.
The time that I arrived at the airport at.
The time I arrived at the airport at.

39. East and West Germany were reunited in 1990.

The year when East and West Germany were reunited.
The year that East and West Germany were reunited.
The year East and West Germany were reunited.
The year which East and West Germany were reunited in.
The year in which East and West Germany were reunited.
The year that East and West Germany were reunited in.
The year East and West Germany were reunited in.

40. The plane will take off from the airport at the scheduled time.

The scheduled time when the plane will take off from the airport.
The scheduled time that the plane will take off from the airport.
The scheduled time the plane will take off from the airport.
The scheduled time which the plane will take off from the airport at.
The scheduled time at which the plane will take off from the airport.
The scheduled time that the plane will take off from the airport at.
The scheduled time the plane will take off from the airport at.

41. 그는 그 순간에 그녀에게 막 전화를 하려던 참이었다.

他在那一刻正要给她打电话。

彼はその瞬間に彼女に電話をしようとしていたところだった。

42. 그녀의 가족은 그때 하와이를 여행하고 있었다.

她的家人当时正在夏威夷旅行。

彼女の家族はその時ハワイを旅していた。

43. 대부분의 사람이 미래에는 100살까지 살 것이다.

大多数人在未来会活到百岁。

ほとんどの人がいつかは100歳まで生きるだろう。

44. 모든 사람이 그때에는 휴대용 식수를 사 마셔야만 할 것이다.

所有人那时都必须购买饮用水喝。

すべての人がその時には携帯用の飲用水を買って飲むべきだろう。

· 290 ·

영어는 **후치수식**, 한중일어는 **전치수식**

41. **He was about to make a phone call to her at the moment.**

The moment when he was about to make a phone call to her.
The moment that he was about to make a phone call to her.
The moment he was about to make a phone call to her.
The moment which he was about to make a phone call to her at.
The moment at which he was about to make a phone call to her.
The moment that he was about to make a phone call to her at.
The moment he was about to make a phone call to her at.

42. **Her family was traveling in Hawaii at that time.**

The time when her family was traveling in Hawaii.
The time that her family was traveling in Hawaii.
The time her family was traveling in Hawaii.
The time which her family was traveling in Hawaii at.
The time at which her family was traveling in Hawaii.
The time that her family was traveling in Hawaii at.
The time her family was traveling in Hawaii at.

43. **Most people will live to be 100 years old in the future.**

The future when most people will live to be 100 years old.
The future that most people will live to be 100 years old.
The future most people will live to be 100 years old.
The future which most people will live to be 100 years old in.
The future in which most people will live to be 100 years old.
The future that most people will live to be 100 years old in.
The future most people will live to be 100 years old in.

44. **Everyone will have to buy potable water at that time.**

The time when everyone will have to buy potable water.
The time that everyone will have to buy potable water.
The time everyone will have to buy potable water.
The time which everyone will have to buy potable water at.
The time at which everyone will have to buy potable water.
The time that everyone will have to buy potable water at.
The time everyone will have to buy potable water at.

45. 내 생활이 그 당시에는 특히 정신없이 바빴다.

我的生活在那些日子特别地忙。

私の生活はその当時、特に何が何だかわからないほど忙しかった。

46. 상황이 그 시절에는 극도로 어려웠다.

在那些日子事情是非常艰难的。

状況がその時期は極度に苦しかった。

47. 우리는 그때 사랑에 빠지기 가장 쉽다.

我们那时最容易陷入爱。

私たちはその時最も恋に落ちやすい。

48. 나는 그날 처음으로 그녀를 만났다.

我在那天第一次见到了她。

私はその日初めて彼女に会った。

45. My life was particularly frantic in those days.

Those days when my life was particularly frantic.
Those days that my life was particularly frantic.
Those days my life was particularly frantic.
Those days which my life was particularly frantic in.
Those days in which my life was particularly frantic.
Those days that my life was particularly frantic in.
Those days my life was particularly frantic in.

46. Things were extremely tough in those days.

Those days when things were extremely tough.
Those days that things were extremely tough.
Those days things were extremely tough.
Those days which things were extremely tough in.
Those days in which things were extremely tough.
Those days that things were extremely tough in.
Those days things were extremely tough in.

47. We are most susceptible to falling in love at the time.

The time when we are most susceptible to falling in love.
The time that we are most susceptible to falling in love.
The time we are most susceptible to falling in love.
The time which we are most susceptible to falling in love at.
The time at which we are most susceptible to falling in love.
The time that we are most susceptible to falling in love at.
The time we are most susceptible to falling in love at.

48. I met her for the first time on the day.

The day when I met her for the first time.
The day that I met her for the first time.
The day I met her for the first time.
The day which I met her for the first time on.
The day on which I met her for the first time.
The day that I met her for the first time on.
The day I met her for the first time on.

49. 커플들이 그때에는 똑같은 옷을 입고 다닌다.

情侣们那时穿着一样的衣服。

カップルたちがその時は同じ服を着て歩いている。

50. 의사소통 능력이 이 시대에는 강조되고 있다.

在这个时代强调沟通能力。

意思疎通の能力がこの時代には強調されている。

49. Couples wear the same clothes at the time.

The time when couples wear the same clothes.
The time that couples wear the same clothes.
The time couples wear the same clothes.
The time which couples wear the same clothes at.
The time at which couples wear the same clothes.
The time that couples wear the same clothes at.
The time couples wear the same clothes at.

50. The communication competence is emphasized in this age.

The age when the communication competence is emphasized.
The age that the communication competence is emphasized.
The age the communication competence is emphasized.
The age which the communication competence is emphasized in.
The age in which the communication competence is emphasized.
The age that the communication competence is emphasized in.
The age the communication competence is emphasized in.

2. 관계 부사 Where

관계 부사도 관계 대명사와 마찬가지로 선행사인 명사를 후치수식하는 형용사절을 이끈다. 관계 대명사는 접속사와 대명사의 역할을 하고, 관계 부사는 접속사와 부사 역할을 한다는 것이 문법적인 특징이며 차이점이라 할 수 있지만, 관계 대명사와 관계 부사가 둘 다 선행사인 명사를 후치수식하는 형용사절을 이끌고 있다는 점에서 본질적으로 같은 기능을 담당하고 있다고 할 수 있다.

관계 부사 where는 선행사가 장소일 때 사용하는 관계 부사이다. 관계 부사는 격변화가 없기 때문에 관계 부사 where 다음에는 항상 '주어 + 동사'가 온다. 그래서 모든 관계 부사들이 다 그렇듯이 관계 부사 where의 구조도 '선행사 + where + 주어 + 동사'의 구조로 되어 있다. 해석은 '주어가 ~하는 장소'로 하면 되겠다. 또한 관계 부사 where는 '전치사 + 관계 대명사'로 바꾸어 쓸 수 있다는 것도 알아두어야 하겠다. 즉 선행사에 따라서 in which, at which, on which, to which 중 하나로 바꾸어 쓸 수 있다.

또 하나 특별히 주의할 것은, 다른 관계 부사들은 관계 부사 that으로 대체할 수 있지만, 관계 부사 where는 일반적으로 관계 부사 that으로 대체하지 않는다는 것과 아울러서 다른 관계 부사들은 생략이 가능한 반면, 관계 부사 where는 생략 현상이 없지는 않지만 빈번하게 일어나지는 않고 선행사가 place인 경우에만 한정적으로 생략되고 있다는 점을 반드시 기억해야 하겠다. 그 이유는 관계 부사 where 대신에 관계 부사 that을 쓰거나 관계 부사 where를 생략했을 경우에는 의미에 혼란을 일으킬 가능성이 매우 크기 때문이다.

관계 부사는 관계 대명사와 비교해서 격변화를 생각할 필요가 없는 단순한 구조이므로 이해하고 사용하기가 훨씬 더 쉽다. 관계 부사도 관계 대명사와 마찬가지로 제한적 용법(restrictive use 또는 defining relative clause)과 계속적 용법(non-restrictive use 또는

non-defining relative clause)이라는 두 가지 용법이 있다. 관계 부사의 제한적 용법은 관계 부사 앞에 콤마가 없는 것으로 관계 부사절이 선행사를 직접 수식하는 형용사절의 기능을 담당하는 용법이고, 관계 부사의 계속적 용법은 관계 부사 where와 관계 부사 when에만 적용되는 것으로서, 관계 부사 앞에 콤마가 있으며, 선행사에 대해서 부가적으로 기술적인(descriptive) 설명을 하는 용법이다. '콤마 where'는 '그런데 거기서', '콤마 when'은 '그런데 그때'라고 물 흐르듯이 계속해서 해석하면 되겠다.

> 여기서 "우리는 이따금 이 카페에서 만난다."라는 문장을 관계 부사 where를 사용해서 '우리가 이따금 만나는 카페'라는 명사 후치수식 구문으로 전환시켜보면 다음과 같이 할 수 있겠다.
>
> We get together in this cafe from time to time.
>
> 1. The cafe where we get together from time to time.
> 2. The cafe which we get together in from time to time.
> 3. The cafe in which we get together from time to time.
> 4. The cafe that we get together in from time to time.
> 5. The cafe we get together in from time to time.
>
> 1. 관계 부사 where
> 2. 관계 대명사 which
> 3. 전치사 + 관계 대명사 which
> 4. 관계 대명사 that
> 5. 관계 대명사 생략

명사 후치수식 구문이 아니라서 여기에서는 언급하지 않았지만 선행사를 생략하고 관계 부사 where만을 사용하는 구문도 구어체에서 많이 쓴다는 것도 동시에 알아두면 좋겠다.

1. 나는 조용한 시골 도시에서 살고 있다.

    我生活在安静的乡村小镇。

    私は静かな田舎町に住んでいる。

2. 그녀는 고등학교에서 영어를 가르친다.

    她在高中教英语。

    彼女は高校で英語を教えている。

3. 그녀의 고양이는 항상 소파 위에서 잠잔다.

    她的猫总是睡在沙发上。

    彼女の猫はいつもソファーの上で眠る。

4. 원자폭탄은 그 지역에서 시험되었다.

    原子弹在该地区被测试。

    原子爆弾はその地域で試された。

5. 우리는 인터넷에서 사업을 할 수 있다.

    我们可以在互联网上做生意。

    私たちはインターネットで事業をすることができる。

영어는 **후치수식**, 한중일어는 **전치수식**

1. **I live in a quiet country town.**

   A quiet country town where I live.
   A quiet country town which I live in.
   A quiet country town in which I live.
   A quiet country town that I live in.
   A quiet country town I live in.

2. **She teaches English at the high school.**

   The high school where she teaches English.
   The high school which she teaches English at.
   The high school at which she teaches English.
   The high school that she teaches English at.
   The high school she teaches English at.

3. **Her cat always sleeps on the sofa.**

   The sofa where her cat always sleeps.
   The sofa which her cat always sleeps on.
   The sofa on which her cat always sleeps.
   The sofa that her cat always sleeps on.
   The sofa her cat always sleeps on.

4. **The atomic bomb was tested in the area.**

   The area where the atomic bomb was tested.
   The area which the atomic bomb was tested in.
   The area in which the atomic bomb was tested.
   The area that the atomic bomb was tested in.
   The area the atomic bomb was tested in.

5. **We can do business on the internet.**

   The internet where we can do business.
   The internet which we can do business on.
   The internet on which we can do business.
   The internet that we can do business on.
   The internet we can do business on.

02 관계 부사 (Relative Adverb)

6. 그녀는 영국에서 태어나고 교육받았다.

   她在英国出生并受到教育。

   彼女は英国で生まれ、教育を受けた。

7. 그는 자신의 개를 데리고 공원에서 산책하는 것을 무척 좋아한다.

   他很喜欢和他的狗一起在公园里漫步。

   彼は自分の犬と一緒に公園で散策するのが大好きだ。

8. 그는 연단 위에서 강연하고 있다.

   他正在讲台上演讲。

   彼は演壇の上で講演をしている。

9. 애완견은 애견카페에서 놀 수 있다.

   宠物狗可以在狗咖啡馆玩儿。

   ペットの犬はドッグカフエで遊ぶことができる。

10. 나는 백화점에서 구두를 한 켤레 샀다.

    我在百货公司买了一双皮鞋。

    私はデパートで靴を一足買った。

영어는 후치수식, 한중일어는 전치수식

6. **She was born and brought up in the UK.**

   The UK where she was born and brought up.
   The UK which she was born and brought up in.
   The UK in which she was born and brought up.
   The UK that she was born and brought up in.
   The UK she was born and brought up in.

7. **He loves to stroll in the park with his dog.**

   The park where he loves to stroll with his dog.
   The park which he loves to stroll in with his dog.
   The park in which he loves to stroll with his dog.
   The park that he loves to stroll in with his dog.
   The park he loves to stroll in with his dog.

8. **He is giving a lecture on the podium.**

   The podium where he is giving a lecture.
   The podium which he is giving a lecture on.
   The podium on which he is giving a lecture.
   The podium that he is giving a lecture on.
   The podium he is giving a lecture on.

9. **Pet dogs can play in the dog cafe.**

   The dog cafe where pet dogs can play.
   The dog cafe which pet dogs can play in.
   The dog cafe in which pet dogs can play.
   The dog cafe that pet dogs can play in.
   The dog cafe pet dogs can play in.

10. **I bought a pair of leather shoes at the department store.**

    The department store where I bought a pair of leather shoes.
    The department store which I bought a pair of leather shoes at.
    The department store at which I bought a pair of leather shoes.
    The department store that I bought a pair of leather shoes at.
    The department store I bought a pair of leather shoes at.

02 관계 부사 (Relative Adverb)

11. 나는 예전에 이 공원 벤치에 앉곤 했다.

我以前经常坐在这个公园的长椅上。

私は以前この公園のベンチに座ったりした。

12. 그 섬에는 아무도 살지 않는다.

那个岛上没有人住。

その島には誰も住んでいない。

13. 나는 그 항구도시에서 살고 싶다.

我想在那个港口城市生活。

私はその港町で暮らしたい。

14. 화재는 처음 그곳에서 시작되었다.

火灾是先从那个地方开始的。

火災は最初そこから始まった。

15. 우리는 다양한 종류의 물건을 이 쇼핑몰에서 산다.

我们在该商场购买各种各样的东西。

私たちは多様な種類の品物をこのショッピングモールで買っている。

11. I used to sit on the park bench.

The park bench where I used to sit.
The park bench which I used to sit on.
The park bench on which I used to sit.
The park bench that I used to sit on.
The park bench I used to sit on.

12. Nobody lives on the island.

The island where nobody lives.
The island which nobody lives on.
The island on which nobody lives.
The island that nobody lives on.
The island nobody lives on.

13. I want to live in the harbor city.

The harbor city where I want to live.
The harbor city which I want to live in.
The harbor city in which I want to live.
The harbor city that I want to live in.
The harbor city I want to live in.

14. The fire started at the place.

The place where the fire started.
The place which the fire started at.
The place at which the fire started.
The place that the fire started at.
The place the fire started at.

15. We buy various kinds of things at the shopping mall.

The shopping mall where we buy various kinds of things.
The shopping mall which we buy various kinds of things at.
The shopping mall at which we buy various kinds of things.
The shopping mall that we buy various kinds of things at.
The shopping mall we buy various kinds of things at.

16. 우리는 공항에서 서로에게 작별인사를 했다.

我们在机场互相道别。

私たちは空港でお互いにお別れの挨拶をした。

17. 보스턴에서는 눈이 많이 내린다.

在波士顿下了很大雪。

ボストンでは雪がたくさん降る。

18. 그는 예전에 그 술집에 다니곤 했었다.

他以前经常去那家酒吧。

彼は以前その酒場へ通ったりしていた。

19. 교통사고는 그 교차로에서 발생했다.

交通事故发生在那个十字路口。

交通事故はその交差点で発生した。

20. 많은 젊은 아가씨들이 해변에서 일광욕을 즐기고 있다.

很多年轻的姑娘们正在海边享受日光浴。

多くの若い女性が海辺で日光浴を楽しんでいる。

16. We said good-bye to each other at the airport.

The airport where we said good-bye to each other.
The airport which we said good-bye to each other at.
The airport at which we said good-bye to each other.
The airport that we said good-bye to each other at.
The airport we said good-bye to each other at.

17. It snows a lot in Boston.

Boston where it snows a lot.
Boston which it snows a lot in.
Boston in which it snows a lot.
Boston that it snows a lot in.
Boston it snows a lot in.

18. He used to go to the barroom.

The barroom where he used to go.
The barroom which he used to go to.
The barroom to which he used to go.
The barroom that he used to go to.
The barroom he used to go to.

19. The traffic accident occurred at the intersection.

The intersection where the traffic accident occurred.
The intersection which the traffic accident occurred at.
The intersection at which the traffic accident occurred.
The intersection that the traffic accident occurred at.
The intersection the traffic accident occurred at.

20. Many young girls are enjoying sunbathing on the beach.

The beach where many young girls are enjoying sunbathing.
The beach which many young girls are enjoying sunbathing on.
The beach on which many young girls are enjoying sunbathing.
The beach that many young girls are enjoying sunbathing on.
The beach many young girls are enjoying sunbathing on.

21. 많은 유명한 그림이 이 미술관에 전시되어 있다.

很多著名的画在该艺术画廊展出。

多くの有名な絵がこの美術館に展示されている。

22. 많은 맹수가 밀림 속을 돌아다닌다.

很多猛兽在密林中转悠。

多くの猛獣が密林の中を歩き回る。

23. 인간은 예전에는 그런 곳들에서는 살 수 없었다.

人以前不能住在那些地方。

人間は以前はそんな所で暮らすことはできなかった。

24. 영어는 이 나라들에서는 모국어이다.

英语是这些国家的母语。

英語はこの国々では母語だ。

25. 그 나라들에서는 결코 눈이 내리지 않는다.

在那些国家绝对不下雪。

その国々では決して雪が降らない。

21. Many famous paintings are exhibited in the art gallery.

The art gallery where many famous paintings are exhibited.
The art gallery which many famous paintings are exhibited in.
The art gallery in which many famous paintings are exhibited.
The art gallery that many famous paintings are exhibited in.
The art gallery many famous paintings are exhibited in.

22. Many ferocious animals are moving around in the jungle.

The jungle where many ferocious animals are moving around.
The jungle which many ferocious animals are moving around in.
The jungle in which many ferocious animals are moving around.
The jungle that many ferocious animals are moving around in.
The jungle many ferocious animals are moving around in.

23. Man could not live in those places before.

The places where man could not live before.
The places which man could not live in before.
The places in which man could not live before.
The places that man could not live in before.
The places man could not live in before.

24. English is the first language in these countries.

The countries where English is the first language.
The countries which English is the first language in.
The countries in which English is the first language.
The countries that English is the first language in.
The countries English is the first language in.

25. It never snows in those countries.

The countries where it never snows.
The countries which it never snows in.
The countries in which it never snows.
The countries that it never snows in.
The countries it never snows in.

26. 우리는 그곳에서 미국 컨트리 음악을 들을 수 있다.

我们在那里可以听到美国乡村音乐。

我々はそこでアメリカのカントリー音楽を聞くことができる。

27. 그 나라에서는 사람들이 생선을 많이 먹는다.

在那个国家人们吃很多鱼。

その国では人々が魚をたくさん食す。

28. 무수히 많은 격렬한 전투가 지금까지 지구상에서 벌어져 왔다.

到目前为止很多激烈的战斗在地球上发生。

無数の激しい戦闘が今まで地球上で展開されてきた。

29. 그 지역에서는 동물이 거의 살 수 없다.

动物们几乎无法在那个地区生存。

その地域では動物がほとんど生きられない。

30. 스위스의 서부지역에서는 불어가 사용된다.

在瑞士西部使用法语。

スイスの西部地域ではフランス語が使われている。

26. We can hear American country music at the place.

The place where we can hear American country music.
The place which we can hear American country music at.
The place at which we can hear American country music.
The place that we can hear American country music at.
The place we can hear American country music at.

27. They eat a lot of fish in the country.

The country where they eat a lot of fish.
The country which they eat a lot of fish in.
The country in which they eat a lot of fish.
The country that they eat a lot of fish in.
The country they eat a lot of fish in.

28. Innumerable fierce battles have been fought on the earth.

The earth where innumerable fierce battles have been fought.
The earth which innumerable fierce battles have been fought on.
The earth on which innumerable fierce battles have been fought.
The earth that innumerable fierce battles have been fought on.
The earth innumerable fierce battles have been fought on.

29. Very few animals can live in the area.

The area where very few animals can live.
The area which very few animals can live in.
The area in which very few animals can live.
The area that very few animals can live in.
The area very few animals can live in.

30. French is spoken in the western part of Switzerland.

The western part of Switzerland where French is spoken.
The western part of Switzerland which French is spoken in.
The western part of Switzerland in which French is spoken.
The western part of Switzerland that French is spoken in.
The western part of Switzerland French is spoken in.

31. 그는 그 가게에서 매일 담배 한 갑을 산다.

　　他每天在那家商店里买一包香烟。

　　彼はその店で毎日タバコを一箱買う。

32. 덥고 습기가 많은 나라에서는 비가 많이 내린다.

　　在炎热和湿气的国家下很多雨。

　　暑く、湿気が多い国では雨がたくさん降る。

33. 아무도 지금까지 이전에 그곳에 가본 적이 없다.

　　从过去到现在从来没有人去过那里。

　　誰も今までそこに行ってみたことがない。

34. 2016년 올림픽 경기는 이 도시에서 개최되었다.

　　2016年奥运会在这个城市举行。

　　2016年オリンピックはこの都市で開催された。

35. 그는 우사에서 소의 젖을 짜고 있다.

　　他正在牛棚里挤牛奶。

　　彼は牛舎で牛の乳をしぼっている。

31. He buys a pack of cigarettes at the shop every day.

The shop where he buys a pack of cigarettes every day.
The shop which he buys a pack of cigarettes at every day.
The shop at which he buys a pack of cigarettes every day.
The shop that he buys a pack of cigarettes at every day.
The shop he buys a pack of cigarettes at every day.

32. It rains a lot in a hot and humid country.

A hot and humid country where it rains a lot.
A hot and humid country which it rains a lot in.
A hot and humid country in which it rains a lot.
A hot and humid country that it rains a lot in.
A hot and humid country it rains a lot in.

33. No one has ever been to the place before.

The place where no one has ever been before.
The place which no one has ever been to before.
The place to which no one has ever been before.
The place that no one has ever been to before.
The place no one has ever been to before.

34. The 2016 Olympic Games were held in the city.

The city where the 2016 Olympic Games were held.
The city which the 2016 Olympic Games were held in.
The city in which the 2016 Olympic Games were held.
The city that the 2016 Olympic Games were held in.
The city the 2016 Olympic Games were held in.

35. He is milking the cows in the barn.

The barn where he is milking the cows.
The barn which he is milking the cows in.
The barn in which he is milking the cows.
The barn that he is milking the cows in.
The barn he is milking the cows in.

36. 모든 청중이 연주회장에서 피아니스트를 기다리고 있다.

所有的听众都在演奏会场等待着钢琴家。

すべての聴衆が演奏会場でピアニストを待っている。

37. 가난하지만 행복한 가족이 이 조그만 집에 살고 있다.

贫困却很幸福的家庭住在这个小房子里。

貧しいながらも幸せな家族がこの小さな家に住んでいる。

38. 동물과 식물이 이 행성에 살고 있다.

动物和植物活在这个星球上。

動物と植物がこの惑星に住んでいる。

39. 현대 세계에서는 인종차별이 있어서는 안 된다.

在现代世界中不应有种族歧视。

現代世界では人種差別はあってはならない。

40. 그 지역에는 많은 모기가 있다.

在那个地区有很多蚊子。

その地域には蚊がたくさんいる。

영어는 후치수식, 한중일어는 전치수식

36. All the audience is waiting for the pianist in the concert hall.

The concert hall where all the audience is waiting for the pianist.
The concert hall which all the audience is waiting for the pianist in.
The concert hall in which all the audience is waiting for the pianist.
The concert hall that all the audience is waiting for the pianist in.
The concert hall all the audience is waiting for the pianist in.

37. A poor but happy family lives in the small house.

The small house where a poor but happy family lives.
The small house which a poor but happy family lives in.
The small house in which a poor but happy family lives.
The small house that a poor but happy family lives in.
The small house a poor but happy family lives in.

38. Animals and plants live on this planet.

The planet where animals and plants live.
The planet which animals and plants live on.
The planet on which animals and plants live.
The planet that animals and plants live on.
The planet animals and plants live on.

39. There should be no racial discrimination in the modern world.

The modern world where there should be no racial discrimination.
The modern world which there should be no racial discrimination in.
The modern world in which there should be no racial discrimination.
The modern world that there should be no racial discrimination in.
The modern world there should be no racial discrimination in.

40. There are a lot of mosquitoes in the area.

The area where there are a lot of mosquitoes.
The area which there are a lot of mosquitoes in.
The area in which there are a lot of mosquitoes.
The area that there are a lot of mosquitoes in.
The area there are a lot of mosquitoes in.

02

관계 부사 (Relative Adverb)

41. 그녀는 그런 상황에서 많은 도움이 필요하다.

她在那种情况下需要很多帮助。

彼女はそのような状況で多くの助けを必要としている。

42. 이 박물관에는 많은 귀중한 문화유물이 있다.

该博物馆有很多宝贵的文化遗物。

この博物館には多くの貴重な文化遺物がある。

43. 그 나라에서는 백인 소수가 한때 흑인 다수를 지배했었다.

在那个国家曾经少数白人统治了多数黑人。

その国では白人少数が一時黒人多数を支配していた。

44. 아주 많은 수의 영화가 이 지역에서 제작된다.

大量的电影在这个区域制作。

とても多くの映画がこの地域で製作される。

45. 나는 일기에 내 생각과 의견을 적어놓을 수 있다.

我可以在日记里写我的想法和意见。

私は日記に自分の考えと意見を書いておくことができる。

41. She needs a lot of help in the situation.

The situation where she needs a lot of help.
The situation which she needs a lot of help in.
The situation in which she needs a lot of help.
The situation that she needs a lot of help in.
The situation she needs a lot of help in.

42. There are many valuable cultural relics in the museum.

The museum where there are many valuable cultural relics.
The museum which there are many valuable cultural relics in.
The museum in which there are many valuable cultural relics.
The museum that there are many valuable cultural relics in.
The museum there are many valuable cultural relics in.

43. The white minority once ruled the black majority in the country.

The country where the white minority once ruled the black majority.
The country which the white minority once ruled the black majority in.
The country in which the white minority once ruled the black majority.
The country that the white minority once ruled the black majority in.
The country the white minority once ruled the black majority in.

44. A large number of movies are made in this area.

The area where a large number of movies are made.
The area which a large number of movies are made in.
The area in which a large number of movies are made.
The area that a large number of movies are made in.
The area a large number of movies are made in.

45. I can write my thoughts and opinions in the diary.

The diary where I can write my thoughts and opinions.
The diary which I can write my thoughts and opinions in.
The diary in which I can write my thoughts and opinions.
The diary that I can write my thoughts and opinions in.
The diary I can write my thoughts and opinions in.

46. 우리는 그곳에서 사람들의 애정과 온정을 느낀다.

我们在那个地方可以感受到人们的爱心和温情。
我々はそこで人々の愛情と温情を感じる。

47. 그들은 거실에서 함께 모여 단란한 한때를 즐기고 있다.

他们在客厅里聚在一起享受着温馨一刻。
彼らは居間に集まって幸せなひとときを楽しんでいる。

48. 우리는 그곳에서 술 마시고 휴식을 취할 수 있다.

我们可以在那个地方喝酒放松。
我々はそこでお酒を飲んで休息を取ることができる。

49. 어떤 물고기도 그런 오염된 강에서는 살아남을 수가 없다.

没有鱼可以在那种污染的河里生存。
どんな魚もそんな汚染された川では生き残れない。

50. 이 도시에는 많은 외국 특파원이 주재하고 있다.

很多外国记者驻扎在这个城市。
この都市には多くの外国特派員が駐在している。

46. We can feel the love and warmth of people at the place.

The place where we can feel the love and warmth of people.
The place which we can feel the love and warmth of people at.
The place at which we can feel the love and warmth of people.
The place that we can feel the love and warmth of people at.
The place we can feel the love and warmth of people at.

47. They are enjoying each other's company in the living room.

The living room where they are enjoying each other's company.
The living room which they are enjoying each other's company in.
The living room in which they are enjoying each other's company.
The living room that they are enjoying each other's company in.
The living room they are enjoying each other's company in.

48. We can drink and relax at the place.

The place where we can drink and relax.
The place which we can drink and relax at.
The place at which we can drink and relax.
The place that we can drink and relax at.
The place we can drink and relax at.

49. No fish can survive in the polluted river.

The polluted river where no fish can survive.
The polluted river which no fish can survive in.
The polluted river in which no fish can survive.
The polluted river that no fish can survive in.
The polluted river no fish can survive in.

50. Many foreign correspondents are stationed in this city.

The city where many foreign correspondents are stationed.
The city which many foreign correspondents are stationed in.
The city in which many foreign correspondents are stationed.
The city that many foreign correspondents are stationed in.
The city many foreign correspondents are stationed in.

3. 관계 부사 How

　관계 부사도 관계 대명사와 마찬가지로 선행사인 명사를 후치수식하는 형용사절을 이끈다. 관계 대명사는 접속사와 대명사의 역할을 하고, 관계 부사는 접속사와 부사 역할을 한다는 것이 문법적인 특징이며 차이점이라 할 수 있지만, 관계 대명사와 관계 부사가 둘 다 선행사인 명사를 후치수식하는 형용사절을 이끌고 있다는 점에서 본질적으로 같은 기능을 담당하고 있다고 할 수 있다.

　관계 부사 how는 선행사가 방법일 때 사용하는 관계 부사이다. 관계 부사는 격변화가 없기 때문에 관계 부사 how 다음에는 항상 '주어 + 동사'가 온다. 관계 부사 how를 사용할 때에는 주의할 점이 있는데, 관계 부사 how와 선행사인 the way는 같은 말이라는 인식이 강해서 같은 말을 두 번 반복해서 사용하지 않는다는 것이다. 즉 관계 부사 how 없이 선행사인 the way만 사용하든지, 아니면 선행사인 the way를 생략하고 관계 부사 how만 사용하든지, 아니면 관계 부사 that을 이용해서 the way that을 사용하든지, 아니면 '전치사 + 관계 대명사'를 이용해서 the way in which를 사용할 수 있다는 것이다. 참고로 위에 있는 네 가지 경우 중에서 관계 부사 how 없이 선행사인 the way만 사용하는 것이 가장 일반적인 경우라는 것도 알아두면 좋겠다.

여기에서 간단한 한 예문을 통해서 관계 부사 how를 설명해 보겠다. "많은 학생이 수학을 그런 식으로 공부한다."라는 문장을 '많은 학생들이 수학을 공부하는 방식'이라는 명사 후치수식 구문으로 전환시켜보면 다음과 같이 할 수 있겠다.

Many students study math in the way.

1. The way many students study math.
2. How many students study math.
3. The way that many students study math.
4. The way which many students study math in.
5. The way in which many students study math.
6. The way that many students study math in.
7. The way many students study math in.

1. 관계 부사 how 생략
2. 선행사 the way 생략
3. 관계 부사 that
4. 관계 대명사 which
5. 전치사 + 관계 대명사 which
6. 관계 대명사 that
7. 관계 대명사 생략

위의 예문들 중 어느 예문을 사용할 것인지는 사용자 개인의 선택의 문제겠지만, 빈도수로 보았을 때 단연 관계 부사 how를 생략한 1번 예문이 가장 많이 사용된다. 본 교재에서는 명사 후치수식을 다루고 있으므로 관계 부사 how의 선행사 the way를 생략한 2번의 경우는 다루고 있지 않지만 이 구문도 구어체에서는 많이 쓴다는 것도 동시에 알아두면 좋겠다.

여기서 우리가 기억해야 할 중요한 점은 문법이라는 틀과 구조의 문제를 뛰어넘어서 어떤 한 문장을 명사 후치수식 구조의 구문으로 자유자재로 만들 수 있느냐 없느냐의 문제라는 것이다. 이러한 후치수식 구문의 구사능력을 발휘하지 못하면 영어를 자유롭게 구사한다는 것은 도저히 불가능하다는 것을 깊이 인식하고 충분한 연습을 해주기 바란다.

1. 나는 너에 대해서 그런 식으로 느낀다.

   我对你有那样的感觉。

   私はあなたに対してそんなふうに感じる。

2. 그것은 그런 식으로 이루어진다.

   那是以那种方式实现的。

   それはそんなふうに行われる。

3. 조사는 그런 식으로 진행된다.

   调查以那种方式进行。

   調査はそんなふうに行われる。

4. 나는 그것을 그런 식으로 바라본다.

   我以那种方式看待它。

   私はそれをそんなふうに眺めている。

1. **I feel about you in the way.**

   The way I feel about you.
   The way that I feel about you.
   The way which I feel about you in.
   The way in which I feel about you.
   The way that I feel about you in.
   The way I feel about you in.

2. **It is done in the way.**

   The way it is done.
   The way that it is done.
   The way which it is done in.
   The way in which it is done.
   The way that it is done in.
   The way it is done in.

3. **The investigation goes in the way.**

   The way the investigation goes.
   The way that the investigation goes.
   The way which the investigation goes in.
   The way in which the investigation goes.
   The way that the investigation goes in.
   The way the investigation goes in.

4. **I see it in the way.**

   The way I see it.
   The way that I see it.
   The way which I see it in.
   The way in which I see it.
   The way that I see it in.
   The way I see it in.

5. 고래는 그런 식으로 헤엄친다.

   鲸鱼以那种方式游泳。

   鯨はそんなふうに泳ぐ。

6. 그녀는 그런 식으로 춤춘다.

   她以那种方式跳舞。

   彼女はそんなふうに踊る。

7. 사랑은 그런 식으로 진행된다.

   爱以那样的方式进行。

   愛はそんなふうに行われる。

8. 그는 자신의 학생을 그런 식으로 다룬다.

   他以那样的方式对待自己的学生。

   彼は自分の学生をそんなふうに扱っている。

5. **The whale swims in the way.**

   The way the whale swims.
   The way that the whale swims.
   The way which the whale swims in.
   The way in which the whale swims.
   The way that the whale swims in.
   The way the whale swims in.

6. **She dances in the way.**

   The way she dances.
   The way that she dances.
   The way which she dances in.
   The way in which she dances.
   The way that she dances in.
   The way she dances in.

7. **Love goes in the way.**

   The way love goes.
   The way that love goes.
   The way which love goes in.
   The way in which love goes.
   The way that love goes in.
   The way love goes in.

8. **He treats his students in the way.**

   The way he treats his students.
   The way that he treats his students.
   The way which he treats his students in.
   The way in which he treats his students.
   The way that he treats his students in.
   The way he treats his students in.

9. **삶은 그런 식으로 계속 진행된다.**

    人生以那样的方式不断地进行下去。

    人生はそんなふうにずっと続く。

10. **그녀에 대한 그의 사랑은 그런 식으로 시작되었다.**

    他对她的爱以那样的方式开始了。

    彼女に対する彼の愛はそんなふうに始まった。

11. **그녀는 자신의 아이들을 그런 식으로 가르친다.**

    她以那样的方式教自己的孩子们。

    彼女は自分の子供たちをそんなふうにしつけている。

12. **뱀은 그런 식으로 앞으로 기어간다.**

    蛇以那种方式向前爬。

    蛇はそんなふうに前へ這って行く。

9. **Life goes on in the way.**

The way life goes on.
The way that life goes on.
The way which life goes on in.
The way in which life goes on.
The way that life goes on in.
The way life goes on in.

10. **His love for her began in the way.**

The way his love for her began.
The way that his love for her began.
The way which his love for her began in.
The way in which his love for her began.
The way that his love for her began in.
The way his love for her began in.

11. **She teaches her children in the way.**

The way she teaches her children.
The way that she teaches her children.
The way which she teaches her children in.
The way in which she teaches her children.
The way that she teaches her children in.
The way she teaches her children in.

12. **Snakes crawl forward in the way.**

The way snakes crawl forward.
The way that snakes crawl forward.
The way which snakes crawl forward in.
The way in which snakes crawl forward.
The way that snakes crawl forward in.
The way snakes crawl forward in.

13. 기러기는 그런 식으로 날아간다.

大雁以那种方式飞。

雁はそんなふうに飛んでいく。

14. 많은 학생이 그런 식으로 영어를 공부한다.

很多学生以那种方式学习英语。

多くの学生がそんなふうに英語を勉強する。

15. 나는 일을 그런 식으로 끝낸다.

我以那种方式结束工作。

私は仕事をそんなふうに終える。

16. 그녀는 그런 식으로 영어 단어와 숙어를 암기한다.

她以那样的方式记住英语单词和惯用语。

彼女はそんなふうに英単語と熟語を暗記する。

13. Geese fly in the way.

The way geese fly.
The way that geese fly.
The way which geese fly in.
The way in which geese fly.
The way that geese fly in.
The way geese fly in.

14. Many students study English in the way.

The way many students study English.
The way that many students study English.
The way which many students study English in.
The way in which many students study English.
The way that many students study English in.
The way many students study English in.

15. I get things done in the way.

The way I get things done.
The way that I get things done.
The way which I get things done in.
The way in which I get things done.
The way that I get things done in.
The way I get things done in.

16. She memorizes English words and phrases in the way.

The way she memorizes English words and phrases.
The way that she memorizes English words and phrases.
The way which she memorizes English words and phrases in.
The way in which she memorizes English words and phrases.
The way that she memorizes English words and phrases in.
The way she memorizes English words and phrases in.

17. 많은 10대가 그런 식으로 행동한다.

很多青少年以那种方式行动。

多くの10代がそんなふうに行動する。

18. 우리는 많은 정보를 그런 식으로 얻는다.

我们以那样的方式得到大量的信息。

私たちは多くの情報をそんなふうに得る。

19. 그녀는 어려운 사람을 그런 식으로 돕고 있다.

她以那种方式帮助困难的人。

彼女は貧しい人をそんなふうに助けている。

20. 나는 예전에 일을 그런 식으로 처리하곤 했었다.

我以前经常以那种方式处理事情。

私は以前仕事をそんなふうに処理したりした。

17. **Many teenagers behave in the way.**

The way many teenagers behave.
The way that many teenagers behave.
The way which many teenagers behave in.
The way in which many teenagers behave.
The way that many teenagers behave in.
The way many teenagers behave in.

18. **We get a lot of information in the way.**

The way we get a lot of information.
The way that we get a lot of information.
The way which we get a lot of information in.
The way in which we get a lot of information.
The way that we get a lot of information in.
The way we get a lot of information in.

19. **She helps people in need in the way.**

The way she helps people in need.
The way that she helps people in need.
The way which she helps people in need in.
The way in which she helps people in need.
The way that she helps people in need in.
The way she helps people in need in.

20. **I used to take care of things in the way.**

The way I used to take care of things.
The way that I used to take care of things.
The way which I used to take care of things in.
The way in which I used to take care of things.
The way that I used to take care of things in.
The way I used to take care of things in.

21. 그녀는 그런 식으로 레스토랑을 운영하고 있다.

　　她以那种方式经营餐厅。

　　彼女はそんなふうにレストランを運営している。

22. 펭귄은 그런 식으로 걷는다.

　　企鹅以那种方式走。

　　ペンギンはそんなふうに歩く。

23. 우리는 상황을 그런 식으로 바라본다.

　　我们以那种方式看情况。

　　私たちは状況をそんなふうに見ている。

24. 그는 지금까지 그런 식으로 많은 돈을 벌었다.

　　他一直以那种方式赚了很多钱。

　　彼は今までそんなふうに多くの金を稼いだ。

21. She is running a restaurant in the way.

The way she is running a restaurant.
The way that she is running a restaurant.
The way which she is running a restaurant in.
The way in which she is running a restaurant.
The way that she is running a restaurant in.
The way she is running a restaurant in.

22. Penguins walk in the way.

The way penguins walk.
The way that penguins walk.
The way which penguins walk in.
The way in which penguins walk.
The way that penguins walk in.
The way penguins walk in.

23. We see things in the way.

The way we see things.
The way that we see things.
The way which we see things in.
The way in which we see things.
The way that we see things in.
The way we see things in.

24. He has made a lot of money in the way.

The way he has made a lot of money.
The way that he has made a lot of money.
The way which he has made a lot of money in.
The way in which he has made a lot of money.
The way that he has made a lot of money in.
The way he has made a lot of money in.

25. 그는 그 어려운 수학 문제를 그런 식으로 풀었다.

他以那个方式解决了那个困难的数学问题。

彼はその難しい数学問題をそんなふうに解いた。

26. 우리 조상은 500년 전에 그런 식으로 살았다.

我们的祖先在五百年前以那样的方式生活。

私たちの祖先は500年前そんなふうに生きていた。

27. 오리는 그런 식으로 빠르게 헤엄친다.

鸭子以那样的方式快速地游泳。

アヒルはそんなふうに速く泳ぐ。

28. 자연은 지금까지 그런 식으로 훼손되었다.

自然到现在为止以那种方式被破坏了。

自然は今までそんなふうに壊された。

25. **He solved the difficult math problem in the way.**

The way he solved the difficult math problem.
The way that he solved the difficult math problem.
The way which he solved the difficult math problem in.
The way in which he solved the difficult math problem.
The way that he solved the difficult math problem in.
The way he solved the difficult math problem in.

26. **Our forefathers lived in the way 500 years ago.**

The way our forefathers lived 500 years ago.
The way that our forefathers lived 500 years ago.
The way which our forefathers lived in 500 years ago.
The way in which our forefathers lived 500 years ago.
The way that our forefathers lived in 500 years ago.
The way our forefathers lived in 500 years ago.

27. **Ducks swim fast in the way.**

The way ducks swim fast.
The way that ducks swim fast.
The way which ducks swim fast in.
The way in which ducks swim fast.
The way that ducks swim fast in.
The way ducks swim fast in.

28. **Nature has been abused in the way.**

The way nature has been abused.
The way that nature has been abused.
The way which nature has been abused in.
The way in which nature has been abused.
The way that nature has been abused in.
The way nature has been abused in.

29. 그들은 그런 식으로 감옥에서 탈출했다.

    他们以那种方式从监狱逃脱。

    彼らはそんなふうに牢屋から脱出した。

30. 그녀는 세상을 그런 식으로 바라보고 있다.

    她以那种方式看待世界。

    彼女は世の中をそんなふうに眺めている。

31. 모든 컴퓨터는 그런 식으로 작동된다.

    所有的计算机都以那种方式运转。

    全てのコンピューターはそんなふうに作動する。

32. 그녀는 그들에게 그런 식으로 영어를 가르치고 있다.

    她以那种方式教他们英语。

    彼女は彼らにそんなふうに英語を教えている。

29. They escaped from the prison in the way.

The way they escaped from the prison.
The way that they escaped from the prison.
The way which they escaped from the prison in.
The way in which they escaped from the prison.
The way that they escaped from the prison in.
The way they escaped from the prison in.

30. She looks at the world in the way.

The way she looks at the world.
The way that she looks at the world.
The way which she looks at the world in.
The way in which she looks at the world.
The way that she looks at the world in.
The way she looks at the world in.

31. Every computer operates in the way.

The way every computer operates.
The way that every computer operates.
The way which every computer operates in.
The way in which every computer operates.
The way that every computer operates in.
The way every computer operates in.

32. She teaches them English in the way.

The way she teaches them English.
The way that she teaches them English.
The way which she teaches them English in.
The way in which she teaches them English.
The way that she teaches them English in.
The way she teaches them English in.

33. 회사는 그런 식으로 운영되고 있다.

公司被以那样的方式运营。

会社はそんなふうに運営されている。

34. 그는 그런 식으로 생활비를 벌고 있다.

他以那种方式赚取生活费。

彼はそんなふうに生活費を稼いでいる。

35. 그 질병은 100년 전에 그런 식으로 치료되었다.

那种疾病100多年前以那样的方式进行治疗。

その病気は100年前はそんなふうに治療されていた。

36. 그녀는 그런 식으로 다른 사람을 대한다.

她以那种方式对待其他人。

彼女はそんなふうに人と接する。

영어는 **후치수식**, 한중일어는 **전치수식**

33. The company is managed in the way.

The way the company is managed.
The way that the company is managed.
The way which the company is managed in.
The way in which the company is managed.
The way that the company is managed in.
The way the company is managed in.

34. He is making a living in the way.

The way he is making a living.
The way that he is making a living.
The way which he is making a living in.
The way in which he is making a living.
The way that he is making a living in.
The way he is making a living in.

35. The disease was cured in the way 100 years ago.

The way the disease was cured 100 years ago.
The way that the disease was cured 100 years ago.
The way which the disease was cured in 100 years ago.
The way in which the disease was cured 100 years ago.
The way that the disease was cured in 100 years ago.
The way the disease was cured in 100 years ago.

36. She treats other people in the way.

The way she treats other people.
The way that she treats other people.
The way which she treats other people in.
The way in which she treats other people.
The way that she treats other people in.
The way she treats other people in.

관계 부사 (Relative Adverb)

37. 그녀는 그런 식으로 바로 본론으로 들어갔다.

　　她以那种方式直接进入了正题。

　　彼女はそんなふうにさっそく本題に入った。

38. 그녀는 그런 식으로 나에게 그 일을 도와달라고 요청했다.

　　她以那种方式要求我帮助那件事。

　　彼女はそんなふうに私にその仕事を手伝ってほしいと要求した。

39. 맹도견은 그런 식으로 자기 주인이 길을 건너는 것을 도와준다.

　　导盲犬以那种方式帮助他的主人过马路。

　　盲導犬はそんなふうに自分の主人が道を渡るのを助ける。

40. 사람들은 사랑에 대해서 그런 식으로 느낀다.

　　人们对爱情有那样的感觉。

　　人々は愛についてそんなふうに感じる。

37. She got right down to business in the way.

The way she got right down to business.
The way that she got right down to business.
The way which she got right down to business in.
The way in which she got right down to business.
The way that she got right down to business in.
The way she got right down to business in.

38. She asked me to help with the work in the way.

The way she asked me to help with the work.
The way that she asked me to help with the work.
The way which she asked me to help with the work in.
The way in which she asked me to help with the work.
The way that she asked me to help with the work in.
The way she asked me to help with the work in.

39. The seeing eye dog helps its master cross the road in the way.

The way the seeing eye dog helps its master cross the road.
The way that the seeing eye dog helps its master cross the road.
The way which the seeing eye dog helps its master cross the road in.
The way in which the seeing eye dog helps its master cross the road.
The way that the seeing eye dog helps its master cross the road in.
The way the seeing eye dog helps its master cross the road in.

40. People feel about love in the way.

The way people feel about love.
The way that people feel about love.
The way which people feel about love in.
The way in which people feel about love.
The way that people feel about love in.
The way people feel about love in.

41. 그는 그런 식으로 자신의 신발 끈을 묶는다.

他以那种方式系他的鞋带。

彼はそんなふうに自分の靴の紐を結ぶ。

42. 그녀는 그런 식으로 다른 사람을 칭찬한다.

她以那种方式称赞其他人。

彼女はそんなふうに人を褒めている。

43. 우리는 그런 식으로 어떤 있을 수 있는 사고를 예방한다.

我们以那种方式预先防止任何可能的事故。

私たちはそんなふうに起こり得る事故を未然に防止する。

44. 우리는 그런 식으로 가장 복잡한 문제를 이해하려고 노력한다.

我们以那种方式努力理解最复杂的问题。

私たちはそんなふうに最も複雑な問題を理解しようと努力する。

41. He ties up his shoestrings in the way.

The way he ties up his shoestrings.
The way that he ties up his shoestrings.
The way which he ties up his shoestrings in.
The way in which he ties up his shoestrings.
The way that he ties up his shoestrings in.
The way he ties up his shoestrings in.

42. She praises other people in the way.

The way she praises other people.
The way that she praises other people.
The way which she praises other people in.
The way in which she praises other people.
The way that she praises other people in.
The way she praises other people in.

43. We prevent any possible accident in advance in the way.

The way we prevent any possible accident in advance.
The way that we prevent any possible accident in advance.
The way which we prevent any possible accident in advance in.
The way in which we prevent any possible accident in advance.
The way that we prevent any possible accident in advance in.
The way we prevent any possible accident in advance in.

44. We try to figure out the most complex problems in the way.

The way we try to figure out the most complex problems.
The way that we try to figure out the most complex problems.
The way which we try to figure out the most complex problems in.
The way in which we try to figure out the most complex problems.
The way that we try to figure out the most complex problems in.
The way we try to figure out the most complex problems in.

45. 지진은 그런 식으로 땅 밑에서 발생한다.

地震以那样的方式在地面下方发生。

地震はそんなふうに地面の下で発生する。

46. 많은 학생이 수학을 그런 식으로 공부한다.

很多学生以那种方式学习数学。

多くの学生が数学をそんなふうに勉強する。

47. 대부분의 서양 주택은 그런 식으로 난방한다.

大多数西式房子都以那种方式供暖。

欧米のほとんどの住宅はそんなふうに暖房をしている。

48. 그녀는 그런 식으로 한자 쓰는 연습을 한다.

她以那种方式练习写汉字。

彼女はそんなふうに漢字書く練習をしている。

45. An earthquake occurs under the ground in the way.

The way an earthquake occurs under the ground.
The way that an earthquake occurs under the ground.
The way which an earthquake occurs under the ground in.
The way in which an earthquake occurs under the ground.
The way that an earthquake occurs under the ground in.
The way an earthquake occurs under the ground in.

46. Many students study math in the way.

The way many students study math.
The way that many students study math.
The way which many students study math in.
The way in which many students study math.
The way that many students study math in.
The way many students study math in.

47. Most western houses are heated in the way.

The way most western houses are heated.
The way that most western houses are heated.
The way which most western houses are heated in.
The way in which most western houses are heated.
The way that most western houses are heated in.
The way most western houses are heated in.

48. She practices writing Chinese characters in the way.

The way she practices writing Chinese characters.
The way that she practices writing Chinese characters.
The way which she practices writing Chinese characters in.
The way in which she practices writing Chinese characters.
The way that she practices writing Chinese characters in.
The way she practices writing Chinese characters in.

49. 그 병원은 모든 암 환자를 그런 식으로 관리한다.

那家医院以那种方式管理所有癌症患者。

その病院はすべてのガン患者をそんなふうに管理する。

50. 박쥐는 그런 식으로 생존 문제에 대처한다.

蝙蝠以那种方式应付生存问题。

コウモリはそんなふうに生存問題に対処する。

49. The hospital manages every cancer patient in the way.

The way the hospital manages every cancer patient.
The way that the hospital manages every cancer patient.
The way which the hospital manages every cancer patient in.
The way in which the hospital manages every cancer patient.
The way that the hospital manages every cancer patient in.
The way the hospital manages every cancer patient in.

50. Bats cope with the problems of existence in the way.

The way bats cope with the problems of existence.
The way that bats cope with the problems of existence.
The way which bats cope with the problems of existence in.
The way in which bats cope with the problems of existence.
The way that bats cope with the problems of existence in.
The way bats cope with the problems of existence in.

4. 관계 부사 Why

관계 부사도 관계 대명사와 마찬가지로 선행사인 명사를 후치수식하는 형용사절을 이끈다. 관계 대명사는 접속사와 대명사의 역할을 하고, 관계 부사는 접속사와 부사 역할을 한다는 것이 문법적인 특징이며 차이점이라 할 수 있지만, 관계 대명사와 관계 부사가 둘 다 선행사인 명사를 후치수식하는 형용사절을 이끌고 있다는 점에서 본질적으로 같은 기능을 담당하고 있다고 할 수 있다.

관계 부사 why는 선행사가 이유일 때 사용하는 관계 부사이다. 관계 부사는 격변화가 없기 때문에 관계 부사 다음에는 항상 '주어 + 동사'가 온다. 따라서 관계 부사 why도 다른 관계 부사와 마찬가지로 '선행사 + why + 주어 + 동사'의 구조로 되어 있다. 해석은 '주어가 ~하는 이유'로 하면 되겠다.

관계 부사 why도 주의할 점이 몇 가지 있는데, 첫째, 관계 부사 why는 생략할 수 있다는 점이다. 둘째, 관계 부사 why 대신에 관계 부사 that을 쓸 수 있다는 점이고, 마지막으로 관계 부사 why는 '전치사 + 관계 대명사'로 바꾸어 쓸 수 있는데, 즉, why 대신에 'for which'로 바꾸어 쓸 수 있다.

> 여기서 "그는 그런 이유로 모임에 오지 못했다."라는 문장을 '그가 모임에 오지 못한 이유'라는 명사 후치수식 구문으로 전환시켜보면 다음과 같이 할 수 있겠다.
>
> He didn't come to the meeting for the reason.
>
> 1. The reason why he didn't come to the meeting.
> 2. The reason that he didn't come to the meeting.
> 3. The reason he didn't come to the meeting.
> 4. The reason which he didn't come to the meeting for.
> 5. The reason for which he didn't come to the meeting.
> 6. The reason that he didn't come to the meeting for.
> 7. The reason he didn't come to the meeting for.
>
> 1. 관계 부사 why
> 2. 관계 부사 that
> 3. 관계 부사 생략
> 4. 관계 대명사 which
> 5. 전치사 + 관계 대명사 which
> 6. 관계 대명사 that
> 7. 관계 대명사 생략

관계 부사 why의 선행사도 'the reason'밖에 없으므로 the reason why를 같이 쓰는 것은 같은 말을 중복해서 말한다는 느낌이 들어서 원어민들이 피하는 경향이 있고 또한 격을 생각해야 하는 관계 대명사를 쓰는 것은 번거롭다는 생각이 들어서 2번의 관계 부사 that을 사용하는 구문과 3번의 관계 부사를 생략하는 구문을 사용하는 것이 일반적이다. 또한 명사 후치수식 구문이 아니라서 여기에서는 언급하지 않았지만, 선행사인 the reason을 생략하고 관계 부사 why만을 사용하는 구문도 구어체에서 많이 쓴다는 것도 동시에 알아두면 좋겠다.

영어를 외국어로 배우고 있는 우리로서는 위에 있는 어떠한 후치수식 구문이든, 특히 관계 대명사를 자유자재로 쓸 수 있도록 충분한 연습을 해주기 바란다.

1. 그는 그런 이유로 나에게 그 질문을 했다.

    他以那样的理由问我那个问题。
    彼はそういう理由で私にその質問をした。

2. 그녀는 지금까지 그런 이유로 존경을 받아 왔다.

    她一向以那样的理由受到尊敬。
    彼女は今までそういう理由で尊敬されてきた。

3. 대부분의 사람은 그런 이유로 죽음을 두려워한다.

    大多数人因那样的理由害怕死亡。
    大部分の人はそういう理由で死を恐れている。

4. 그녀는 그런 이유로 소풍을 갈 수 없었다.

    她因那样的理由不能去野游。
    彼女はそういう理由でピクニックに行くことができなかった。

1. **He asked me the question for the reason.**

   The reason why he asked me the question.
   The reason that he asked me the question.
   The reason he asked me the question.
   The reason which he asked me the question for.
   The reason for which he asked me the question.
   The reason that he asked me the question for.
   The reason he asked me the question for.

2. **She has been admired for the reason.**

   The reason why she has been admired.
   The reason that she has been admired.
   The reason she has been admired.
   The reason which she has been admired for.
   The reason for which she has been admired.
   The reason that she has been admired for.
   The reason she has been admired for.

3. **Most people are afraid of death for the reason.**

   The reason why most people are afraid of death.
   The reason that most people are afraid of death.
   The reason most people are afraid of death.
   The reason which most people are afraid of death for.
   The reason for which most people are afraid of death.
   The reason that most people are afraid of death for.
   The reason most people are afraid of death for.

4. **She couldn't go on a picnic for the reason.**

   The reason why she couldn't go on a picnic.
   The reason that she couldn't go on a picnic.
   The reason she couldn't go on a picnic.
   The reason which she couldn't go on a picnic for.
   The reason for which she couldn't go on a picnic.
   The reason that she couldn't go on a picnic for.
   The reason she couldn't go on a picnic for.

5. 그녀는 그런 이유로 학교에 결석했다.

　　她以那样的理由缺课。
　　彼女はそういう理由で学校を欠席した。

6. 그녀는 지금까지 그런 이유로 울었다.

　　她一向以那样的理由哭。
　　彼女は今までそういう理由で泣いた。

7. 너는 그런 이유로 거기에 가서는 안 된다.

　　你不能以那样的理由去那里。
　　あなたはそういう理由でそこに行ってはいけない。

8. 그들은 그런 이유로 행복해한다.

　　他们由于那样的理由很幸福。
　　彼らはそういう理由で幸せだ。

5. **She is absent from school for the reason.**

The reason why she is absent from school.
The reason that she is absent from school.
The reason she is absent from school.
The reason which she is absent from school for.
The reason for which she is absent from school.
The reason that she is absent from school for.
The reason she is absent from school for.

6. **She has cried for the reason.**

The reason why she has cried.
The reason that she has cried.
The reason she has cried.
The reason which she has cried for.
The reason for which she has cried.
The reason that she has cried for.
The reason she has cried for.

7. **You should not go there for the reason.**

The reason why you should not go there.
The reason that you should not go there.
The reason you should not go there.
The reason which you should not go there for.
The reason for which you should not go there.
The reason that you should not go there for.
The reason you should not go there for.

8. **They are happy for the reason.**

The reason why they are happy.
The reason that they are happy.
The reason they are happy.
The reason which they are happy for.
The reason for which they are happy.
The reason that they are happy for.
The reason they are happy for.

9. 나는 그런 이유로 그를 좋아하지 않는다.

   我因那样的原因不喜欢他。
   私はそういう理由で彼を好きじゃない。

10. 그는 그런 이유로 몹시 속상해했다.

    他因那样的理由非常伤心。
    彼はそういう理由でひどくむしゃくしゃした。

11. 그녀는 그런 이유로 이것을 제기했다.

    她以那样的理由提出了这个建议。
    彼女はそういう理由でこれを提起した。

12. 나는 그런 이유로 그에게 이것을 언급했다.

    我以那样的理由对他谈到了这个。
    私はそういう理由で彼にこれを言及した。

9. I don't like him for the reason.

The reason why I don't like him.
The reason that I don't like him.
The reason I don't like him.
The reason which I don't like him for.
The reason for which I don't like him.
The reason that I don't like him for.
The reason I don't like him for.

10. He was very upset for the reason.

The reason why he was very upset.
The reason that he was very upset.
The reason he was very upset.
The reason which he was very upset for.
The reason for which he was very upset.
The reason that he was very upset for.
The reason he was very upset for.

11. She brought this up for the reason.

The reason why she brought this up.
The reason that she brought this up.
The reason she brought this up.
The reason which she brought this up for.
The reason for which she brought this up.
The reason that she brought this up for.
The reason she brought this up for.

12. I mentioned this to him for the reason.

The reason why I mentioned this to him.
The reason that I mentioned this to him.
The reason I mentioned this to him.
The reason which I mentioned this to him for.
The reason for which I mentioned this to him.
The reason that I mentioned this to him for.
The reason I mentioned this to him for.

13. 그녀는 그런 이유로 의사가 되었다.

她以那样的理由成为医生。

彼女はそういう理由で医者になった。

14. 그는 그런 이유로 그렇게 일찍 일어났다.

他以那样的理由起得那么早。

彼はそういう理由でそんなに早く起きた。

15. 그는 그런 이유로 학교에 일찍 갔다.

他因那样的理由早就上学去了。

彼はそういう理由で学校に早く行った。

16. 그는 그런 이유로 걸어 다니는 사전이라고 불린다.

他因那样的理由被称为活词典。

彼はそういう理由で歩く辞典と呼ばれる。

13. She became a doctor for the reason.

The reason why she became a doctor.
The reason that she became a doctor.
The reason she became a doctor.
The reason which she became a doctor for.
The reason for which she became a doctor.
The reason that she became a doctor for.
The reason she became a doctor for.

14. He got up so early for the reason.

The reason why he got up so early.
The reason that he got up so early.
The reason he got up so early.
The reason which he got up so early for.
The reason for which he got up so early.
The reason that he got up so early for.
The reason he got up so early for.

15. He went to school early for the reason.

The reason why he went to school early.
The reason that he went to school early.
The reason he went to school early.
The reason which he went to school early for.
The reason for which he went to school early.
The reason that he went to school early for.
The reason he went to school early for.

16. He is called a walking dictionary for the reason.

The reason why he is called a walking dictionary.
The reason that he is called a walking dictionary.
The reason he is called a walking dictionary.
The reason which he is called a walking dictionary for.
The reason for which he is called a walking dictionary.
The reason that he is called a walking dictionary for.
The reason he is called a walking dictionary for.

17. 나는 그런 이유로 그의 제안을 받아들였다.

我以那样的理由接受了他的提议。

私はそういう理由で彼の提案を受け入れた。

18. 그는 그런 이유로 이런 수고를 하지 않는다.

他以那样的理由不受这种麻烦。

彼はそういう理由でこういう苦労をしない。

19. 그녀는 그런 이유로 그를 좋아한다.

她因那样的理由喜欢他。

彼女はそういう理由で彼が好きだ。

20. 그녀는 그런 이유로 여름을 좋아하지 않는다.

由于那种原因她不喜欢夏天。

彼女はそういう理由で夏が好きじゃない。

17. **I accepted his offer for the reason.**

The reason why I accepted his offer.
The reason that I accepted his offer.
The reason I accepted his offer.
The reason which I accepted his offer for.
The reason for which I accepted his offer.
The reason that I accepted his offer for.
The reason I accepted his offer for.

18. **He does not take this trouble for the reason.**

The reason why he does not take this trouble.
The reason that he does not take this trouble.
The reason he does not take this trouble.
The reason which he does not take this trouble for.
The reason for which he does not take this trouble.
The reason that he does not take this trouble for.
The reason he does not take this trouble for.

19. **She likes him for the reason.**

The reason why she likes him.
The reason that she likes him.
The reason she likes him.
The reason which she likes him for.
The reason for which she likes him.
The reason that she likes him for.
The reason she likes him for.

20. **She does not like summer for the reason.**

The reason why she does not like summer.
The reason that she does not like summer.
The reason she does not like summer.
The reason which she does not like summer for.
The reason for which she does not like summer.
The reason that she does not like summer for.
The reason she does not like summer for.

21. 그는 그런 이유로 항상 머리가 아프고 메스꺼움을 느낀다.

由于那种原因他总是头痛而且感到恶心。

彼はそういう理由でいつも頭痛と吐き気を感じる。

22. 너는 그런 이유로 그녀를 사랑하는구나.

你因那样的理由爱她啊。

あなたはそういう理由で彼女を愛しているんだな。

23. 그는 그런 이유로 내 집에 건너왔다.

他以那样的理由来到了我家。

彼はそういう理由で私の家に来た。

24. 사람들은 그런 이유로 명상하는 것을 무척 좋아한다.

人们因那样的理由非常喜欢冥想。

人々はそういう理由で瞑想するのが大好きだ。

21. He always has a headache and feels nauseous for the reason.

The reason why he always has a headache and feels nauseous.
The reason that he always has a headache and feels nauseous.
The reason he always has a headache and feels nauseous.
The reason which he always has a headache and feels nauseous for.
The reason for which he always has a headache and feels nauseous.
The reason that he always has a headache and feels nauseous for.
The reason he always has a headache and feels nauseous for.

22. You love her for the reason.

The reason why you love her.
The reason that you love her.
The reason you love her.
The reason which you love her for.
The reason for which you love her.
The reason that you love her for.
The reason you love her for.

23. He came over to my house for the reason.

The reason why he came over to my house.
The reason that he came over to my house.
The reason he came over to my house.
The reason which he came over to my house for.
The reason for which he came over to my house.
The reason that he came over to my house for.
The reason he came over to my house for.

24. People love to practice meditation for the reason.

The reason why people love to practice meditation.
The reason that people love to practice meditation.
The reason people love to practice meditation.
The reason which people love to practice meditation for.
The reason for which people love to practice meditation.
The reason that people love to practice meditation for.
The reason people love to practice meditation for.

25. 그녀는 그런 이유로 지금까지 나에게 오랫동안 편지를 하지 못했다.

　　她因那样的理由至今很长时间没能给我写信。

　　彼女はそういう理由で今まで長い間私に手紙を出せなかった。

26. 그는 그런 이유로 더 이상 내 도움을 필요로 하지 않는다.

　　他因那样的理由不再需要我的帮助。

　　彼はそういう理由でこれ以上私の助けを必要としない。

27. 그는 그런 이유로 지금까지 빌린 돈을 갚지 못했다.

　　他因那样的理由至今没能偿还借款。

　　彼はそういう理由で今まで借りたお金を返済できなかった。

28. 나는 그런 이유로 지금까지 그 책을 반납하지 못했다.

　　我因那样的理由至今还没能退还那本书。

　　私はそういう理由で今までその本を返却できなかった。

25. She has not written to me for a long time for the reason.

The reason why she has not written to me for a long time.
The reason that she has not written to me for a long time.
The reason she has not written to me for a long time.
The reason which she has not written to me for a long time for.
The reason for which she has not written to me for a long time.
The reason that she has not written to me for a long time for.
The reason she has not written to me for a long time for.

26. He does not need my help any more for the reason.

The reason why he does not need my help any more.
The reason that he does not need my help any more.
The reason he does not need my help any more.
The reason which he does not need my help any more for.
The reason for which he does not need my help any more.
The reason that he does not need my help any more for.
The reason he does not need my help any more for.

27. He has failed to pay back the borrowed money for the reason.

The reason why he has failed to pay back the borrowed money.
The reason that he has failed to pay back the borrowed money.
The reason he has failed to pay back the borrowed money.
The reason which he has failed to pay back the borrowed money for.
The reason for which he has failed to pay back the borrowed money.
The reason that he has failed to pay back the borrowed money for.
The reason he has failed to pay back the borrowed money for.

28. I have not returned the book for the reason.

The reason why I have not returned the book.
The reason that I have not returned the book.
The reason I have not returned the book.
The reason which I have not returned the book for.
The reason for which I have not returned the book.
The reason that I have not returned the book for.
The reason I have not returned the book for.

29. 그녀는 그런 이유로 자신의 돈을 돌려받고 싶어 한다.

她想以那样的理由收回自己的钱。

彼女はそういう理由で自分のお金を返してもらうことを望んでいる。

30. 그는 그런 이유로 저 스마트 폰을 선택했다.

他以那样的理由选择了那个智能手机。

彼はそういう理由であのスマートフォンを選んだ。

31. 나는 그런 이유로 어젯밤 한숨도 자지 못했다.

我因那样的理由昨天晚上没合眼。

私はそういう理由で昨夜一睡もできなかった。

32. 그는 그런 이유로 천문학자가 되기로 결심했다.

他因那样的理由决心成为天文学家。

彼はそういう理由で天文学者になろうと決心した。

29. **She wants her money back for the reason.**

The reason why she wants her money back.
The reason that she wants her money back.
The reason she wants her money back.
The reason which she wants her money back for.
The reason for which she wants her money back.
The reason that she wants her money back for.
The reason she wants her money back for.

30. **He chose that smart phone for the reason.**

The reason why he chose that smart phone.
The reason that he chose that smart phone.
The reason he chose that smart phone.
The reason which he chose that smart phone for.
The reason for which he chose that smart phone.
The reason that he chose that smart phone for.
The reason he chose that smart phone for.

31. **I didn't sleep a wink last night for the reason.**

The reason why I didn't sleep a wink last night.
The reason that I didn't sleep a wink last night.
The reason I didn't sleep a wink last night.
The reason which I didn't sleep a wink last night for.
The reason for which I didn't sleep a wink last night.
The reason that I didn't sleep a wink last night for.
The reason I didn't sleep a wink last night for.

32. **He decided to be an astronomer for the reason.**

The reason why he decided to be an astronomer.
The reason that he decided to be an astronomer.
The reason he decided to be an astronomer.
The reason which he decided to be an astronomer for.
The reason for which he decided to be an astronomer.
The reason that he decided to be an astronomer for.
The reason he decided to be an astronomer for.

33. 나는 그런 이유로 이 국제기구에서 일하고 싶다.

我因那样的理由想在这个国际机构工作。

私はそういう理由でこの国際機構で働きたい。

34. 그녀는 그런 이유로 우리에게 동참하지 못했다.

她因那样的理由没能参与我们。

彼女はそういう理由で我々に参加できなかった。

35. 그는 그런 이유로 더 이상 골프를 즐기지 않는다.

他因那样的缘故不再享受高尔夫运动了。

彼はそういう理由でこれ以上ゴルフを楽しまない。

36. 공기가 그런 이유로 그렇게 오염되어 있다.

空气因那样的缘故被污染了。

空気がそういう理由でそんなに汚染されている。

33. I want to work for the international organization for the reason.

The reason why I want to work for the international organization.
The reason that I want to work for the international organization.
The reason I want to work for the international organization.
The reason which I want to work for the international organization for.
The reason for which I want to work for the international organization.
The reason that I want to work for the international organization for.
The reason I want to work for the international organization for.

34. She did not join us for the reason.

The reason why she did not join us.
The reason that she did not join us.
The reason she did not join us.
The reason which she did not join us for.
The reason for which she did not join us.
The reason that she did not join us for.
The reason she did not join us for.

35. He no longer enjoys playing golf for the reason.

The reason why he no longer enjoys playing golf.
The reason that he no longer enjoys playing golf.
The reason he no longer enjoys playing golf.
The reason which he no longer enjoys playing golf for.
The reason for which he no longer enjoys playing golf.
The reason that he no longer enjoys playing golf for.
The reason he no longer enjoys playing golf for.

36. The air is so polluted for the reason.

The reason why the air is so polluted.
The reason that the air is so polluted.
The reason the air is so polluted.
The reason which the air is so polluted for.
The reason for which the air is so polluted.
The reason that the air is so polluted for.
The reason the air is so polluted for.

37. 그들은 그런 이유로 영어를 그렇게 열심히 공부한다.

他们以那样的理由努力学习英语。

彼らはそういう理由で英語をそんなに一生懸命に勉強する。

38. 그의 신발은 그런 이유로 닳아 해졌다.

他的鞋子因那样的理由磨损了。

彼の靴はそういう理由ですり減った。

39. 우리는 그런 이유로 영어를 공부하지 않을 수 없다.

我们因那样的理由不得不学习英语。

私たちはそういう理由で英語を勉強せざるを得ない。

40. 그는 그런 이유로 대학입학 시험에서 떨어졌다.

他因那样的缘故没有通过大学入学考试。

彼はそういう理由で大学入学試験に落ちた。

37. They study English so hard for the reason.

The reason why they study English so hard.
The reason that they study English so hard.
The reason they study English so hard.
The reason which they study English so hard for.
The reason for which they study English so hard.
The reason that they study English so hard for.
The reason they study English so hard for.

38. His shoes are worn out for the reason.

The reason why his shoes are worn out.
The reason that his shoes are worn out.
The reason his shoes are worn out.
The reason which his shoes are worn out for.
The reason for which his shoes are worn out.
The reason that his shoes are worn out for.
The reason his shoes are worn out for.

39. We cannot help studying English for the reason.

The reason why we cannot help studying English.
The reason that we cannot help studying English.
The reason we cannot help studying English.
The reason which we cannot help studying English for.
The reason for which we cannot help studying English.
The reason that we cannot help studying English for.
The reason we cannot help studying English for.

40. He failed the entrance examination for college for the reason.

The reason why he failed the entrance examination for college.
The reason that he failed the entrance examination for college.
The reason he failed the entrance examination for college.
The reason which he failed the entrance examination for college for.
The reason for which he failed the entrance examination for college.
The reason that he failed the entrance examination for college for.
The reason he failed the entrance examination for college for.

41. 그는 그런 이유로 폐암으로 사망했다.

他因那样的理由死于肺癌。

彼はそういう理由で肺癌で死亡した。

42. 우리는 그런 이유로 그 문제를 해결하는 데 집중해야만 한다.

我们以那样的理由必须集中精力解决那个问题。

私たちはそういう理由でその問題を解決することに集中しなければならない。

43. 그는 그런 이유로 내 질문에 대답하기를 주저한다.

他因那样的理由犹豫着回答我的问题。

彼はそういう理由で私の質問に答えることを躊躇する。

44. 그들은 그런 이유로 우리한테서 도움을 받지 못하고 있다.

他们因那样的缘故没能得到我们的帮助。

彼らはそういう理由で私たちから助けを得られないでいる。

41. He died of lung cancer for the reason.

The reason why he died of lung cancer.
The reason that he died of lung cancer.
The reason he died of lung cancer.
The reason which he died of lung cancer for.
The reason for which he died of lung cancer.
The reason that he died of lung cancer for.
The reason he died of lung cancer for.

42. We have to concentrate on solving the problem for the reason.

The reason why we have to concentrate on solving the problem.
The reason that we have to concentrate on solving the problem.
The reason we have to concentrate on solving the problem.
The reason which we have to concentrate on solving the problem for.
The reason for which we have to concentrate on solving the problem.
The reason that we have to concentrate on solving the problem for.
The reason we have to concentrate on solving the problem for.

43. He hesitates to answer my question for the reason.

The reason why he hesitates to answer my question.
The reason that he hesitates to answer my question.
The reason he hesitates to answer my question.
The reason which he hesitates to answer my question for.
The reason for which he hesitates to answer my question.
The reason that he hesitates to answer my question for.
The reason he hesitates to answer my question for.

44. They don't get help from us for the reason.

The reason why they don't get help from us.
The reason that they don't get help from us.
The reason they don't get help from us.
The reason which they don't get help from us for.
The reason for which they don't get help from us.
The reason that they don't get help from us for.
The reason they don't get help from us for.

45. 나는 그런 이유로 밤에 자지 못한다.

我因那样的理由晚上睡不着觉。

私はそういう理由で夜に眠れない。

46. 나는 그런 이유로 더 이상 여기에 머물 수 없다.

我因那样的理由不能再留在这里。

私はそういう理由でこれ以上ここに滞在できない。

47. 인간은 그런 이유로 지금까지 우주를 탐험했다.

至今为止人类以那样的理由探索宇宙。

人間はそういう理由でこれまで宇宙を探検した。

48. 사람들은 그런 이유로 남극대륙에 간다.

人们因那样的理由去南极大陆。

人々はそういう理由で南極大陸に行く。

45. I don't sleep at night for the reason.

The reason why I don't sleep at night.
The reason that I don't sleep at night.
The reason I don't sleep at night.
The reason which I don't sleep at night for.
The reason for which I don't sleep at night.
The reason that I don't sleep at night for.
The reason I don't sleep at night for.

46. I can't stay here any longer for the reason.

The reason why I can't stay here any longer.
The reason that I can't stay here any longer.
The reason I can't stay here any longer.
The reason which I can't stay here any longer for.
The reason for which I can't stay here any longer.
The reason that I can't stay here any longer for.
The reason I can't stay here any longer for.

47. Human beings have explored space for the reason.

The reason why human beings have explored space.
The reason that human beings have explored space.
The reason human beings have explored space.
The reason which human beings have explored space for.
The reason for which human beings have explored space.
The reason that human beings have explored space for.
The reason human beings have explored space for.

48. People go to Antarctica for the reason.

The reason why people go to Antarctica.
The reason that people go to Antarctica.
The reason people go to Antarctica.
The reason which people go to Antarctica for.
The reason for which people go to Antarctica.
The reason that people go to Antarctica for.
The reason people go to Antarctica for.

49. 제비는 그런 이유로 남쪽으로 날아간다.

燕子因那样的理由飞向南方。

ツバメはそういう理由で南に飛んでいく。

50. 우리는 그런 이유로 핵전쟁을 두려워한다.

我们因那样的理由害怕核战争。

私たちはそういう理由で核戦争を恐れている。

49. Swallows fly south for the reason.

The reason why swallows fly south.
The reason that swallows fly south.
The reason swallows fly south.
The reason which swallows fly south for.
The reason for which swallows fly south.
The reason that swallows fly south for.
The reason swallows fly south for.

50. We are afraid of a nuclear war for the reason.

The reason why we are afraid of a nuclear war.
The reason that we are afraid of a nuclear war.
The reason we are afraid of a nuclear war.
The reason which we are afraid of a nuclear war for.
The reason for which we are afraid of a nuclear war.
The reason that we are afraid of a nuclear war for.
The reason we are afraid of a nuclear war for.

03

영어는 **후치수식**, 한중일어는 **전치수식**

분사
Participle

1. 현재분사
(Present Participle)

　현재분사는 동사의 원형에 'ing' 형태를 취하고 동사의 기능과 형용사의 기능을 동시에 갖고 있다. 즉, 현재분사는 문장의 구성 요소인 보어와 목적어를 수반할 수 있고 부사나 부사구나 부사절의 수식을 받는 동사적인 성격을 갖고 있으면서 동시에 명사를 수식할 수 있는 형용사적인 성격을 지니고 있다.

　현재분사가 명사를 수식하는 형용사의 기능을 담당하고 있으므로 현재분사도 형용사와 같이 한정적 용법(attributive use)과 서술적 용법(predicative use)이 있다. 즉, 현재분사가 명사를 앞이나 뒤에서 바로 수식하는 경우를 한정적 용법이라 하고 현재분사가 2형식의 주격 보어나 5형식의 목적격 보어 역할을 하면서 문장의 구성 요소로 사용되는 경우를 서술적 용법이라고 한다.

　여기서 특히 주의할 점이 두 가지 있는데, 하나는 우리가 익히 알고 있듯이 현재분사는 능동과 진행의 뜻을 내포하고 있다는 사실이고, 다른 하나는 현재분사가 명사를 뒤에서 후치수식하는 구조는 모두 관계 대명사와 be 동사가 생략되어 있는 구조라는 점이다. 현재분사의 명사 후치수식 구조는 관계 대명사로 이루어진 명사 후치수식 구조를 더 짧고 더 간단하게 말하고 쓰기 위한 구조라고 이해하면 되겠다. 많은 예문들을 통해서 자유롭게 활용할 수 있도록 충분히 익혀주기 바란다.

여기서 "거미는 사냥하기 위해서 거미줄을 친다."라는 문장을 '사냥하기 위해서 거미줄을 치는 거미'라는 명사 후치수식 구문으로 전환시켜보면 다음과 같이 할 수 있겠다.

The spider spins a web for hunting.

1. The spider spinning a web for hunting.
2. The spider which spins a web for hunting.
3. The spider that spins a web for hunting.
4. The spider which is spinning a web for hunting.
5. The spider that is spinning a web for hunting.

1. 현재분사
2. 관계 대명사 which
3. 관계 대명사 that
4. 관계 대명사 which
5. 관계 대명사 that

훌륭한 영어 구사력을 갖기 위해서는 명사를 후치수식하는 구문을 자유자재로 사용할 줄 아는 것이 절대적으로 중요하다는 점을 인식하고 충분한 연습을 해주기 바란다.

1. 새벽 동이 트고 있다.

    早晨天正渐渐变亮。
    夜が明けている。

2. 한 사람이 도와달라고 소리치고 있다.

    一个人正呼吁要求帮助。
    一人の人が助けてくれと叫んでいる。

3. 대부분의 에너지 음료는 다량의 카페인을 함유하고 있다.

    大多数功能饮料含有大量的咖啡因。
    ほとんどのエネルギードリンクは多量のカフエインを含有している。

4. 신종 독감 바이러스가 유행하고 있다.

    新型流感病毒正在流行。
    新型インフルエンザウイルスが流行している。

5. 많은 피난민이 보트를 타고 지중해를 건너고 있다.

    很多难民正乘船穿越地中海。
    多くの避難民がボートに乗って地中海を渡っている。

6. 사람들이 극장에 들어가려고 기다리고 있다.

    人们正在等待进入剧场。
    人々が劇場に入ろうと待っている。

영어는 후치수식, 한중일어는 전치수식

1. **Dawn is breaking the night.**

   Dawn breaking the night.
   Dawn which is breaking the night.
   Dawn that is breaking the night.

2. **A man is calling for help.**

   A man calling for help.
   A man who is calling for help.
   A man that is calling for help.

3. **Most energy drinks contain a large amount of caffeine.**

   Most energy drinks containing a large amount of caffeine.
   Most energy drinks which contain a large amount of caffeine.
   Most energy drinks that contain a large amount of caffeine.

4. **A new flu virus is going around.**

   A new flu virus going around.
   A new flu virus which is going around.
   A new flu virus that is going around.

5. **A lot of refugees are crossing the Mediterranean Sea by boat.**

   A lot of refugees crossing the Mediterranean Sea by boat.
   A lot of refugees who are crossing the Mediterranean Sea by boat.
   A lot of refugees that are crossing the Mediterranean Sea by boat.

6. **People are waiting to get into the theater.**

   People waiting to get into the theater.
   People who are waiting to get into the theater.
   People that are waiting to get into the theater.

03

분사 (Participle)

7. 그 사람은 무능하다고 비판받고 있다.

那个人被批评无能。

彼は無能だと批判されている。

8. 아이들이 해변에서 놀고 있다.

孩子们正在海边玩耍。

子供たちが海辺で遊んでいる。

9. 그 집은 항구를 마주하고 있다.

那座房子面向港口。

その家は港に面している。

10. 노신사들이 나비넥타이를 매고 있다.

老先生们戴着蝴蝶领结。

老紳士が蝶ネクタイを締めている。

11. 많은 오리가 물 위를 떠다니고 있다.

很多鸭子漂浮在水面上游来游去。

多くのアヒルが水上に浮いている。

12. 사나운 폭풍이 다가오고 있다.

猛烈的暴风雨即将来临。

荒々しい暴風が迫っている。

7. **He is being criticized for incompetence.**

   The person being criticized for incompetence.
   The person who is being criticized for incompetence.
   The person that is being criticized for incompetence.

8. **The children are playing on the beach.**

   The children playing on the beach.
   The children who are playing on the beach.
   The children that are playing on the beach.

9. **The house faces the port.**

   The house facing the port.
   The house which faces the port.
   The house that faces the port.
   The house which is facing the port.
   The house that is facing the port.

10. **Old gentlemen are wearing bow ties.**

    Old gentlemen wearing bow ties.
    Old gentlemen who are wearing bow ties.
    Old gentlemen that are wearing bow ties.

11. **Many ducks are floating on the water.**

    Many ducks floating on the water.
    Many ducks which are floating on the water.
    Many ducks that are floating on the water.

12. **A bad storm is coming in.**

    A bad storm coming in.
    A bad storm which is coming in.
    A bad storm that is coming in.

13. 올빼미가 들쥐를 노려보고 있다.

　　猫头鹰正盯着田鼠。
　　フクロウが野ねずみをねらっている。

14. 여덟 개의 행성이 태양 주위를 돌고 있다.

　　八个行星围绕着太阳旋转。
　　八つの惑星が太陽の周りを回っている。

15. 대부분의 십 대는 모든 것을 자신의 부모에게 의존하고 있다.

　　大多数十几岁的少年一切都依靠着他们的父母。
　　10代のほとんどがすべてのことで自分の親に依存している。

16. 한 아가씨가 티셔츠와 반바지를 입고 있다.

　　一个姑娘穿着一件T-恤和短裤。
　　ひとりのお嬢さんがTシャツと半ズボンを着ている。

17. 그 작업은 대단한 에너지와 열정을 요구한다.

　　那项工作需要很大的精力和热情。
　　その作業は大変なエネルギーと熱情を要求する。

18. 수억 명의 사람이 깨끗한 물을 마시지 못하고 있다.

　　数亿人无法喝上干净的水。
　　数億人の人が清潔な水を飲めていない。

13. An owl is glaring at a field mouse.

An owl glaring at a field mouse.
An owl which is glaring at a field mouse.
An owl that is glaring at a field mouse.

14. Eight planets are moving around the sun.

Eight planets moving around the sun.
Eight planets which are moving around the sun.
Eight planets that are moving around the sun.

15. Most teenagers are depending on their parents for everything.

Most teenagers depending on their parents for everything.
Most teenagers who are depending on their parents for everything.
Most teenagers that are depending on their parents for everything.

16. A girl is wearing a T-shirt and shorts.

A girl wearing a T-shirt and shorts.
A girl who is wearing a T-shirt and shorts.
A girl that is wearing a T-shirt and shorts.

17. The task requires great energy and enthusiasm.

The task requiring great energy and enthusiasm.
The task which requires great energy and enthusiasm.
The task that requires great energy and enthusiasm.

18. Hundreds of millions of people do not drink clean water.

Hundreds of millions of people not drinking clean water.
Hundreds of millions of people who do not drink clean water.
Hundreds of millions of people that do not drink clean water.
Hundreds of millions of people who are not drinking clean water.
Hundreds of millions of people that are not drinking clean water.

19. 많은 환자가 의사를 보기 위해서 기다리고 있다.

很多病人都在等着看医生。

多くの患者が医者に診察を受けるために待っている。

20. 그들은 산을 뚫어서 터널을 내고 있다.

他们正在凿山修隧道。

彼らは山を貫いてトンネルを掘っている。

21. 배가 바람을 헤치고 나아가고 있다.

一艘船正在逆风前进。

船が風に逆らって進んでいる。

22. 많은 차가 교차로에서 움직이지 않은 상태로 서 있다.

很多汽车堵在十字路口走不动。

多くの車が交差点で動かない状態で止まっている。

23. 철새는 더 따뜻한 기후를 찾아서 남쪽으로 날아간다.

候鸟为寻找更温暖的气候飞往南方。

渡り鳥はより暖かい気候を求めて南に飛んでいく。

19. **Lots of patients are waiting to see the doctor.**

Lots of patients waiting to see the doctor.
Lots of patients who are waiting to see the doctor.
Lots of patients that are waiting to see the doctor.

20. **They are digging a tunnel through a mountain.**

People digging a tunnel through a mountain.
People who are digging a tunnel through a mountain.
People that are digging a tunnel through a mountain.

21. **A ship is making its way against the wind.**

A ship making its way against the wind.
A ship which is making its way against the wind.
A ship that is making its way against the wind.

22. **Many cars are standing still at the crossroad.**

Many cars standing still at the crossroad.
Many cars which are standing still at the crossroad.
Many cars that are standing still at the crossroad.

23. **Migratory birds fly south in search of warmer climate.**

Migratory birds flying south in search of warmer climate.
Migratory birds which fly south in search of warmer climate.
Migratory birds that fly south in search of warmer climate.
Migratory birds which are flying south in search of warmer climate.
Migratory birds that are flying south in search of warmer climate.

24. 사람들은 다양한 자원봉사 활동에 참여한다.

    人们参加各种志愿活动。
    人々は多様なボランティア活動に参加する。

25. 많은 남자가 그녀와 같은 현명한 아가씨를 찾고 있다.

    很多男人正在找像她一样明事理的姑娘。
    多くの男性が彼女のような賢明な娘を探している。

26. 나뭇잎이 길 위에 떨어지고 있다.

    树叶掉落在路上。
    木の葉が道の上に落ちている。

27. 많은 사람이 쌍쌍이 그리고 무리 지어 걸어가고 있다.

    很多人成双成对和成群地走着。
    多くの人が二人ずつ、または群がって歩いている。

28. 그 온순한 어린이는 주로 혼자 지낸다.

    那个温顺的孩子大多是自己生活。
    そのおとなしい子供は主に一人で過ごしている。

24. People take part in various volunteer activities.

People taking part in various volunteer activities.
People who take part in various volunteer activities.
People that take part in various volunteer activities.
People who are taking part in various volunteer activities.
People that are taking part in various volunteer activities.

25. A lot of men are looking for a wise girl like her.

A lot of men looking for a wise girl like her.
A lot of men who are looking for a wise girl like her.
A lot of men that are looking for a wise girl like her.

26. The leaves are falling on the streets.

The leaves falling on the streets.
The leaves which are falling on the streets.
The leaves that are falling on the streets.

27. Many people are walking in pairs and groups.

Many people walking in pairs and groups.
Many people who are walking in pairs and groups.
Many people that are walking in pairs and groups.

28. The gentle child stays much to himself.

The gentle child staying much to himself.
The gentle child who stays much to himself.
The gentle child that stays much to himself.
The gentle child who is staying much to himself.
The gentle child that is staying much to himself.

29. 추위가 내 몸을 뚫고 들어오고 있다.

    寒冷刺穿着我的身体。

    寒さが私の体を突き抜けて入ってきている。

30. 그 추레한 노신사는 닳아 해진 모자를 쓰고 있다.

    那位褴褛的老绅士戴着一顶破旧的帽子。

    その小汚い老紳士は破れた帽子をかぶっている。

31. 눈이 봄 햇살에 녹고 있다.

    雪在春天的阳光下融化着。

    雪が春の日差しに溶けている。

32. 많은 갈매기가 배 주위를 날고 있다.

    很多海鸥在船周围飞。

    多くのカモメが船の周りを飛んでいる。

33. 학생들은 인문학과 자연과학을 전공한다.

    学生们专攻人文学和自然科学。

    学生たちは人文学と自然科学を専攻する。

29. The cold is piercing through my body.

The cold piercing through my body.
The cold which is piercing through my body.
The cold that is piercing through my body.

30. The shabby old gentleman is wearing a worn-out hat.

The shabby old gentleman wearing a worn-out hat.
The shabby old gentleman who is wearing a worn-out hat.
The shabby old gentleman that is wearing a worn-out hat.

31. Snow is melting in spring sunshine.

Snow melting in spring sunshine.
Snow which is melting in spring sunshine.
Snow that is melting in spring sunshine.

32. Many sea gulls are flying around the ship.

Many sea gulls flying around the ship.
Many sea gulls which are flying around the ship.
Many sea gulls that are flying around the ship.

33. The students major in humanities and natural sciences.

The students majoring in humanities and natural sciences.
The students who major in humanities and natural sciences.
The students that major in humanities and natural sciences.
The students who are majoring in humanities and natural sciences.
The students that are majoring in humanities and natural sciences.

34. 하얀 구름이 파란 하늘 여기저기에서 떠다닌다.

白色的云彩漂浮在蓝天的任何地方。

白い雲が青い空のあちらこちらで漂っている。

35. 다섯 대의 헬리콥터가 대도시 상공을 일렬로 날고 있다.

五架直升机正在大城市上空排成一列飞行。

五機のヘリコプターが大都市の上空を一列に飛んでいる。

36. 열차는 매시 정각에 시카고를 출발한다.

火车每小时整点从芝加哥出发。

列車は毎時定刻にシカゴを出発する。

37. 많은 이름 모를 들꽃이 숲 속에서 자라고 있다.

很多无名的野花生长在丛林中。

名前も知らない多くの野花が森の中で育っている。

38. 산업 폐수는 다량의 독성 화학 물질을 함유하고 있다.

工业污水含有大量有毒化学物质。

産業廃水は多量の毒性化学物質を含有している。

34. White clouds float here and there in the blue sky.

White clouds floating here and there in the blue sky.
White clouds which float here and there in the blue sky.
White clouds that float here and there in the blue sky.
White clouds which are floating here and there in the blue sky.
White clouds that are floating here and there in the blue sky.

35. Five helicopters are flying in a row over the large city.

Five helicopters flying in a row over the large city.
Five helicopters which are flying in a row over the large city.
Five helicopters that are flying in a row over the large city.

36. A train leaves Chicago every hour on the hour.

A train leaving Chicago every hour on the hour.
A train which leaves Chicago every hour on the hour.
A train that leaves Chicago every hour on the hour.
A train which is leaving Chicago every hour on the hour.
A train that is leaving Chicago every hour on the hour.

37. Many unknown wild flowers are growing in the woods.

Many unknown wild flowers growing in the woods.
Many unknown wild flowers which are growing in the woods.
Many unknown wild flowers that are growing in the woods.

38. Industrial sewage contains a large amount of toxic chemicals.

Industrial sewage containing a large amount of toxic chemicals.
Industrial sewage which contains a large amount of toxic chemicals.
Industrial sewage that contains a large amount of toxic chemicals.

39. 그는 정해진 시간보다 30분 뒤에 도착한다.

　　他比规定的时间晚30分钟到达。
　　彼は決まった時間より30分後に到着する。

40. 괄목할만한 발전이 지금 그 나라에서 이루어지고 있다.

　　那个国家目前正在实现着令人瞩目的发展。
　　目覚しい発展が今その国で遂げられている。

41. 많은 다른 부류의 사람이 많은 다른 종류의 일을 한다.

　　很多不同种类的人做着很多不同种类的工作。
　　多くの異なる部類の人が多くの異なる種類の仕事をしている。

42. 한 어머니가 자신의 팔에 아이를 안고 있다.

　　一位母亲用自己的胳膊抱着孩子。
　　ある母親が自分の腕に子供を抱えている。

43. 노란 수선화가 바람에 흔들리고 있다.

　　黄色的水仙在风中挥舞着。
　　黄色い水仙が風に揺れている。

영어는 후치수식, 한중일어는 전치수식

39. He arrives 30 minutes after the set time.

The person arriving 30 minutes after the set time.
The person who arrives 30 minutes after the set time.
The person that arrives 30 minutes after the set time.
The person who is arriving 30 minutes after the set time.
The person that is arriving 30 minutes after the set time.

40. The remarkable progress is now being made in the country.

The remarkable progress now being made in the country.
The remarkable progress which is now being made in the country.
The remarkable progress that is now being made in the country.

41. Many different kinds of people do many different kinds of things.

Many different kinds of people doing many different kinds of things.
Many different kinds of people who do many different kinds of things.
Many different kinds of people that do many different kinds of things.
Many different kinds of people who are doing many different kinds of things.
Many different kinds of people that are doing many different kinds of things.

42. A mother is carrying a child in her arms.

A mother carrying a child in her arms.
A mother who is carrying a child in her arms.
A mother that is carrying a child in her arms.

43. The yellow daffodils are waving in the wind.

The yellow daffodils waving in the wind.
The yellow daffodils which are waving in the wind.
The yellow daffodils that are waving in the wind.

분사 (Participle)

44. 사람들이 현재의 금융위기와 힘겹게 싸우고 있다.

　　　人们正在艰辛地抗争着和当前的金融危机。
　　　人々は現在の金融危機と何とか戦っている。

45. 70억 명 이상의 사람이 지구에 살고 있다.

　　　70亿以上的人在地球上生活着。
　　　70億以上の人が地球に住んでいる。

46. 두 외국인이 서로에게 영어로 얘기하고 있다.

　　　两个外国人正在用英语交谈。
　　　2人の外国人がお互いに英語で話している。

47. 태양 광선이 창문을 통해서 안으로 흘러들어온다.

　　　太阳的光线通过窗户透入到里面。
　　　太陽光線が窓を通じて中に流れ込んでくる。

48. 오존층은 해로운 자외선으로부터 지구를 보호해준다.

　　　臭氧层保护地球免受有害的紫外线。
　　　オゾン層は有害な紫外線から地球を保護してくれる。

영어는 후치수식, 한중일어는 전치수식

44. People are struggling with the current financial crisis.

People struggling with the current financial crisis.
People who are struggling with the current financial crisis.
People that are struggling with the current financial crisis.

45. More than seven billion people live on the earth.

More than seven billion people living on the earth.
More than seven billion people who live on the earth.
More than seven billion people that live on the earth.
More than seven billion people who are living on the earth.
More than seven billion people that are living on the earth.

46. Two foreigners are speaking to each other in English.

Two foreigners speaking to each other in English.
Two foreigners who are speaking to each other in English.
Two foreigners that are speaking to each other in English.

47. The rays of the sun stream in through the window.

The rays of the sun streaming in through the window.
The rays of the sun which stream in through the window.
The rays of the sun that stream in through the window.
The rays of the sun which are streaming in through the window.
The rays of the sun that are streaming in through the window.

48. The ozone layer protects the earth from harmful ultraviolet rays.

The ozone layer protecting the earth from harmful ultraviolet rays.
The ozone layer which protects the earth from harmful ultraviolet rays.
The ozone layer that protects the earth from harmful ultraviolet rays.
The ozone layer which is protecting the earth from harmful ultraviolet rays.
The ozone layer that is protecting the earth from harmful ultraviolet rays.

03 분사 (Participle)

49. 무수히 많은 사람이 자신의 영어를 향상시키려고 노력하고 있다.

无数的人正在努力提高自己的英语。

多くの人が自分の英語を向上させようと努力している。

50. 그 여가수는 녹색 스카프와 어울리는 녹색 신발을 착용하고 있다.

那位女歌手戴着绿色围巾穿着合适的绿色鞋子。

その女性歌手は緑色のスカーフに合う緑色の靴を着用している。

49. **Innumerable people try to improve their English.**

Innumerable people trying to improve their English.
Innumerable people who try to improve their English.
Innumerable people that try to improve their English.
Innumerable people who are trying to improve their English.
Innumerable people that are trying to improve their English.

50. **The female singer wears a green scarf and matching green shoes.**

The female singer wearing a green scarf and matching green shoes.
The female singer who wears a green scarf and matching green shoes.
The female singer that wears a green scarf and matching green shoes.
The female singer who is wearing a green scarf and matching green shoes.
The female singer that is wearing a green scarf and matching green shoes.

2. 과거분사
(Past Participle)

　과거분사는 말 그대로 동사의 과거분사형이며 동사의 기능과 형용사의 기능을 동시에 갖고 있다. 즉 과거분사는 문장의 구성 요소인 보어와 목적어를 수반할 수 있고 부사나 부사구나 부사절의 수식을 받는 동사적인 성격을 갖고 있으면서 동시에 명사를 수식할 수 있는 형용사적인 성격을 띠고 있다.

　과거분사가 명사를 수식하는 형용사의 기능을 담당하고 있으므로 과거분사도 한정적 용법(attributive use)과 서술적 용법(predicative use)이 있다. 즉 과거분사가 명사를 앞이나 뒤에서 바로 수식하는 경우를 한정적 용법이라 하고 과거분사가 2형식의 주격 보어나 5형식의 목적격 보어 역할을 하면서 문장의 구성 요소로 사용되는 경우를 서술적 용법이라고 한다.

　여기서 특히 주의할 점이 두 가지 있는데, 하나는 우리가 익히 알고 있듯이 과거분사는 대체로 수동의 뜻을 내포하고 있다는 사실이다. 하지만 모든 과거분사가 다 수동의 의미를 내포하고 있는 것은 아니라는 것이다. 일반적으로 말해서, 타동사의 과거분사가 수동의 뜻을 나타내는 것은 당연하다고 말할 수 있지만, 자동사의 과거분사는 능동의 뜻을 나타낸다는 것도 반드시 알아두어야 하겠다.

　우리가 주의해야 할 또 다른 하나는, 과거분사가 명사를 뒤에서 후치수식하는 구조는 모두 관계 대명사와 be 동사가 생략되어 있는 구조라는 점이다. 과거분사의 명사 후치수식 구조는 관계 대명사로 이루어진 명사 후치수식 구조를 더 짧고 더 간단하게 말하고 쓰기 위한 구조라고 이해하면 되겠다. 본 교재에 있는 예문들을 통해서 자유롭게 활용할 수 있도록 충분히 익혀주기 바란다.

여기서 "이 나라는 극동의 심장부에 위치하고 있다."라는 문장을 '극동의 심장부에 위치하고 있는 나라'라는 명사 후치수식 구문으로 전환시켜보면 다음과 같이 할 수 있겠다.

The country is located in the heart of the Far East.

1. The country located in the heart of the Far East.
2. The country which is located in the heart of the Far East.
3. The country that is located in the heart of the Far East.

1. 과거분사
2. 관계 대명사 which
3. 관계 대명사 that

우리말과 영어 사이에 여러 가지 구문론적인 차이점들이 있지만, 우리가 영어를 학습하는 데 있어서 난관인 동시에 열쇠가 될 수 있는 것이 명사를 수식하는 영어의 후치수식 구조를 빨리 터득하는 것이라고 필자는 지금까지 많이 강조해왔다. 우리가 문장을 구문론적으로 분류할 때, 주어 동사가 하나로 되어 있는 단문(simple sentence)과 두 개 이상의 단문이 등위접속사에 의해서 연결된 중문(compound sentence), 그리고 주절과 종속절로 이루어진 복문(complex sentence)으로 분류한다. 영어를 외국어로 배우고 있는 우리로서는 구조적으로 봤을 때, 복문 때문에 영어가 어렵고 정복하기 힘들다고 볼 수 있다. 명사절과 형용사절과 부사절을 종속절로 갖고 있는 복문 중에서 명사 후치수식 구조가 없는 우리에게는 형용사절을 가진 복문이 가장 어렵다고 하지 않을 수 없다. 다시 말해서 본 교재가 다루고 있는 명사 후치수식 구조를 자유롭게 사용할 수 있다면 영어에 완전히 적응했다고 봐도 무난할 것이다. 아무쪼록 더욱 품위 있는 영어를 구사할 수 있도록 여러분의 끊임없는 연습을 요구하는 영어 학습에 많은 성과와 기쁨과 만족이 있기를 기원한다.

1. 좋았던 옛 시절은 영원히 지나가 버렸다.

   好的旧时光永远地消失了。

   昔懐かしい時代は永遠に過ぎ去ってしまった。

2. 많은 돈이 이번 사건과 관련되어 있다.

   很多钱与本次事件有关。

   多くのお金がこの事件と関わっている。

3. 그 닭들은 조류 독감 바이러스에 감염된 것으로 밝혀졌다.

   那些鸡被发现感染了禽流感病毒。

   その鶏は鳥インフルエンザウイルスに感染したことが分かった。

4. 이 커피는 그녀가 요청한 대로 카페인을 제거한 것이다.

   这咖啡是按照她的要求去除咖啡因的。

   このコーヒーは彼女が注文したとおりカフェインを抜いたものだ。

5. 따뜻한 도움의 손길이 난민들에게 제공되고 있다.

   温暖的援手正在向难民提供。

   暖かい助けの手が難民たちに提供されている。

6. 그 화재는 그녀의 부주의로 인해서 일어났다.

   那次火灾起因于她的粗心。

   その火災は彼女の不注意によって起きた。

영어는 후치수식, 한중일어는 전치수식

1. **The good old days are gone forever.**

   The good old days gone forever.
   The good old days which are gone forever.
   The good old days that are gone forever.

2. **A lot of money is involved in this incident.**

   A lot of money involved in this incident.
   A lot of money which is involved in this incident.
   A lot of money that is involved in this incident.

3. **The chickens are found to be infected with the bird flu virus.**

   The chickens found to be infected with the bird flu virus.
   The chickens which are found to be infected with the bird flu virus.
   The chickens that are found to be infected with the bird flu virus.

4. **The coffee is decaffeinated as she asked.**

   The coffee decaffeinated as she asked.
   The coffee which is decaffeinated as she asked.
   The coffee that is decaffeinated as she asked.

5. **A warm helping hand is extended to the refugees.**

   A warm helping hand extended to the refugees.
   A warm helping hand which is extended to the refugees.
   A warm helping hand that is extended to the refugees.

6. **The fire was caused by her carelessness.**

   The fire caused by her carelessness.
   The fire which was caused by her carelessness.
   The fire that was caused by her carelessness.

03 분사 (Participle)

7. 막대한 피해가 그 화재로 인해서 초래되었다.

   巨大的伤害是由那次火灾造成的。

   莫大な被害がその火災によってもたらされた。

8. 이 정원은 가을이면 다채로운 나뭇잎으로 덮인다.

   这个庭院一到秋天就被五颜六色的树叶覆盖。

   この庭園は秋になると多彩な木の葉に覆われる。

9. 대부분의 것은 교육과 밀접하게 관련되어 있다.

   大多数事情与教育密切相关。

   ほとんどのものは教育と密接に関連している。

10. 대부분의 가정은 TV가 지배하고 있다.

    大多数家庭由电视支配。

    ほとんどの家庭ではTVが支配している。

11. 합의안이 지금 양당에 의해서 마련되었다.

    协议案现在由两党制定。

    合意案が今両党によって作られた。

12. 면책특권이 국회의원에게 부여되어 있다.

    国会议员被授予免责特权。

    免責特権が国会議員に付与されている。

7. **Huge damage was caused by the fire.**

   Huge damage caused by the fire.
   Huge damage which was caused by the fire.
   Huge damage that was caused by the fire.

8. **The garden is covered with colorful leaves in autumn.**

   The garden covered with colorful leaves in autumn.
   The garden which is covered with colorful leaves in autumn.
   The garden that is covered with colorful leaves in autumn.

9. **Most of the things are closely related with education.**

   Most of the things closely related with education.
   Most of the things which are closely related with education.
   Most of the things that are closely related with education.

10. **Most of the homes are dominated by TV.**

    Most of the homes dominated by TV.
    Most of the homes which are dominated by TV.
    Most of the homes that are dominated by TV.

11. **An agreement has been worked out by both parties.**

    An agreement worked out by both parties.
    An agreement which has been worked out by both parties.
    An agreement that has been worked out by both parties.

12. **Parliamentary privilege is given to the lawmakers.**

    Parliamentary privilege given to the lawmakers.
    Parliamentary privilege which is given to the lawmakers.
    Parliamentary privilege that is given to the lawmakers.

13. 그의 손은 많은 일을 해서 모양이 일그러져있다.

　　他的手由于做了很多活都变形了。
　　彼の手は多くの仕事によって曲がっている。

14. 그들은 자신의 목표를 이룰 결심이 서 있다.

　　他们决心实现自己的目标。
　　彼らは自分の目標を達成する決心ができている。

15. 그 승리는 지금까지 필사적인 투쟁으로 얻었다.

　　那胜利是通过殊死的斗争赢得的。
　　その勝利は今までの必死な闘争で得たものだ。

16. 엄청난 양의 에너지가 태양에 의해서 방출되고 있다.

　　巨大的能量被太阳释放出来。
　　膨大な量のエネルギーが太陽によって放出されている。

17. 최고의 권한은 국민에게 부여되어 있다.

　　人民被赋予最高的权限。
　　最高の権限は国民に付与されている。

18. 그 아름다운 정원은 모든 종류의 꽃으로 가득 차 있다.

　　那美丽的庭园被所有种类的花填满了。
　　その美しい庭園はあらゆる種類の花でいっぱいだ。

13. His hands are disfigured by much work.

His hands disfigured by much work.
His hands which are disfigured by much work.
His hands that are disfigured by much work.

14. They are determined to achieve their goals.

People determined to achieve their goals.
People who are determined to achieve their goals.
People that are determined to achieve their goals.

15. The victory has been won by a desperate struggle.

The victory won by a desperate struggle.
The victory which has been won by a desperate struggle.
The victory that has been won by a desperate struggle.

16. A huge amount of energy is released by the sun.

A huge amount of energy released by the sun.
A huge amount of energy which is released by the sun.
A huge amount of energy that is released by the sun.

17. The supreme authority is vested in the people.

The supreme authority vested in the people.
The supreme authority which is vested in the people.
The supreme authority that is vested in the people.

18. The beautiful garden is filled with all kinds of flowers.

The beautiful garden filled with all kinds of flowers.
The beautiful garden which is filled with all kinds of flowers.
The beautiful garden that is filled with all kinds of flowers.

19. 몇 가지 단서가 범죄 현장에서 발견되었다.

几个线索在犯罪现场被发现了。

いくつかの手がかりが犯罪現場で発見された。

20. 그 학생들은 시험결과에 만족하지 못하고 있다.

那些学生对考试结果不满意。

その学生たちは試験結果に満足していない。

21. 그 아이는 더위에 짜증이 났다.

那孩子对热感到厌烦。

その子供は暑さにいらだった。

22. 아주 많은 돈이 지금까지 이런 식으로 모금되었다.

至今用这种方式已经募集到了很大的一笔钱。

とてもたくさんのお金が今までこのような方法で募金された。

23. 그들은 파티에 올 것으로 예상된다.

他们预计将来参加聚会。

彼らはパーティーに来るものと予想される。

24. 세상은 크고 작은 우연의 일치로 가득 차 있다.

世界上充满了大大小小的巧合。

世界は大小の偶然の一致にあふれている。

19. Some clues were found at the crime scene.

Some clues found at the crime scene.
Some clues which were found at the crime scene.
Some clues that were found at the crime scene.

20. The students are not satisfied with the test results.

The students not satisfied with the test results.
The students who are not satisfied with the test results.
The students that are not satisfied with the test results.

21. The child was irritated by the heat.

The child irritated by the heat.
The child who was irritated by the heat.
The child that was irritated by the heat.

22. A great deal of money has been raised in this way.

A great deal of money raised in this way.
A great deal of money which has been raised in this way.
A great deal of money that has been raised in this way.

23. They are expected to come to the party.

People expected to come to the party.
People who are expected to come to the party.
People that are expected to come to the party.

24. The world is filled with little and big coincidences.

The world filled with little and big coincidences.
The world which is filled with little and big coincidences.
The world that is filled with little and big coincidences.

25. 번개 섬광이 있고서 천둥소리가 뒤이어졌다.

先有闪电闪光接着有打雷的声音。

雷の光の後に、雷の音が続いた。

26. 속담은 우리 조상의 오랜 경험에서 이끌어낸 것이다.

谚语来自我们祖先的长久经验。

諺は私たちの先祖の長年の経験から導き出されたものだ。

27. 이 약은 비염을 치료하기 위해서 의사 선생님이 처방해줬다.

该药为了治疗鼻炎由医生给开的处方。

この薬は鼻炎を治療するために医者が処方してくれた。

28. 그 도시는 지중해 해안에 있는 해변 휴양지로 알려져 있다.

那个城市被称为地中海沿岸的海滩度假村。

その都市は地中海海岸のリゾート地として知られている。

29. 이 이야기들은 지금까지 구전으로 전해져왔다.

这些故事至今一直都是口传下来的。

これらの話は今まで口伝えで伝わってきた。

30. 태풍으로 심각한 피해를 입었다.

台风造成了严重的损害。

台風で深刻な被害を被った。

25. The flash of lightning was followed by the sound of thunder.

The flash of lightning followed by the sound of thunder.
The flash of lightning which was followed by the sound of thunder.
The flash of lightning that was followed by the sound of thunder.

26. Proverbs are drawn from our ancestors' long experiences.

Proverbs drawn from our ancestors' long experiences.
Proverbs which are drawn from our ancestors' long experiences.
Proverbs that are drawn from our ancestors' long experiences.

27. The medicine was prescribed by the doctor to treat rhinitis.

The medicine prescribed by the doctor to treat rhinitis.
The medicine which was prescribed by the doctor to treat rhinitis.
The medicine that was prescribed by the doctor to treat rhinitis.

28. The city is known as a beach resort on the Mediterranean coast.

The city known as a beach resort on the Mediterranean coast.
The city which is known as a beach resort on the Mediterranean coast.
The city that is known as a beach resort on the Mediterranean coast.

29. The stories have been passed down by word of mouth.

The stories passed down by word of mouth.
The stories which have been passed down by word of mouth.
The stories that have been passed down by word of mouth.

30. Serious damage was done by the typhoon.

Serious damage done by the typhoon.
Serious damage which was done by the typhoon.
Serious damage that was done by the typhoon.

31. 유전 물질은 우리 몸의 모든 세포 안에서 발견된다.

    遗传物质在我们身体内的任何细胞中都会被发现。

    遺伝物質は私たちの体のすべての細胞の中で発見される。

32. 이 유리잔은 김이 모락모락 피어오르는 뜨거운 음료로 가득 차 있다.

    这个玻璃杯充满了热气腾腾的饮料。

    このグラスは湯気がゆらゆらと立ち上る暖かい飲み物で満たされている。

33. 양해각서가 오늘 파리에서 체결되었다.

    谅解备忘录今天在巴黎签署了。

    了解覚書が今日パリで締結された。

34. 학생들은 때때로 시험장에서 부정행위를 하고 싶은 유혹을 받는다.

    学生们有时会受到想在考场不正行为的诱惑。

    学生たちは時に試験会場で不正行為をしたい誘惑に陥る。

35. 이 기호는 생물학자들에 의해서 암컷으로 사용된다.

    该符号是生物学家们用于雌性。

    この記号は生物学者たちによって雌として使用される。

36. 많은 명승지가 전국에 산재해 있다.

    很多景点分散在全国各地。

    多くの名所が全国に点在している。

31. **The genetic material is found inside every cell of our body.**

The genetic material found inside every cell of our body.
The genetic material which is found inside every cell of our body.
The genetic material that is found inside every cell of our body.

32. **The glass is filled with a steaming hot drink.**

The glass filled with a steaming hot drink.
The glass which is filled with a steaming hot drink.
The glass that is filled with a steaming hot drink.

33. **The memorandum of understanding was signed in Paris today.**

The memorandum of understanding signed in Paris today.
The memorandum of understanding which was signed in Paris today.
The memorandum of understanding that was signed in Paris today.

34. **Students are sometimes tempted to cheat on the test.**

Students sometimes tempted to cheat on the test.
Students who are sometimes tempted to cheat on the test.
Students that are sometimes tempted to cheat on the test.

35. **The symbol is used by biologists for female.**

The symbol used by biologists for female.
The symbol which is used by biologists for female.
The symbol that is used by biologists for female.

36. **Many scenic spots are scattered across the country.**

Many scenic spots scattered across the country.
Many scenic spots which are scattered across the country.
Many scenic spots that are scattered across the country.

37. 그 결정은 주의 깊게 생각하지 않고 이루어졌다.

那一决定没有仔细思考制成。

その決定は注意深く考えずに行われた。

38. 허파는 흡연으로 가장 심각하게 손상을 받는다.

肺部因吸烟而受到严重损害。

肺は喫煙によって最も深刻に損傷を受ける。

39. 많은 시간을 직장에 통근하면서 보낸다.

大量的时间花在通勤途中。

多くの時間を職場に通勤しながら消費している。

40. 우리의 일상생활은 경쟁의식으로 가득 차있다.

我们的日常生活充满了竞争意识。

私たちの日常生活は競争意識に満ちている。

41. 영어는 세계 모든 곳에서 사용되고 이해된다.

英语在世界各地被使用和理解。

英語は世界のすべての所で使われ、理解される。

42. 그 경기는 스포츠 광팬의 행동으로 망쳤다.

那场比赛被体育狂热者的行为破坏了。

その試合は熱狂的なサポーターの行動によって台無しになった。

37. The decision was made without careful thought.

The decision made without careful thought.
The decision which was made without careful thought.
The decision that was made without careful thought.

38. The lungs are most seriously damaged by smoking.

The lungs most seriously damaged by smoking.
The lungs which are most seriously damaged by smoking.
The lungs that are most seriously damaged by smoking.

39. Much time is spent commuting to work.

Much time spent commuting to work.
Much time which is spent commuting to work.
Much time that is spent commuting to work.

40. Our daily lives are filled with a rival consciousness.

Our daily lives filled with a rival consciousness.
Our daily lives which are filled with a rival consciousness.
Our daily lives that are filled with a rival consciousness.

41. English is spoken and understood everywhere in the world.

English spoken and understood everywhere in the world.
English which is spoken and understood everywhere in the world.
English that is spoken and understood everywhere in the world.

42. The game was spoiled by the behavior of sports fanatics.

The game spoiled by the behavior of sports fanatics.
The game which was spoiled by the behavior of sports fanatics.
The game that was spoiled by the behavior of sports fanatics.

43. 여름휴가는 중국 고전을 읽으면서 보냈다.

暑假是读中国经典度过的。

夏休みは中国の古典を読んで過ごした。

44. 그 질병은 지금까지 치료 불가능하다고 여겨져 왔다.

那种疾病一直被认为不可能治愈。

その病気はこれまで治療不可能だと考えられてきた。

45. 많은 재미있는 질문을 학생들이 자주 묻는다.

学生们经常问很多有趣的问题。

たくさんの面白い質問を生徒たちがよく問う。

46. 변호사의 주장은 단지 정황증거에만 기반을 두고 있다.

律师的主张只基于间接证据。

弁護士の主張はただ状況証拠だけに基盤を置いている。

47. 아름다운 한시(漢詩) 하나가 병풍에 쓰여 있다.

一首美丽的中国诗写在一个屏风上。

美しい一つの漢詩が屏風に書かれている。

48. 그는 음주 운전 중에 한 사람을 사망케 한 것으로 유죄판결을 받았다.

他因酒后驾车导致一人死亡受到了有罪判决。

彼は飲酒運転で一人を死亡させたことで有罪判決を受けた。

43. The summer vacation was spent reading Chinese classics.

The summer vacation spent reading Chinese classics.
The summer vacation which was spent reading Chinese classics.
The summer vacation that was spent reading Chinese classics.

44. The disease has been considered impossible to cure.

The disease considered impossible to cure.
The disease which has been considered impossible to cure.
The disease that has been considered impossible to cure.

45. Many interesting questions are frequently asked by students.

Many interesting questions frequently asked by students.
Many interesting questions which are frequently asked by students.
Many interesting questions that are frequently asked by students.

46. The lawyer's assertion is based on only circumstantial evidence.

The lawyer's assertion based on only circumstantial evidence.
The lawyer's assertion which is based on only circumstantial evidence.
The lawyer's assertion that is based on only circumstantial evidence.

47. A beautiful Chinese poem is written on a folding screen.

A beautiful Chinese poem written on a folding screen.
A beautiful Chinese poem which is written on a folding screen.
A beautiful Chinese poem that is written on a folding screen.

48. He was convicted of killing a man while driving drunk.

The person convicted of killing a man while driving drunk.
The person who was convicted of killing a man while driving drunk.
The person that was convicted of killing a man while driving drunk.

49. 엄청난 양의 정보가 인터넷에서 제공되고 있다.

互联网上提供了非常大量的信息。

膨大な量の情報がインターネットで提供されている。

50. 급속한 발전이 지난 30년에 걸쳐서 이루어졌다.

在过去三十年里取得了快速进展。

急速な発展が過去30年にわたって遂げられた。

49. A huge amount of information is provided on the internet.

A huge amount of information provided on the internet.
A huge amount of information which is provided on the internet.
A huge amount of information that is provided on the internet.

50. The rapid progress has been made over the last thirty years.

The rapid progress made over the last thirty years.
The rapid progress which has been made over the last thirty years.
The rapid progress that has been made over the last thirty years.